The Criminalization of Immigration

The Criminalization
of Immigration
Contexts and Consequences

EDITED BY

Alissa R. Ackerman
UNIVERSITY OF WASHINGTON, TACOMA

AND

Rich Furman
UNIVERSITY OF WASHINGTON, TACOMA

CAROLINA ACADEMIC PRESS
Durham, North Carolina

Ackerman, Alissa.
 The Criminalization of immigration : contexts and consequences /
edited by Alissa Ackerman and Rich Furman.
     pages cm
Includes bibliographical references and index.
 ISBN 978-1-61163-356-6 (alk. paper)
1. Illegal aliens--United States. 2. Immigration
enforcement--United States. 3. United States--Emigration and
immigration--Government policy. I. Furman, Rich. II. Title.

JV6483.A25 2013
325'.1--dc23

                            2013030174

Carolina Academic Press
700 Kent Street
Durham, North Carolina 27701
Telephone (919) 489-7486
Fax (919) 493-5668
www.cap-press.com

Printed in the United States of America
2017 Printing

To my boys, Logan and Trevor …
you have stolen my heart!
A.A.

To Slick, (1998–2013)
What it is …
R.F.

Contents

Section 2: State Laws

Chapter Four · Undocumented Immigration Policy in Arizona   49
Susanna Jones

Chapter Five · Undocumented Immigrant Policy in Alabama   61
María Pabón López and Natasha Ann Lacoste

SECTION 1

Introductory Chapters

Chapter One

Introduction: The Changing Tide of America and the Criminalization of Immigration

Alissa R. Ackerman & Rich Furman

Immigration has become one of the hottest topics in our national discourse (Fryberg et al, 2011). Few other topics lead to such passionate opinions. Indeed, the topic of immigration is so emotional that it so often transcends facts and knowledge, and leads us directly into key values about what it means to be "an American" (Nevins, 2010). While this is certainly not new, the development of the Internet and other mass media have allowed social conditions that have been complex and emotional to be greatly heightened in the public eye.

In many ways, the emotional and value laden aspect of immigration has served our country and its immigrant population well. For most of our history, one of our nation's important narratives has been that we are a country that was built by and for immigrants, and that each generation of immigration has added a new level of richness and possibility to the American landscape. This narrative has been a powerful influence on how the United States handles immigrants, refugees, and asylum seekers. However, coexisting with this narrative has been another emotional and value driven story. In this story, America is a country for Americans, and is threatened by a nefarious other; the immigrant (Furman, Negi & Cisneros-Howard, 2008). This is not a new narrative, and in many ways, has existed for nearly the entire life of the nation. As political, social and economic trends shift and transform, the immigrant is often viewed as a threat to our physical and moral survival (Werner, 2011). While this narrative has long been part of our collective unconscious, it has recently risen from the depths of our unconscious to the tip of our collective tongues. Indeed, the America of the 21st century is in a dynamic and fluid state; new realities and how they are reflected in new narratives are rapidly being constructed (Nielson, 2009).

September 11th, 2001, has, perhaps, forever altered our relationship to "the other." (Mittelstadt, Speaker, Meissner, & Chisti, 2011). For the first time since Pearl Harbor, an attack on American soil threatened our personal and public sense of security. However, the rise of the Internet and its cacophony of bombarding images made this a far more powerful assault in the minds of many Americans. Not only did this shock our sense of safety, security and well being, Americans were attacked from inside America by those perceived as other. The actual and symbolic power of this event, combined with long-standing nativist and racist sentiments, were inflamed by President George W. Bush's violent, aggressive rhetoric. Soon after, this "other" that we once welcomed with open arms (according to the first narrative), who once would become us, had now become the enemy.

America was soon at war, two wars in fact. Both of these physical wars, and our own recession, required a means of calming the American people, of blaming something other than ourselves (Sekhon, 2003). What was needed, Sanchez, Furman and Ackerman explore in Chapter Two, was a pacification strategy that could quell our restless, aching hearts. This strategy, which has many other functions besides pacification, is known as the criminalization of immigration (Furman et al. 2012). As we shall see, the power of these forces, their global nature, and other unfortuitous factors has lead to a series of policies, programs and mechanisms for contending with the "problem" of undocumented immigration (Aman, & Rehrig, 2011). The response to these forces has been a powerful rise of nativism in the United States, a nativism that has long existed, but has now shifted in response to new global realities (Jacobson, 2008). The America of the 21st century is not the undisputed world's superpower. Our economic and political hegemony are now being challenged. We find our per capita income slipping, or military reach stretched, and our sense of identity fractured and confused. "What is America in the 21st, postmodern, global century?" and "What is an American?" are questions more frequently asked than in our previous century. The criminalization of immigration, in a very real sense, has been the codification of policies and laws that reflect an extreme response to our own fears of our future, of our own retrenchment into nativism and xenophobia (Bosworth & Kaufman, 2011).

This nativism, this profound fear of the forces of globalization, of threats against our safety and well being have led to calls for comprehensive immigration reform at the federal level (Furman & Sanchez, 2012). Indeed, the Supreme Court has consistently ruled that immigration policy rests solely in the purview of the federal government (Nielsen, 2009). Yet, the federal government has been bogged down by partisan debates and other legal challenges over what to do about immigration. Additionally, the federal notion of the nature of the illegality is often not of the liking (or often misunderstood) by anti-immigration advocates. According to federal law, crossing the border and entering the United States without proper documentation and permission is considered an administrative, not criminal violation. Administrative violations, such as a citizen paying their taxes late, are not considered the same type of offense as criminal violations, and typically are not dealt with by the criminal justice system. For example, the police do not come after citizens who are late on their taxes.

In response to the lack of movement by the federal government to change the nature of immigration related offenses, states have begun passing draconian, and often unconstitutional, state laws that aim to criminalize many aspects of the lives of the undocumented (Provine & Sanchez, 2011). Just in the last several years the number of immigration related bills introduced at the state level has skyrocketed from approximately 300 bills in 2005 to 1500 in 2009 (Immigration Policy Center, 2011).

The editors designed the structure of the sections of this book with these realities in mind. We sought chapters that help the reader understand the local, state, national and global dynamics of the criminalization of immigration. In this book, you will find chapters written by scholars from various disciplines: social work, law, sociology, anthropology, criminology as well as other fields. You will also find chapters written by non academics. Regardless, we sought chapters that would provide you with a comprehensive understanding of the phenomenon. We want you to understand the criminalization of immigrants from multiple vantage points, from multiple theoretical and disciplinary lenses, and also from the lived experiences of those who work, and literally live, in this arena. We believe we have succeeded, and welcome you to discover a rich, intriguing, and sometimes painful world; for ultimately, the criminalization of immigration is the criminalization of humans. The immigrants who are the pawns in this complex, global battle are hardly criminals, but instead are usually poor, uneducated, hard working people who wish to make better lives for themselves and their families. It is this reality that is often neglected in policy debates, but is not neglected here. We hope that the chapters not only educate you, but inspire you to act.

Section and Chapter Introductions

The book before you is divided into several sections. The chapters in Part One of the book introduce key concepts and dilemmas pertaining to the criminalization of immigration. This section is designed to familiarize readers with the broad-scale, macro-level and theoretical issues implicated in criminalizing immigrant populations. In this section, the chapters compel us to question the notion of immigration as a social problem. Each questions key assumptions that we make about the nature of immigration as a social problem.

Chapter Two, by Sanchez, Furman and Ackerman, explores the problematization of undocumented immigration and how it is used as a pacification strategy. The authors explore three specific and strategic ways in which immigration policy is used as a pacification strategy: the construction of the undocumented immigrant as a "threat" and the cause of various social and economic "problems," state laws that criminalize immigration and increase the surveillance of all Latinos, and the increased detention and incarceration of immigrants. The authors explore the ways in which pacification strategies fail to address real problems and consequences of undocumented immigrants being perceived as the source of the "problem" is examined. From this chapter, we assess various ways immigration is used in social discourse, and watch for ways in which immigration is blamed as a cause, for conditions in which it is a symptom.

In his compelling chapter, "Immigration as Theater of the Absurd," David Brotherton presents us with a powerful metaphor that provides us with an additional analytical tool. Chapter Three deftly and dramatically calls into question many of the, too often taken for granted, assumptions about the sociopolitical context of immigration. His chapter challenges us to pay careful attention to the meaning of the behavior of various actors, and to carefully deconstruct key aspects of the immigration discourse. We hope readers will explore and take in both of these chapters which provide, along with this introduction, a more "mile high" view of key dynamics of the overall immigration context.

The three chapters of Section Two explore specific examples of how individual states are engaging in policies that seek to criminalize immigration. Each explores the nature of state's rights and responsibilities and how these intersect with federal immigration jurisdiction. They describe the intersection of the two, and describe the complex relationship between the federal government's historic responsibility for immigration policy, and various states laws that challenge this.

In Chapter Four, Susanna Jones presents a powerful exploration of the history of immigration law in Arizona. She connects this history to nativism forces, and demonstrates the manner in which race, ethnicity, immigration, and criminalization intersect. Dr. Jones presents an in-depth exploration of SB 1070, one of the nation's most extreme and influential immigration laws. Arizona is a particularly important example, as it is the site where some of the most anti-immigration policing efforts have occurred. Dr. Jones not only explores the nature of the laws and policies, but also discusses the important role that immigration advocates have in shaping the implementation of public policy. One of the important lessons from this chapter is that policy practice is not only about how laws are written, but how they are implemented where the rubber meets the road.

Chapter Five, by Dr. Maria Lopez and Natasha Lacoste, addresses the various means by which a recent Alabama law has sought to criminalize the lives of undocumented citizens. Alabama is a fascinating case study, due to the history of human and civil rights struggles within the state, the role that undocumented immigrants have played in the relative health of this growing Southern economy, and the diversity of the discourses engaged in by various constituents. Alabama has moved beyond, in many respects, previous laws, and has created a constellation of restrictions that seek to not only criminalize immigration, but the actual lives of undocumented immigrants.

Sujey Vega's chapter provides a discussion of immigration policy in Indiana. It begins with the story of Soccoro, an undocumented immigrant, and her children, who find themselves in a state that is inhospitable to their struggles. By introducing Socorro and her struggles and then linking this case to Indiana immigration policy, Dr. Vega paints a vivid picture of the lived experience and consequences of the state's law. SB 590 was signed into law by Governor Mitch Daniels in mid-2011 and has been likened to Arizona's SB 1070 due to the punitive nature of the law. This chapter shows an important example of how immigration policy is being "performed" in states that are not traditional receiving sites for Latino immigrants. Such states represent important "battlegrounds" for various players in the immigration debate.

The third section of the book is titled "Actors and Players: The Socio-Political Context of the Criminalization of Immigration." It may seem obvious, but it is worth noting that laws and policies do not occur outside of contemporary political debates, trends, and conflicts. The first two chapters in this section provide specific examples of the effect of contemporary issues on the criminalization of immigration while the second two chapters examine right leaning groups or political parties and their beliefs about immigration and immigration policy.

Professor Kati Griffith discusses the impact of the criminalization of immigration on labor standards enforcement in Chapter Seven. As we shall see in a later chapter by Negi and her colleague, as labor is criminalized, undocumented immigrants suffer various psychosocial problems. This chapter explores the manner in which immigration law has been formed, but more importantly, the ways in which it is regulated and the standard by which it is enforced. Encouragement standards impact the hourly rate by which undocumented immigrants are paid, their health and safety within and outside the workplace, protections from workplace discrimination, and collective activity protections. The author cogently describes how the criminalization of immigration erodes many of the workplace and labor protections that we have come to view as givens within the United States. This becomes an additional example of how this criminalization is another assault on what can be viewed as basic human rights.

In Chapter Eight Ackerman, Furman, Judy, and Cohen discuss the private prison industry and it's stake in the immigration debate. The industry is always looking to increase revenue which means it is constantly seeking out ways to expand it's services. In 2010, the United States saw its first decrease in state prison populations in nearly 40 years. If this trend continues, the private prison industry will begin to lose revenue. As Ackerman et al. outline, the private prison industry has an extensive lobbying effort to persuade state and federal lawmakers to vote on bills that support their cause. Immigrant detention is the newest profit stream for this industry. The authors discuss how and why the private prison industry has been successful in this endeavor and the risks and consequences associated with the detention of the undocumented in privately run facilities.

Dr. Chebel D'Appollonia applies a transatlantic lens to the immigration debate in her chapter "The Right and Undocumented Immigration: A Transatlantic Perspective". Here, she compares the conservative movements on both sides of the Atlantic, the rule of law, and various stances on immigration policy. The political dilemmas and consequences posed by Conservative ideologies and immigration on either side of the Atlantic are divergent. In the United States, where the Hispanic population continues to grow, Republicans are hard pressed to find solutions for immigration reform. As Chebel D'Appollonia states, Hispanic voters turned out to vote for President Barack Obama in extraordinary numbers. The GOP will either cave to its largely white, restrictionist base, or it will begin conversations around immigration reform. A

Republican can no longer win the highest office in the country without the Hispanic vote, which clearly is leaning toward the Democrats. In Europe, the Rightist parties have no incentive to view ethnic voters as a political resource because the pool of ethnic voters is low. The extreme right wing parties have secured a more prominent place in politics, positing a political threat to the mainstream right. The chapter adeptly compares and contrasts the politics of immigration from two very different perspectives and therefore shows the reader that the criminalization of immigration is not an "American" problem.

Next, Drs. Stanislav Vysotsky and Eric Madfis present a clear example of how the immigration discourse becomes a mechanism for a larger aim. In this case, the authors demonstrate how white supremacist groups utilize anti-immigration sentiments as a means of galvanizing support. By playing into deep seated fears and insecurities, these groups create a polarization between this threatening "other" and what are often categorized as patriotic, even mainstream American values. The criminalization of immigration serves the aims of this population, and they have been active through Internet discussion forums, both internally and in the popular media. This chapter reminds us that while some of these views are extreme, they are not diametrically opposed to the views held by a great many Americans.

The fourth section of the book, Immigration, Transmigration, and the International Context, contains chapters that situate criminalization within a global context. Social problems or policy concerns are influenced by, or influences, globalization. This is perhaps more true for immigration than it is for most other social phenomenon. Immigration, and the more recently conceptualized transmigration, are part and parcel of globalization. Immigration is fueled by global forces, and creates new necessities, opportunities and dilemmas for the organization of social life.

Charges of human rights violations are typically leveled by the United States against governments that we view as totalitarian and oppressive. The American public is often not used to, and perhaps comfortable with, concerns about human rights being leveled by our government, policies and laws. However, the human rights implications of immigration laws and policies, both here and internationally, are profound. David Androff's chapter helps us understand the fundamental ethical and human rights dilemmas implicated by our new state-level human rights laws. The article challenges us to view immigration policy through a lens that we typically reserve for others. As you shall note, this powerful analytic tool has significant implications for our credibility as a nation. At no time in U.S. history have questions of national security been more closely tied to perceptions about the way that the US treats people, both here and abroad. As such, understanding the implications of a human rights critique has implications for policy and law beyond the domain of immigration policy.

In "Transnational Dimensions of Mexican Migration at the Cusp of Immigration Reform," Dr. William Haller helps situate the most salient issues of immigrant policy within a transnational framework. The relationship between Mexico and the United States, and the dynamics that characterize it, has had profound implications for various social problems. Haller asserts that the nature of the dysfunctional dynamics between our nations, along with immigration policy that has often been myopic, has lead to the development of powerful criminal forces, including human trafficking, drug smuggling, and the proliferation of arms. The chapter highlights the powerful flaw of developing national, state, and local laws without attending transnational law and policy.

Perhaps no better example exists about the transnational nature of crime, and the potential negative consequences of domestic policy, than the case of the Maras. The Maras are violent gangs of El Salvadoran youth that began in Los Angeles during the 1980s. Some of the Mara were trained during the violent civil war in El Salvador. Most were extremely poor and lived lives characterized by violence, marginalization, and alienation. The Maras were started as a means of youth protecting their neighborhoods against other gangs in Los Angeles, but soon became the most violent gang in the city. As the Maras increasingly were deported for their crimes, they exported their gangs back to the streets of San Salvador, the capital of El Salvador. Dr. Sonya Wolf describes the evolution of this gang from a local gang to a transnational criminal organization that threatens regional stability. We can begin to gain a complex understanding of the consequences of criminalizing immigration without paying clear attention to potential unknown consequences.

Too frequently, national specific examples of the criminalization of immigration focus on the North American context. Dr. Ana Aliverti helps us change this dynamic through her highly detailed and analytic chapter on the criminalization of immigration in the United Kingdom. Through viewing the criminalization of immigration through the historical and political lenses of the United Kingdom, we are encourage to challenge some of the assumptions that we make, and to deconstruct some of what we view as givens.

The final section of the book is "Case Examples: The Human Cost of the Criminalization of Immigration." The social forces and policies explored in this book cannot be viewed merely from a macro, social perspective. Each of the policies, laws and trends discussed were lived by real people. In this section, we present a variety of case examples that hopefully make the major themes of this book come alive. While many of the chapters contain vignette stories of real people, the explicit purpose of this section is to help the reader connect to the emotional, lived experiences of real people.

Tien Ung documents the plight of the Asian American community and Intimate Partner Violence (IPV). Typically, IPV becomes exacerbated for victims in immigrant communities based solely on one's legal status. Ung discusses the historical aspects of the Violence Against Women Act (VAWA) and the protections for immigrant women contained within the Act and demonstrates the impact of the VAWA expiring in 2011. Dr. Ung notes that criminalizing immigration has negative, unintended consequences for all women, including those who work with them. It leaves individuals who work with this population of victims less empowered and unable to understand the complexities of the lives these women lead. While Ung's chapter highlights a specific type of abuse within one community, the lessons learned from her work resonate with various others' lived experiences.

Mark Grey's case study explores Latino meatpacking workers in Iowa. This fascinating case study explores the sociocultural context of older sets of white immigrants integrating newer nonwhite populations. Meatpacking plants found willing workers from Central Mexico, who provided a pool of hard working, reliable labor during a time of labor scarcity. His study explores various social perceptions about this population, some based upon misunderstandings, some based upon myth, some upon fear. Grey situates the complex social dynamics of this heartland state within the context of local and immigration policy. He helps us understand how national and even transnational issues are played out in the context of small town, rural American lives.

While not technically relying upon case study, Suarez-Orozco and colleagues present a compelling chapter of one of the most vulnerable populations impacted by the criminalization of immigration: children. In their chapter, "Children of the Unauthorized: Domains of Compromise in their Development," the authors analyze a wide range of current research that presents a grim picture of the outcomes for children of undocumented immigrants. The authors explore educational and psychosocial problems that put these children at current risk, and present a compelling case for how not attending to the plight of their parents may lead to significant personal and social consequences. The vast majority of these children are American citizens, who start life with increased risk of educational failure, emotional problems, and increased behavioral issues. Our already overwhelmed schools and social service institutions are put at risk by the threat of, or actual deportation of their parents.

Drs. Nalini Negi and Neely Mahapatra explore one of the most vulnerable, and often overlooked populations—immigrant day laborers. Day laborers are a population that has been historically marginalized. They have been blamed for the degradation of neighborhoods, scapegoated for our nation's economic woes, and have been unfairly blamed for committing a disproportionate number of crimes, including sex offenses. What we learn from this powerful chapter, however, is that day laborers are far more at risk of various psychosocial maladies than they are a cause of distress for others. The increased criminalization of immigration has placed these workers at greater risk, making it more difficult to obtain and keep work. Given that these economic transmigrants often support families on both sides of the border, their increased risks also increase the vulnerability of many women and children.

The criminalization of immigration not only affects immigrants and their families, but also people who work within the criminal justice system. Certainly, immigrants and their families experience the most severe and devastating consequences, yet existing within often oppressive, dehumanizing contexts impacts all who operate. This is most certainly true of all who encounter immigration detention centers. In the final chapter of the book, Douglas Epps presents a personal narrative of his experience as a prison guard within the Northwest Detention Center. His evocative narrative hints at the psychological costs of the thousands who serve as agents of criminalization. The author explores the cognitive dissonance he experiences as his own personal values are challenged from all sides. He struggles to make sense of the anti-immigrant sentiments of some of the detention center personnel, and of his own feelings as he attempts to integrate the humanity of the detainees into a set of beliefs that allow him to function each and every day. Through his narrative we begin to understand the mechanisms by which criminal justice personnel detach and dissociate from key aspects of their own emotions. From reading his narrative, it is difficult to not feel both empathy for and concern about the humanity not only of the immigrants, but the workers who are dehumanized through the very process of their work.

We intentionally close our book with this set of chapters, as it is through the lived experiences and stories of those whose lives are most impacted by immigration policy that wen ca truly learn what these policies mean and do. Policies are not merely laws, and laws are not merely numbered passages in state and federal registries. Policies and laws are lived each day; they are performed as living acts of real people. They empower and embolden, or restrict and oppress. As you read the following chapters of this book, we encourage you to view the criminalization of immigration in this manner.

References

Aman, A. C., & Rehrig, G. (2011). *The domestic face of globalization: Law's role in the integration of immigrants in the United States.* Legal Studies Research Paper, #196, Indiana University School of Law. Bloomington, Indiana: University of Indiana.

Bosworth, M., & Kaufman, E. (2011). Foreigners in a carceal age: Immigration and imprisonment in the U. S. Legal Research Paper Series, No. 34. Oxford University. Retrieved on April 2, 2012 at http://papers.ssrn.com/sol3/papers.cfm?abstract_id=1852196.

Fryberg, S. A., Stephens, N.M., Covarrubias, R., Markus, H. R., Carter, E. D., Laiduc, G. A., & Salido, A. J. (2011). How the media frames the immigration debate. The critical role of location and politics. *Analysis of Social Issues and Public Policy,* 13 JUL 2011. DOI:10.1111/j.1530–2415.2011.01259.

Furman, R., Ackerman, A., Loya, M., Jones, S., & Negi, N. (2012). The Criminalization of immigration: Value conflicts for the social work profession. *Journal of Sociology and Social Welfare, 39*(1), 169–185.

Furman, R., Negi, N. J., & Cisneros-Howard, A. L. (2008). The immigration debate: Lessons for social work. *Social Work, 53*(3), 283–285.

Furman, R. & Sanchez, M. (2012). The impossible flaw of natavism: The need for transnational social policy. *Transnational Social Support. 2*(2), 40–43.

Jacobson, R. D. (2008). *The new nativism: Proposition 187 and the debate over immigration.* Minneapolis, MN: University of Minnesota Press.

Nielsen, J. (2009). Locking down our borders: How anti-immigration sentiment led to unconstitutional legislation and the erosion of fundamental principles of American government. *Journal of Law and Policy.18*(1), 459–502.

Mittelstadt, M. Speaker, B., Meissner, D. & Chisti, M. (2011). *Through the prism of national security: Major immigration policy and program changes in the decade since 9/11.* Washington, DC: Migration Policy Institute.

Nielsen, J. (2009). Locking down our borders: How anti-immigration sentiment led to unconstitutional legislation and the erosion of fundamental principles of American government. *Journal of Law and Policy. 18*(1), 459–502.

Nevins, J. (2010). *Operation Gatekeeper: The rise of the "Illegal Alien" and the making of the U.S. Mexico boundary.* New York: Routledge.

Provine, M. D., & Sanchez, G. (2011). Suspecting immigrants: Exploring links between racialist anxieties and expanded police power in Arizona. *Policing & Society, 21*(4), 468–479.

Sekhon, V. (2003). The civil rights of "others": Anti-terrorism, the Patriot Act, and Arab and South Asian American rights in post-9/11 American society. *Texas Journal on Civil Liberties & Civil Rights, 8*(1), 117–148.

Werner, D. (2011). SPCL ready for long legal battle over Alabama's harsh anti-immigrant law. *Southern Poverty Law Center.* Retrieved April 3, 2013 from http://www.splcenter.org/get informed/news/. http://www.splcenter.org/get-informed/news/.

Chapter Two

The Problematization of Immigration as a Pacification Strategy

Michelle Sanchez, Rich Furman & Alissa R. Ackerman

Introduction

Perhaps no social issue is as controversial and contested as undocumented immigration. Even as the Supreme Court's recent decision reaffirmed that immigration policy rests within the domain of federal policy (Edsall, 2012), the nuances and subtleties of their decision remains highly debated. Republicans and Democrats alike are claiming "victory," and are using the Supreme Court's decision toward their political aims in a highly "strategic" way. This notion of immigration as a potential strategy in the political process is not new. Numerous presidential campaigns have focused on the "problem" of immigration (Hetherington & Weiler, 2009), and have focused more on what their opponents have done or not done than articulate a coherent, policy driven plan (Freeman, 2011).

These political strategies coincide with the problematization of immigration, and further lends support for the notion of how immigration has been utilized as a tool to meet various aims and means. Nevins (2002) addresses the way that immigration related "problems" are strategically constructed by political and other actors:

> A variety of federal government officials and national politicians, along with a compliant media, helped to construct the perception of crisis and to stoke public fears. But what one society deems a "problem" or a "crisis" and how it understands that problem is far from inevitable.

> Why one particular issue becomes especially salient—as opposed to a whole host of other potential "problems"—is a matter that requires an explanation that not only contextualizes the putative problem, but also establishes the social actors that construct its popular image. Nevins (2002).

The means by which immigration is utilized in strategic terms warrants further exploration. As immigration continues to be problematized, the ways in which it has been utilized as a vehicle to meet various aims and objectives must be understood.

Politicians and political parties have linked immigration policy to national security (Aman & Rehrig, 2011), terrorism (Bacon, 2010; Tumlin, 2004), job creation and loss (Martin, 2012), the overall health of the economy (Nevins, 2002), general crime (Furman, Ackerman, Loya, Jones, & Negi, 2012; Higgins, Gabbidon, Martin, 2010), and even sex crimes (Ducat, Thomas, & Blood, 2009). What these political debates and discourses seem to have in common is that they serve the powerful function of attempting to pacify the American public. That is, they serve to keep the American public from critically evaluating the structural problems within society as a whole, and within certain institutions and structures, by using immigration as a strategy of pacification. The word "use" perhaps connotes a far more causal and consciously nefarious process than we intend; indeed, immigration becomes a strategy whereby citizens are disciplined toward the performance of blaming social inequities and social problems upon undocumented immigrants. This disciplining process is embedded within the structural arrangements and agendas of various political constituents, and operates, sometimes within and sometimes beyond, the conscious intentions of those implicated in social power dynamics (Guevarra, 2010). That is, the manner in which undocumented immigration serves as this disciplining mechanism, or a mechanism for the pacification of various constituents, may at times be an intentional strategy, and at other times is far more subtle, and arguably insidious.

The purpose of this article is to explore the problematization of undocumented immigration as a pacification strategy. To meet the aims of this article, we support our argument in several ways. First, we examine the work of Gramsci (1971) and how his work explains the power dynamics of pacification strategies. Next, we explore the notion of pacification, with a special focus on the way it is utilized by Neocleous (2011A). While he applies the concept of pacification to issues related to security, pacification has considerable explanatory value for other social phenomena, including the problematization of immigration. After examining these scholars' work as it applies to pacification, we present several ways in which the problematization and criminalization of un-documented immigration in the United States are utilized as pacification strate-gies. We explore each of these pacification strategies, the function they serve, who seems to benefit, and the impact of each of these strategies in the phe-nomenon of immigration. In conclusion, we explore the significance of these ideas, and explore their implications for other countries, transnational social supports, and transnational social work.

Pacification as a Strategy

In this section, we include a discussion of more general notions of pacifi-cation, in addition to other authors' applications of the term pacification. We look at the work of Gramsci (1971) that discusses several fundamental aspects of pacification strategies before moving on to the work of Mark Neocleous (Neocleous, 1996; 2010, 2011A & 2011B). His work represents one of the most complex and comprehensive explorations of the strategic uses of pacification.

In Latin, to pacify translates as *pacificare*, derived from the root pax, mean-ing peace, and facre, to make. Thus, to pacify is to make peace. This is in-structive, as the concept of peace connotes a lack of aggression, a lack of action, and is often separated from views of what is "right." This is typified by the slo-gan, "no justice, no peace." This slogan makes it clear that the notion of peace is not implicit within notions of justice. Pacification then, in this sense, is to create a sense of peace and order void of the realm of values, justice, and moral-ity. This amoral notion of pacification can be found within a definition taken from an analysis of pacification strategies of the Vietnam War (Maclear, as found in Pinard, 2006):

> ... the military, political, economic, and social process of establish-ing or reestablishing local government response to and involving the participation of the people. It includes the provision of sustained, credible territorial security, the enemy's underground government, the assertion or re-assertion of political control and involvement of the people in government, and the initiation of economic and social activity capable of self-sustenance and expansion. (p. 255)

A simple family object demonstrates a related but different way of concep-tualizing pacification. A baby's pacifier is an object that is placed in the baby's mouth to stop their crying. Note, this action of pacifying does not solve any of the myriad of biopsychosocial needs that prompted the baby to cry in the first place. The pacifier seeks to mollify or quell the baby, to give the parent some "peace." A pacified baby is a quiet one, one that does not pay attention to its actual needs and to the operations of the world around them. The use of a pacifier in many ways encourages a blindness to, or the denial of the analysis of, the etiology of the baby's problem or issue. This notion of pacification, as a tool for providing distraction from the real source of a problem, is a central strategy in utilizing immigration as a vehicle for pacification that we shall later explore. Similar to pacifying a crying baby, the pacification mechanisms discussed below do not address any real source of a problem, nor do they provide any solutions, other than to mollify the American public. Indeed, these mechanisms seem to serve the interest of the dominant member of the relationship; in this case, with the child, and in the case of immigration, various dominant players reap benefits from the mechanisms of pacification.

Various scholars have explored how individuals and societies can be pacified and conquered (Byler, 2005) as well as how internal conflicts are resolved (Negi & Furman, 2010). For our purposes, we will examine the work of Gramsci (1971) and Neocleous (2011) to further explore different dimensions of pacification and to lay the foundation for our arguments. Gramsci (1971) explained how conflicts are resolved in a society and his explanation can be thought of as a pacification strategy. According to Gramsci, in society, there are two levels that operate to construct consciousness and to organize human relationships. The first is 'civil society,' or the private, nonpolitical sphere of society, and 'political society' which includes legal, political and institutional forces. Gramsci argued that 'civil society' is ruled by hegemony, but on the other hand, 'political society' is ruled by 'direct domination' or control. Gramsci's definition of 'political society' is a concept that combines politics and force which Neocleous provides an in-depth analysis of.

Neocleous explores, in Gramsci's terminology, the concept of 'political society' by viewing 'direct domination' as a pacification strategy. One of the main themes of the work of Neocleous (2011A and B) is to explore the politics of security and how this serves as a vehicle for pacification. Pacification, according to Neocleous, contains two interrelated approaches: construction and reconstructing, or also referred to as politics and force. Means of achieving security depend heavily on a society's idea of what is insecure and how and when security is achieved. Neocleous focuses on three ways in which security is used as a way of achieving pacification: restoring security through political and economic force, deconstruction and reconstruction, and social reconstruction through military and/or police force. These mechanisms have been used historically to control certain populations and to secure insecurities, culturally, economically, politically and socially. He cogently explores the relationship between police power, law and order, when he asserts (2011B):

> Holding onto the idea of war as a form of conflict in which enemies face each other in clearly defined militarized ways, and the idea of police as dealing neatly with crime, distracts us from the fact that it is far more the case that the war power has long been a rationale for the imposition of international order and the police power has long been a wide-ranging exercise in pacification. (p. 157)

This notion has powerful explanatory value for understanding immigration and border policing. The U.S.-Mexico border has served several purposes for the U.S. and is a mechanism in which pacification has been achieved throughout its history in several different ways. For most of the history of the United States, the boundary was only periodically enforced, and was done so normally in response to single events that lead to especially strong public outcry (Andreas, 2000). In the early 1990s, the social construction of immigration became a problem that was widely accepted and supported by the American public. Attention and funding increased to meet the need to prove the security of the border, or to secure insecurities that were perceived to exist. The border as a territorial boundary was deconstructed, and in its place, the border was reconstructed as, in Nevins' (2002) terminology, a territorial state ideal, or the institutionalization of state power over national space. This process of institutionalizing the border has required the use of social, political, and economic control over the "problem" of immigration.

Consequently, increased funding for border patrol and the expansion of a physical barrier has evolved from a public problem to a normalized process of pacification. This dynamic is evident in the various "wars on" that have been the focus of social fear and hysteria, and have culminated in the war on drugs (Chin, 2011), war on terror (Nielsen, 2009), and war on immigrants (Furman, Langer, Sanchez, Negi, 2007). Each of these "wars" represent a powerful confluence of various pacification strategies. The use of the word war, which is defined as "a conflict carried on by force," works to deflect attention away from the fact that "the war on drugs," "the war on immigration," and "the war on terrorism" are all pacification strategies. These "wars" marshall social resources and power around common enemies. As in times of war, those who deny the existence of enemies are often viewed as traitors; the views on what constitutes social problems are largely marginalized (Ashdown, 2006). As Ashdown contends:

These are the folks who are generally on the periphery of the culture where it intersects with the criminal justice system. It is thus possible for the mainstream culture to either miss or ignore the overall loss in civil liberties until its members themselves are individually impacted. (p. 802)

Because boundary policing, border surveillance and the detention and criminalization of immigrants has become normalized, those who question or oppose legislation and funding that supports border security are often marginalized. The rational behind this normalized process is created when a "problem" is equated to an insecurity. For example, because the "problem" of immigration became increasingly evident in the 1990s, pacification strategies were needed and utilized to pacify the public and to show that political and governmental control over the problem could be achieved; however, this pacification strategy culminated in a specific race, class, social status, and location becoming the scapegoat.

The war on drugs, the war on immigration, and the war on terrorism have all successfully pacified public fears. Neocleous (2011) argues that security is the key to pacification and that the primary way to achieve pacification is through the restoration of security; when a problem becomes an insecurity, pacification strategies are needed to show that security can be achieved. Since at least the 1990s, political campaigns, media sensationalism and institutional forces have promoted the idea that security can be restored through aggressive legislation that ultimately criminalizes various forms of behavior, including immigration, and through constantly addressing the problem and debating which political strategies will best control the particular problem. The way in which a problem becomes a politicized strategy will be explored next.

Undocumented Immigration as a Tool of Pacification

Pacification Mechanism 1 — "Threats" of Illegal Immigrants

Neocleous uses the work of Marx to reflect how security is a means of controlling capital and how a permanent insecurity exists in bourgeois society. Applied to immigration policy, the permanent insecurity is the ability of the "other" to invade societies occupied by "us." In other words, the increased policing of borders separating one population from another is instigated and achieved by the country with more capital, and with more insecurities of losing that capital. In regards to the U.S.-Mexico border, this is reflected in the way that goods are exchanged but legislation has become directed at immigrants crossing the border—especially illegally—and by the criminalization of aspects of immigrants' lives. For example, in 1994, the year Operation Gatekeeper was established, trade between the U.S. and Mexico totaled $80 billion, and by 2000 that amount had increased to 200 billion Nevins (2002). These figures reflect how the flow of goods has increased during the same period when criminalizing immigration also increased. From 1995 to 2003, the incarceration of immigrants rose by 394 percent (Watson, 2005), rising from 3,420 in 1995 to 16,903 in 2003. In other words, trade has increased and goods cross the U.S.-Mexico border at an ever increasing rate, but to protect capital and U.S. society from the "problem" of immigration, it is policed and scrutinized through legislation.

The perceived threats of "illegal" immigrants serves as responses to economic and social problems. If we get to blame the "other" for the structural problems within American society, then citizens will not notice these structural problems. Blaming undocumented immigrants for a host of problems serves as a means of pacifying citizens; instead of venting their anger, and perhaps rebelling, the undocumented immigrant becomes a convenient and easy scapegoat. Gusfield (1981) explains how "ownership constitutes one piece of the structure of public problems. It indicates the power to define and describe the problem. It tells us who but not what" (p. 13). In this sense, the illegal immigrant is the cause of the "problem," but there has been a failure in explaining what the problem is.

It is not a coincidence that the rapid expansion of anti-immigrant sentiment coincided with the worst economic downturn since the great depression. Most recently, President Barack Obama issued an executive order lifting the threat of deportation for young people brought to the United States as children. According to Obama, these young people will be given temporary relief from deportation to apply for legal work authorization. The ensuing response from skeptics was to perpetuate anti-immigrant sentiment for political gain. For example, a Fox News opinion column reported the following:

> The unavoidable fact is that Mr. Obama's announced executive amnesty will increase the supply of legal workers to compete for jobs with the 20 million Americans who can't find a job or have been forced into part-time work … And the increase in the labor supply will not be small. Most news reports at first suggested that around 800,000 il-

legal aliens would benefit from the president's offer of job permits. But that is a misinterpretation of estimates in 2010 ... There were nearly 2 million illegal aliens who could qualify for the provisional part of the amnesty because they were in high school, in college or had already graduated from college. But only about 800,000 were expected to actually end up as college graduates and qualify for the permanent amnesty. Because the new Obama amnesty would not require college graduation, the 800,000 figure is no longer valid. All 2 million would qualify. In addition, the Obama amnesty would not require a person to even go to college which would add hundreds of thousands more illegal aliens to the beneficiary list. (Beck, 2012)

While many mark the increased problematization of anti-immigrant sentiments to 9/11, and it certainly did exacerbate this phenomenon, some evidence exists for its occurrence in the 1990s. The early 1990s saw the outbreak of what would soon become a historically unparalleled level of official and public concern about the U.S. government's ability—or the lack thereof—to police the U.S.-Mexico boundary and to prevent unauthorized or "illegal" immigration from Mexico (Nevins, 2). The establishment of Operation Gatekeeper in 1994 was a direct response to public opinion of immigration as a threat socially, economically and culturally. Immigration was a key issue and debate after the 1992 presidential election and leading up Clinton's re-election campaign in 1996. The change in discourse surrounding immigration and illegal immigrants leading up to and after Operation Gatekeeper both normalized and necessitated this trend.

Hall (1997) argued that "we use the principles of similarity and difference to establish relationships between concepts or to distinguish them from one another." The crisis of illegal immigration called for distinguishing the similarity and difference of people on either side of the U.S.-Mexico border (Nevins, 2002). Through the institutionalization of border policing and a change in public discourse, the labeling of immigrants as the "other" became essentially anyone entering a certain space without authorization and who had the potential to be a threat once inside of that space. Further, the emergence of the term "illegal" works to criminalize crossing the border without authorization and also to shift public opinion of illegal immigrants to the perspective that illegal equates to threats and crime. The term illegal, as well as legal, resident, citizen and alien, are "the discursive manifestations of the perceived necessity to maintain territorial purity" and to create difference between "us" and "them" (Nevins, 120). While public discourse is influenced by political actors and other institutional forces, it is also largely responsible for strengthening nativist sentiment in the U.S. and normalizing the build-up of the boundary as a way to create spatial and racial distance from the "other."

Pacification Mechanism 2—Criminalizing Immigration

Criminalizing undocumented immigrants and immigration serves to pacify undocumented immigrants and documented immigrants alike. If a state law requires that police check the identification of anyone they suspect of being undocumented, they will undoubtedly increase their attention and surveillance over all Latinos, as it is impossible to phenotypically distinguish between those who are documented and those who are not. As a result of state laws that allow for the detention of anyone suspected of being an undocumented immigrant until their status can be verified, many immigrants and nationals are detained as a result. The detention of immigrants is, in and of itself, a pacification mechanism; however, making it mandatory for law enforcement to check immigration status at encounters where there is probable cause to believe an individual is undocumented, specifically pacifies members of the public.

Another way to achieve pacification is by criminalizing key aspects of immigrants' lives by utilizing political power at the state level. Several states have used anti-immigration laws as a pacification strategy that addresses citizens' fears of crimes that may be committed by undocumented immigrants. One example is Alabama's H.B. 56 law that makes it a felony for an undocumented immigrant to enter into contracts with the state (Werner, 2011). Such contracts include applying for a business or driver's license or receiving public utilities for a residence. Another example is Arizona's S.B. 1070 law, which encourages law enforcement to verify the immigration status of anyone suspected of being an "illegal." It is important to note that being in the U.S. illegally is not a criminal act but is only an administrative violation; this type of violation rests solely in the purview of federal jurisdiction, not at the state level (Jacobson, 2008). The United States Supreme Court upheld federal jurisdiction for immigration in June 2012 in Arizona et al. v. United States. However, by creating state level laws that do not encumber federal jurisdiction, but do criminalize certain aspects of immigration, states are able to circumvent federal law and pacify fears of illegal immigration. This pacification strategy works to limit the actions of undocumented immigrants and to criminalize aspects of their lives that are necessary to meet basic needs. In doing so, public fear is addressed and rights are removed from immigrants who cannot produce documentation. This trend in anti-immigration laws at the state level has accelerated in recent years. According to the Immigration Policy Center (2011), only 300 immigration bills came before state legislators in 2005 but by 2009, that number increased to 1500.

The chilling effect on immigration policy has not only been on the behavior of undocumented immigrants and transmigrants, but on Latinos themselves. This is a relatively new development and arguably one that has evolved from a new definition of what the "problem" is, as well as, what level of policing immigration will achieve "security." "What is at stake in pacification is the kind of security measure that lies at the heart of social order" (Neocleous, 2010). The criminalization of immigration and political strategies thus serve as a pacification strategy that not only deflects attention from the real source of economic or social problems, but it also labels immigrants as an economic and social threat.

Certainly in recent history, U.S. presidents, as well as numerous states, have attempted to deflect attention from real "problems" by pacifying the public instead of dealing with the root cause of the specific issue. As previously noted, the war on drugs, the war on immigration and the war on terrorism have all culminated in marking the "problem," and a specific race, class, social status and location. For example, the War on Drugs, which began under the Nixon Administration, worked as a pacification strategy, because members of the public believed that the federal government had a plan to decrease the production, distribution, and consumption of narcotics (Lusane, 1991). However, the War on Drugs, which spanned nearly forty years, culminated in a large failure. For instance, over one trillion U.S. tax dollars was spent on this war, but while reports of high school students trying illicit drugs have ebbed and flowed since the 1970s, the rate of daily drug use for marijuana, opiates, and cocaine have remained unchanged over this forty-year span (Szalavitz, 2011). Over the same time period crack and crystal meth became more popular, despite the belief that these drugs were the cause of the War on Drugs. Research now shows that these drugs were actually the result of Nixon's policy because they are more potent in smaller amounts and are more easily concealed. Finally, the War on Drugs has resulted in the United States having the highest incarceration rate in the world. When Nixon's policy began, the U.S. housed inmates at a rate of 110 per 100,000 people. Today, the U.S. incarceration rates stands at 743 per 100,000, with over 50% of federal inmates being imprisoned on a drug related conviction. As for the racial effects of the War on Drugs, ample evidence exists that points to people of color being the scapegoat of this pacification strategy. For instance, according to the Drug Policy Alliance, African-Americans make up approximately 14% of the total U.S. population of regular drug users, but account for 37% of those incarcerated for drugs.

Similarly, in 2007, 10.5% of whites and 12.2% of blacks in Washington, D.C. reported smoking marijuana; however, 91% of those arrested for marijuana crimes in that jurisdiction were black (Kain, 2011). Scholars have argued that these actions do nothing to address the real problem of drug use and abuse in this country. One could argue the same about current immigration related policy.

Pacification Mechanism 3—Immigration Detention and the Incarcerative Industrial Complex

The criminalization of immigration further justifies the building up of the criminal industrial complex, thereby providing further expansion of one of the key mechanisms of pacification. While the connection between immigration and the criminal justice system dates back to the war of 1812 (Daniels, 2006), there has been a significant expansion of for-profit corporations involved in the incarceration of immigrants during the last 30 years (Simon, 1998). Originally, the impetus for the involvement of for-profit prisons was spurred by states' desires for cost cutting; the belief was that the private sector would operate various levels of incarceration facilities more efficiently than the states (Mason, 2012). In fact, given that the purpose of for-profit companies is to maximize profits in each fiscal quarter, these corporations have sought to find new populations in need of incarceration; hence their involvement in immigration detention.

While for-profit prison corporations have denied lobbying or involvement in the political process in regard to immigration policy, this is not the case. Just one example of the relationship between for-profit prison corporations and the legislative process is the fact that two of the largest private prison companies are current paying members of the American Legislative Exchange Council (ALEC). ALEC is an organization that is involved with state legislators, the federal government, and other institutions to form private-public relationships that have played a distinct role in the creation of legislation related to the criminalization of immigration. In addition, several key players from the private prison corporations Corrections Corporation of America and The GEO Group were in meetings with legislators and ALEC during the creation of Arizona's S.B. 1070 which became a model of legislation for several states considering similar laws. In addition, a recent investigation found that two of Arizona Governor Jan Brewer's top aids had previously been employed as lobbyists for the private prison industry (Sullivan, 2010).

Further evidence of the nature of for-profit prisons being motivated to fill bed space and turn a profit, is the lower quality of services and advocacy detained individuals receive compared to non-profit prisons. Blakely and Bumphus (2004) found that private prison workers earn less and are trained less than prison workers in public prisons. In addition, these authors found that those who were incarcerated in privately run facilities experience more violence than those housed in public prisons or jails. The long-term consequences of detention in privately run facilities are not completely known. However, similar to other pacification mechanisms, the detention of undocumented immigrants is a strategy that mollifies the public, allowing for the disregard of the actual issues at hand.

Conclusion

In this article, we explored the various ways in which immigration is "utilized" and how its problematization has lead toward a pacification of the American populous. This is not meant to imply that a unidirectional relationship exists between those in power and those not in power. Through various political processes and the problematization of immigration, the blaming of immigration for a host of problems has become something of a national pastime. These strategies serve as mechanisms for pacification, whereby other explanations for various social problems and dilemmas are not fully explored. Instead, the processes of pacification and constructing undocumented immigration as a fundamental cause of America's economic decline, and a host of social problems, can rest squarely on undocumented migration and transmigration.

The impact of this pacification is powerful and pervasive. Most significantly, major structural problems within the American and global economies are left largely unexplained by large segments of the population who view immigration as the root of unemployment. In a related issue, by criminalizing undocumented immigrants, new realities of globalization and transnationalism are not fully explored in the mainstream media. Since the focus of discourse is on the "criminal behavior" of immigrants, it's not on structural and political factors that have contributed to undocumented immigration. For instance, the role of the North American Free Trade Agreement (Wellman, 2012) and the creation of the network of maquiladoras on the U.S.-Mexico border have had profound impacts on the flow of undocumented immigrants, as do shortages of agricultural labor in the American South (Cobb, Molina & Sokulsky, 1989). In short, this pacification leads to a curtailment of national debate around issues of extreme importance. Additionally, this focus on the problematized other, the undocumented immigrant, serves to deter more Americans from learning about transnational and global realities. Such isolationism does not serve the American populous and our integration into a global community.

As the problematization of undocumented and documented immigration alike is not a problem unique to the North American context, this work has relevance for all countries where political forces blame undocumented immigrants for a host of social problems. Social workers working with transmigration populations must understand the pervasiveness of this system of pacification, and the potential psychosocial impacts on their clients. It would be impossible for undocumented immigrants to not internalize these sentiments. This is lamentable, as transmigrants are especially at risk for a host of psychosocial ailments (Furman & Negi, 2007). As transnationally oriented social workers begin to further conceptualize transnational social services, they must build into their interventions methods to help contend with the effects of this systemic alienation. Those who encourage and work with natural transnational social supports and social development programs should also consider the impact of depression caused by these forces, and consider alliances with mental health and other professionals. In conclusion, social workers and others must advocate for the use of a transnational, global lens when exploring social policy. Helping to encourage global and transnational thinking will help to caste a more holistic, less punitive means of understanding the plight of undocumented migrants.

Discussion Question

1. What is meant by the term pacification?
2. What are the various pacification strategies described in this chapter?
3. Describe, in detail, the strategy that has been most successful in pacifying the public.

References

Andreas, P. (2000). Border games: Policing the U.S.-Mexico divide. Ithica, NY: Cornell University Press.

Aman, A. C., & Rehrig, G. (2011). The domestic face of globalization: Law's role in the integration of immigrants in the United States. Legal Studies

Research Paper, #196, Indiana University School of Law. Bloomington, Indiana: University of Indiana.

Ashdown, G. G. (2006). The blueing of America: The bridge between the war on drugs and the war on terror. University of Pittsburgh Law Review, 67(4), 753–802.

Bacon, D. (2010). Federal raids against immigrant workers on the rise. Race, poverty and the environment, fall. Retrieved December 28, 2010 from http://urbanhabitat.org/node/5826 http://urbanhabitat.org/node/5826.

Beck, R. (2012, June 15). Obama's move on immigration is an unconstitutional disaster for the unemployed. Retrieved on July 16, 2012 from http://www.foxnews.com/opinion/2012/06/15/obama-move-on-immigration-is-unconstitutional-disaster-for-unemployed/#ixzz20pDM1COQ.

Blakely, C.R. & Bumphus, V.W. (2004). Private and public sector prisons—a comparison of selected characteristics. Federal Probation, 68, 27–33.

Byler, C. (2005). Pacifiying the Moros: American military government in the Southern Phillipines, 1899–1913. Military Review, May/June, 41–45.

Chin, G. J. (2011). Race, the war on drugs and the consequences of criminal conviction. Journal of Gender, Race & Justice, 5(3), 253–262.

Cobb, S. L., Molina, D. J., & Sokulsky, K. (1989). The impact of maquiladoras on commuter flows in the Texas-Mexican Border. Journal of Borderland Studies, 4(1), 71–88.

Daniels, R. (2006, Winter/Spring 2006). Immigration Policy in a Time of War: The United States, 1939–1945. Journal of American Ethnic History, 25(2/3), 107–116. Retrieved July 14, 2008, from Academic Search Premier database.

Ducat, L., Thomas, S., & Blood, W. (2009). Sensationalising sex offenders and sexual recidivism: Impact of the Serious Sex Offender Monitoring Act 2005 on media reportage. Australian Psychologist, 44(3), 156–165.

Drug Policy Alliance (n.d.). Race and the Drug War. Retrieved on July 24, 2012 from http://www.drugpolicy.org/issues/race-and-drug-war.

Edsall, Thomas B. (2012, July 1). Playing It Dangerously Safe. The New York Times. Retrieve from http://campaignstops.blogs.nytimes.com/2012/07/01/playing-it-dangerously-safe/.

Freeman, G. P. (2011). Comparative analysis of immigration politics: A retrospective. American Behavioral Scientist, 55 (12), 1541–1561.

Furman, R., Ackerman, A., Loya, M., Jones, S., & Negi, N. (2012). The criminalization of immigration: Value conflicts for the social work profession. Journal of Sociology and Social Welfare, 39(1), 169–185.

Furman, R., Langer, C. L., Sanchez, T. W., & Negi, N. J. (2007). A qualitative study of immigration policy and practice dilemmas for social work students. Journal of Social Work Education, 43(1), 133–146.

Furman, R., & Negi, N. (2007). Social work practice with transnational Latino populations. International Social Work, 50(1), 107–112.

Guevarra, A. R. (2010). Marketing dreams, manufacturing heroes: The transnational labor brokering of Filipino Workers. New Brunswick, NJ: Rutgers University Press.

Gramsci, Antonio. (1971). Selection from the Prison Notebooks. Translated and edited by Quintin Hoare and Geoffrey Nowell-Smith. New York: International Publishers.

Gusfield, J. R. (1981). The culture of public problems. Chicago: University of Chicago Press.

Hall, Stewart. (1997). Representation: Cultural Representations and Signifying Practices. Thousand Oaks, Calif.: Sage Publications.

Hetherington, M. J., & Weiler, J. D. (2009). Autoritarianism and polarization in American politics. New York: Cambridge University Press.

Higgins, G. E., Gabbidon, S. L., Martin, F. (2010). The role of race/ethnicity and race relations on public opinion related to the immigration and crime link. Journal of Criminal Justice, 38(1), 51–56.

Immigration Policy Center (April, 2011). Q & A guide to state immigration laws: What you need to know if your state is considering Arizona SB 1070-type legislation. Special Report. Retrieved on April 16, 2012 http://www.immigrationpolicy.org/special-reports/qa-guide-state-immigration-laws. Jacobson, R. D. (2008). The new nativism: Proposition 187 and the debate over immigration. Minneapolis, MN: University of Minnesota Press.

Kain, E. (2011, Aug. 19). Race and the War on Drugs. Forbes Online. Retrieved on July 24, 2012 from http://www.forbes.com/sites/erikkain/2011/08/19/race-and-the-war-on-drugs/.

Lusane, C. (1991). Pipe dream blues: Racism and the war on drugs. Boston, MA: South End Press.

Maclear, M. (1981). The ten thousand day war, Vietnam: 1945–1975. New York: Avon.

Martin, P. (2012). Immigration and farm labor: What's next. Choices: The Magazine of Food, Farm and resource issues, 27(1), Retrieved on July 1, 2012, http://www.choicesmagazine.org/magazine/pdf/cmsarticle_216.pdf.

Mason, C. (2012). Too Good to be True: Private Prisons in America. Washington, DC: TheSentencing Project.

Negi, N., & Furman, R. (2010). (eds.). Transnational social work practice. New York: Columbia University Press.

Neocleous, M. (1996). Perpetual war, or 'war and war again': Schmitt, Foucault, fascism. Philosophy & Social Criticism, 22(2), 47–66.

Neocleous, M. (2010) War as Peace, Peace as Pacification. Radical Philosophy, 159(1), 8–17.

Neocleous, M. (2011a). "A brighter and nicer life": Security as pacification. Social & Legal Studies, 20(2), 191–208.

Neocleous, M. (2011b). The police of civilization: The war on terror as civilising offensive. International Political Sociology, 5(2), 144–159.

Nevins, J. (2002). Operation Gatekeeper: The rise of the "Illegal Alien" and the making of the U.S. Mexico boundary. New York: Routledge.

Nielsen, J. (2009). Locking down our borders: How anti-immigration sentiment led to unconstitutional legislation and the erosion of fundamental principles of American government. Journal of Law and Policy. 18(1), 459–502.

Pinard, M. D. (2006). Thesis: The American and South Vietnamese pracification efforts. Ann Arbor, Michigan, University of Michigan.

Simon, J. (1998). Refugees in a carceral age: The rebirth of immigration prisons in the United States. Public Culture, 10(3), 577–607.

Sullivan, L (2010, October 29). Shaping State Laws With Little Scrutiny. National Public Radio. Retreived on April 14, 2012, from http://www.npr.org/2010/10/29/130891396/shaping-state-laws-with-little-scrutiny.

Szalavitz, M. (2011, June 17). Top 10 Unhealthy Side Effects of the War on Drugs: How the War on Drugs Harms American Health. Time: Healthland. Retrieved on July 17, 2012 fromhttp://healthland.time.com/2011/06/17/top-10-unhealthy-side-effects-of-the-war-on-drugs/#richard-m-nixon#ixzz21ZaO1h00.

Tumlin, K. C. (2004). Suspect first: How terrorism policy is reshaping immigration policy. California Law Review, 19(4), 1175–1240.

Watson, D. (2005). Record Numbers in US Prisons: Women, children and immigrants top incarceration increases. Retrieved on July 26, 2012 from http://www.wsws.org/articles/2005/nov2005/pris-n05.shtml.

Wellman, C. H. (2012). Immigration restrictions in the real world. Philosophical Studies, DOI: 10.1007/s11098-012-9901-z.

Werner, D. (2011). SPCL ready for long legal battle over Alabama's harsh anti-immigrant law. Southern Poverty Law Center. Retrieved October 23rd, 2011 from http://www.splcenter.org/get-informed/news/.

Chapter Three

The Criminalization of the Immigrant and Deportation as a Theater of Cruelty

(Presentation Given to the Symposium of Performance and Justice, New York City, March 2013)

David C. Brotherton

Introduction

More than 350,000 non-citizen immigrants are deported from the United States every year (Immigration and Customs Enforcement [ICE] 2012).[1] Of these, many are long time permanent residents who have been socialized by American cultural norms and who leave behind multiple family ties referred to as the "collateral damage" of the immigration/deportation system (International Law Center 2010, Brotherton and Barrios 2011). They are the social detritus of the American Dream, the "wasted lives" to use Bauman's (2004) term for surplus people in late modernity, and the result of the socially bulimic process for so many contemporary immigrants entering "advanced" capitalist societies i.e., the dialectic of cultural inclusion and socio-economic exclusion (Young 2011).

---

1. The problem with this extraordinary outcome/result of our immigration policies is that such outcomes are not at all so abnormal seen over time. According to the legal scholar Dan Kanstroom over 40 million residents in this U.S. have somehow been involved in the deportation process. What is perhaps most strange is the degree to which much of this has not been sufficiently studied, analyzed and theorized. The ever growing prevalence of permanent exile or what Kanstroom (2007) calls "post-entry social control" is a huge oversight by American social science including its disciplines of anthropology, sociology, political science and legal studies.

In this chapter I will approach the phenomenon of deportation in the United States drawing on my participant observations as an expert witness in immigration appeals court dramas over the past six years. Using the dramaturgical license and analytical insights of sociology, criminology and performance studies I will particularly employ the work of the surrealist dramatist Antonin Artaud who in the 1930s developed the notion of a Theater of Cruelty (Artaud 1958, 1971, orig. 1934). It was Artaud's conviction that theater needed to show the vibrant, experiential and disturbing reality of life beneath those symbolic universes of modernity that reproduced "falsehood and illusion" and the "dictatorship of the text."

Immigration Enforcement, Appeals and the Deportee

U.S. immigration/deportation policy has become increasingly restrictive and draconian due to the passing of three acts: the Immigration Reform and Control Act of 1986, the Immigration Act of 1990, and the Illegal Immigration and Immigration Reform Act (IIIAIRA) of 1996. Such policies have in turn been heavily influenced by the war on drugs (especially the Anti-Drug Abuse Act in 1988, which introduced the term "aggravated felony") and the war on terrorism (particularly through the Antiterrorism and Effective Death Penalty Act of 1996 and the Patriot Act of 2001). Under the Obama regime, more than 400,000 immigrants are deported yearly with around 50% of these called "removals," i.e., immigrants who are more or less permanently residing in the United States having been convicted of a crime rather than a visa violation. In 2011 Congress appropriated nearly $700 million for the government's deportation programs variously called the Criminal Alien Program (CAP), Secure Communities, 278(g) and the National Fugitives Operations Program (NFOP). This investment in increased border control has increased from $23 million seven years prior and represents a dramatic shift from policing the border to the interior control of immigrant communities (Golash-Boza 2013). With the heightened level of expulsion of permanent residents the "collateral damage" among U.S. families is of growing concern with more than 50,000 American children without one or both parents due to deportation (International Law Center 2010).

Once in the deportation/criminal justice administrative system non-citizen immigrants have no constitutional rights and no guaranteed access to legal representation. In general, immigrant communities are a vulnerable community before the law as a result of language differences and the large numbers who lack citizenship and/or legal residency but the extraordinary increase in the judicial powers of ICE and its umbrella organization the Department of Homeland Security since 9/11 has yet to be checked by the U.S.'s division of executive powers (Kanstroom 2007, 2013). Detained immigrants therefore often find themselves without sufficient legal defense and enter a system geared to imprison and punish not simply to contain. A recent media report revealed that every day more than 300 detainees are placed in solitary confinement in camps designed to keep subjects until they are administratively expelled or allowed to remain (Urbina and Rentz 2012).

Under current deportation laws, the only chance of appeal for a deportable male permanent resident, charged with an "aggravated felony," is to successfully claim that agents of the receiving nation will torture him. For a female "deportable alien," an added option is to demonstrate that she faces the risk of death and/or serious injury at the hands of a male assailant as described in the Violence Against Women Act of 1994. The government's commitment to permanently exile deportable immigrants and the inflexibility of the currently laws are shown in New York City where of the 45,000 deportation cases the government was recently asked to review only 1.4% were granted prosecutorial discretion (Chavkin 2012).

Theory, Drama and the Deportee

Scholars have begun to increasingly highlight the use of an array of criminal justice and immigration laws and their apparatuses to socially control immigrant communities (Kanstroom 2007, Coutin 2007, DeGenova and Peutz 2010, Stumpf 2006). This observation accords with those who argue that state threats against immigrants are a particular form of Othering in late modern capitalism, a process of circumscribing or thwarting social citizenship that Young (op cit.) describes as bulimic rather than just exclusionary. This highly charged and contradictory process is carried out through several intersecting dynamics: (i) the pushes and pulls of the political economy with its restructuring of work, redistribution of wealth, irrational reward system, and heightening of class divisions; (ii) the universalism of consumer culture and its promotion of need, individualism, and freedom; (iii) the technological revolution of information generation and dissemination; (iv) the evolution of the social control industry with its expansion of gulags, laws, surveillance systems, and constraints on civil and democratic liberties; and (v) the porous and fluid nature of all physical, social, and cultural borders. Together, these processes make it difficult for individuals to formulate a coherent sense of self and lead to a ubiquitous condition that he calls "ontological insecurity."

This process is typical of late modernity with its heightened need for ordering and order maintenance (Bauman 2004) and is accentuated by the introduction of a "new penology" (Feeley and Simon 1992) and a "culture of control" (Garland 2002) based on a set of beliefs about the pathological nature of criminals and other types of socially constructed human pollutants. In this brave new world of governance through crime and fear, there is a presumed need to take preemptive action and exact extreme punishments to ensure that risks to the good, the pure, and the healthy never materialize (Douglas 1966). Welch (2001) adds that the moral panics used to mediate, rationalize, and frame these strategies reflect the needs of an industry of crime control (Christie 1993) where the deportee has become a source of revenue and an object of financial desire on the part of multinational security corporations. There are few attempts in the literature however to describe the drama of these mass expulsions.

Drama has long been what Jenks (2003) calls a "root metaphor" in the description of human conduct and behavior particularly in the realm of transgression, rule-breaking, and different forms of social control, both coercive and consensus based. The sociologist Ervin Goffman is one of the more famous exponents of this approach through his treatises on total institutions, the representations of self, stigma and the front and back stage performances of the everyday while Shakespeare is routinely invoked in the social sciences to underscore the intrinsic theatricality and pathos of the human condition. Meanwhile Dwight Conquergood was one of the most accomplished exponents of the performativity of everyday life among the subaltern classes, arguing that the asymmetrical power relations between the haves and have-nots are revealed through their rites, rituals and resistances. But it is the provocative ideas of Artaud and his compelling notion of a theater of cruelty that has mostly drawn my attention in this treatment and interpretation of deportation or what I call the *expulsion play.*

For Artaud, theater was a holistic, all-sided dramatic vehicle to uncover the nihilistic essence of the human experience set in a world of chaotic, unexpected and fluid meanings. This type of theater forces the audience to go below the appearance of performance rituals, the inevitability of order and the natural logic of scenes mechanically contrived. Artaud's aim was to shock the audience into feeling and experiencing a new social reality that is much closer to our lived reality and it is in this theatrical compulsion that Artaud uses the term "cruelty."

If we draw on this radical reconsideration of theater and apply it to scenes in an immigration court we see that the multiple on-set and off-set communicative gestures and interactions represent at one level society's reproduced orderliness and bureaucratic rationality but at another level those related "realities" that include all the convulsion, passion, rejection, resistance, and imagination which are the hallmarks of Artaud's approach. Further, in this performance/ criminological interpretation of the court we encounter audiences who cannot simply observe and passively absorb but are thrust into an uncertain realm of dynamic psycho-social tensions and felt contradictions. The resulting transgressions are viewed through a lens that privileges the dialectical agency of historical subjects/objects located within conflicting, merging and cross-cutting material and symbolic forces.

I argue that this critical inter-disciplinary approach is especially appropriate for our immigration courts where people's imaginary shared rights are annulled through laws based on the residual logics of Runaway Slave Acts, Indian Removal Acts, Chinese-Exclusion acts, Japanese internment Executive Orders and Operation "Wetbacks." The contradictions of living in an Immigration/ Deportation Nation are nowhere more manifest than in the absurdities and ironies espied through these expulsion plays.[2]

Theater of Cruelty in the Everyday Immigration Courts

The five scenes below are taken directly from deportation proceedings and are followed by my performance-based and criminological comments. They consist of settings, interactions, courtroom pronunciamentos, acts of defiance, and gestures of would-be submission all noted as I sat and observed as an expert witness. I consider them poignantly dramatic instances of a theatrical criminology of deportation that has striking parallels with Artaud's theater of cruelty.

Corporate Style and the Dictatorship of Texts

We approach a low-rise building in a "business district" not far from the Canadian border. It sits at the end of a newly built ex-urban sub-division that pre-

---

2. Catherine Cole, the performance studies scholar, also makes an interesting analysis of the Truth and Reconciliation Commission hearings in the South Africa, revealing the wide-ranging theatricality of the process played out on a national stage. The presentation of the "unspeakable" and the recollection of traumatic events by both the victims and the perpetrators are deeply emotional and dramatic moments that when staged at this level are collectively experienced rather than the more private and personal experiences of the closed court room (see Cole 2011).

sumably was farm land until recently and is now filled with corporate-like, non-descript franchise hotels such as Embassy Suites, Travel Lodge, the usual fare of mid-level accommodations for travelers and business folk alike—all owned by global leisure corporations. The building in its highly fuctionalist, box-like appearance blends in with the surrounding hotels. I enter with the immigration lawyer having left our cell phones and keys, etc., in the car. I just have a notebook and pen and the lawyer has his laptop and case files. We check in with the guards at the desk, most of whom are white. The exchange is perfunctory. All the guards are wearing knife-proof vests. We pass through a metal detector and then take our seats. There are three dark-skinned women in their 30s and 40s waiting to see their spouses or boyfriends. One woman has a baby in her arms.

Next to the door, behind which is the visiting area for detainees (who sit behind thick Plexiglass), is a large poster with "office of detention and removal operations" emblazoned at the top. Underneath it says "41 Performance-Based National Detention Standards" and lists prominently among them "improved conditions of confinement" and "a safe, humane environment for detainees and detention center employees." On another wall is a similarly large poster with a picture of a library on which is superimposed several white inmates or detainees bent over opened books. Below is a caption that reads: "Electronic access to legal information and publications; special assistance for non-English speaking detainees; a grievance system that allows detainees to appeal their initial classification level."

Comment:

It is impossible to over emphasize the power of the state over the individual in deportation cases. The vast majority of deportable aliens have no legal representation, do not fully understand the laws arraigned against them and do not have sufficient cultural capital to digest complex volumes of law and legal cases. The "dictatorship of the text" is complete. Abstract texts in tomes contain the legitimacy of the internment. Texts as forms of symbolic violence bear down on detained subjects, yet they also are used to give the appearance of human rights for the incarcerated, as if the mere mention of their presence somehow guarantees that a rational, fair, open and natural legal process is at hand. Meanwhile, the corporate architectural style of buildings for imprisonment purposes is another layer of this dictatorial relationship—a seamless reminder of the asymmetrical power relations that are at the basis of deportation.

The Culture of Permanent Exclusion

Frank Madera sits in a wheel chair facing a berobed judge perched on a dais in an immigration appeals court room housed in a deportee detention center deep in upstate New York. Frank, born in the Dominican Republic but now a permanent resident of the United States for the past fifty years, faces permanent removal from the United States due to his conviction on an "aggravated felony" charge.

Frank is 57 years old and blind due to lack of medical attention for cataracts while in Fishkill prison where he has just served three years for burglary (on the orders of local drug dealers). Frank has also endured 5 strokes in the last two years partly related to his Type 1 chronic diabetes and still suffers from paralysis down his right side. Frank's fragile and deteriorating physical and mental state is compounded by the bipolar disorder with which he was diagnosed more than a decade ago. His functional illiteracy only exacerbates his feelings of powerlessness and confusion. Frank is trying to contest the government's order for his removal.

Lawyer (he is summing up his appeal to have the removal order rescinded):

"Your honor, it is clear based on Mr. Madera's testimony and that of our expert witness that if the government's request to have Mr. Madera removed is granted it will be nothing short of a death sentence. He is a sick man, a very sick man. He was effectively blinded by our prison system and he suffers from multiple life-threatening ailments. If deported it will be tantamount to torture because the country that will receive him will not provide him with either the medicines or the treatments he desperately needs. Further, he is a deportee and we have already heard about the terrible stigma suffered by deportees in the Dominican Republic. They are harassed, denied employment, imprisoned, blamed for every ill facing the country, and forced to live in fear. How can Mr. Madera possibly survive under these circumstances? I ask your honor to use your discretion and make the decision to grant Mr. Madera the relief that he has requested. No one benefits from his removal."

Judge: "Thank you both of you for your closing statements. I have listened carefully to your arguments and I have taken into account the statements of the expert witness and Mr. Madera. However, I find that the case you have presented and the arguments therein do not meet the stipulations of the law that would allow me to grant Mr. Madera relief. Mr. Madera, you willfully broke the law in this country not once but several times. Mr. Madera, you knew what you were doing. No one forced you to carry out these acts. They all amount to aggravated felonies under current legislation as well as moral turpitude. I fully understand, Mr. Madera, that life will not be easy for you on your return to your homeland, but I am not convinced that the limitations on health services amount to a form of government torture. It simply is not the same. Mr. Madera, I order you to be removed and, of course, you may consult with you lawyer about the possibility of an appeal...."

Frank stares ahead quite impassively. The translator is explaining the judge's verdict to Frank. A correction officer pulls on his wheel chair and starts to escort Frank out and back to jail. I look at Frank who stares back and I shake my head.

Db: I'm so sorry, Frank. I did my best. I'm so sorry.

Frank: That's OK ... it could have been worse.

Lawyer (we are walking out the Detention Center after he has visited briefly with Frank): This is why I do corporate law ... I just deal with numbers, money, profit and losses. Who gives a fuck? I don't. Ok, I fight hard for my client and do my best to get a good settlement but if we lose, who cares? It's just money. If I lose here someone dies. I go home and I can't sleep for thinking I could have done better.

Comment:

Cruelty comes in many forms and guises in deportation hearings. What possible danger does Frank represent to U.S. society? Or, more appropriately, what does Frank represent to a branch of U.S. society that appears to be acting with more and more irrational verve and intent? Yet, the upholders of the laws are still engaged in and wedded to a form of morality play as if failure to repeat these mantras of good versus evil, deserving versus undeserving, will only lead to some social unraveling. Purity, argued the anthropologist Mary Douglas, was a result of society's penchant for cleansing ourselves of human filth. But what exactly is being expunged? The bad immigrant or the immigrant who goes bad? The redundant immigrant (to use Bauman's phrase)? The punished immigrant who functions as a deterrent to others? And what of the vindictiveness on display? The corporate probono lawyer is correct: the handling of cases that revolve around pure profit motives and abstract data of the ledger book mask the actual social injury involved in the extraction of value. It is easy to distance oneself from such proceedings. In cases like that of Frank the social harm is conspicuous and its causes are equally unambiguous. For anyone with a conscience and a sense of compassion, it is impossible not to be affected and to ask oneself if more could have been done to mitigate the injury. It is not just Frank and his future that is at stake but that of the human condition itself.

The Artaudian Moment

"What do you think faces your son if he is deported to the Dominican Republic?" asks the lawyer.

"Delinquency, nothing but delinquency. Nothing good can come of this. I know he will face terrible things, I know this. My country will harm him, I know this."

"Do you think your son will be tortured if he is returned?" asks the lawyer

The mother just sits after the question is translated. She looks apoplectically at the audience. God knows what's going through her mind; the question is too pointed, too harrowing to be answered.

"Do you understand the questions?" asks the judge.

Again, the mother just looks at the audience and pats her chest. She then begins to talk, as if channeling something from another universe.

"Yes, I believe something terrible will happen to him. I believe the police will hurt him. I can't bear to think about it. I don't want to talk about it. I don't want to think about this evil. Can I say something? May I say something?" the mother asks the judge.

"Yes, you may," replies the judge as he looks down at his feet as if to communicate, "Here we go again."

The mother then gets to her feet and raises her hands in the air as if praying in a Pentecostal church.

"Oh God, Oh Jesus, Oh Maria, I pray to you, release my son from this trial. Oh Judge, please forgive my son. Please have the power, the pity to allow my son to go free. Allow him to come back to his mother and father, that's all we ask. He's a good boy. He doesn't mean ill to anyone. What use is this to take him away from us and his children. Please, please I beg you...."

The mother continues for several more minutes beseeching the judge to release her son. The family members are again sobbing uncontrollably, men and women alike are howling in grief. Even one of the guards, a bulky African-American man, is beginning to break down and I see tears start to run slowly down his cheeks. The mother suddenly stops, turns away from the judge and looking glassy-eyed, collapses into the chair and closes her eyes. There is now pandemonium in the court room and the judge orders one of the guards to call a nurse. After about three minutes the mother comes around, having fainted, and is holding her chest and breathing heavily. One of her daughters runs over and holds her head, stroking her hair gently and whispering softly that "everything's all right," which is about the furthest thing from the truth right now.

Comment:

The torment that underlies much of the deportation process is nowhere more evident than when the family members and the loved ones of the deportable subject are present. Here we see an example of the "convulsion" that Artaud refers to in his manifesto. It is that aspect of the dynamic, chaotic reality that he felt was belied by most dramatic interpretations in the tradition of bourgeois theater. In this scene the mother confronts the insufferability of the moment her tragedy comes full circle. She confronts the power of the state and its agents to take away the child she bore and struggled to raise ... and for what? She knows her son is not a criminal but the victim of a travesty of justice for which there will be no possibility of correction, no innocence project stepping in, no recourse to a higher, more reasonable level of the judiciary ... just the denouement of a legal process that should never have been allowed to begin if democracy had been truly functioning.

A Moment of Resistance

"So, what do you understand by torture?"

"Well, for me, it is the application of extreme forms of pain and punishment to someone in an attempt to get information and just to terrorize someone. This punishment can be physical, it can come from beatings but also from the denial of food to someone. It can also be psychological and emotional." The niece makes an impressive statement and surprises me at how cool, calm and collected she can be under the circumstances.

"Thank you," says the lawyer. "So, do you think that this form of torture that will be facing your uncle when he goes back to his homeland? If so, why do you think this will happen?" asks the lawyer, who is now beginning to regain some of his composure.

"Well, let me see," says the niece. "I can't say for certain that this will happen to him, but I do know how Dominican society feels towards deportees and I do know how violent and brutal the police are. I can tell you that Dominicans think of deportees as less than human. They are nothing to them and are blamed for everything that goes wrong in the country. And if they are thinking this, then you can imagine what the police are thinking. The police simply treat them like dirt. They beat them, kill them, torture them, they do whatever they like to them."

"How do you know this?" asks the defense lawyer.

"Because when I've been back there for holidays, when I've been staying in the capital, I hear what people say about them and I have had dealings with the police just driving around," answers the niece.

"*Now hold on here,*" *says the judge.* "*None of this means anything. This has nothing at all to do with the conditions of torture that need to apply in this case. For a start, your definition of torture is all wrong. As I've said before, it is about pulling fingernails, taking out teeth, attaching electrodes to testicles … that's torture. Not all this talk about being denied food and psychological punishment, that's not what we're talking about under this law. And as for giving testimony on the probability of torture, you've proceeded to talk about how bad the police are and how nasty the people can be toward deportees but that's irrelevant, absolutely irrelevant. You have to be specific, factual. Mr. Crichter, once again I must ask you, have you prepared your witness?*"

"*Yes, judge, as much as I could. I am just trying to show that …*"

"*I know what you are trying to show, Mr. Crichter, and I am trying to keep this trial focused and it is proving impossible.*" *The judge then turns back to Ms. X …*

"*Ms. X., do you understand what I am saying?*"

"*Yes, judge. I understand what you are saying but do you understand what I am saying? I think I understand what torture is and maybe it doesn't satisfy the needs of this court and maybe I have it all wrong but I don't think so. It is this court that has it all wrong. If you want to know what torture is, this is torture. What you are doing to my uncle is torture. Look at it here! Look at what the laws are doing! It is tearing up our family. It is tearing my uncle away from his children, his mother, his father and his loved ones. What justice is there in this? I have done my research. I have studied criminal justice and I don't see any here today. There is torture, yes, and it is here. This is torture but there is no justice.*"

Comment:

Clearly there has to be some kind of push back. For years, however, few immigrant community leaders took up the challenge to shine a light on yet another flagrant abuse of the subjugated by the judicial branch of the host society. Nor did the media, both corporate and public, do much to raise the issues that go to the core of immigration and citizenship. So overwhelmed did the immigrant community feel, so aware of the negative stereotypes constantly foisted on it by the white-dominated power structure that it felt afraid to expose its darker side any more. Consequently, it focused most of its energy and resources on promoting the integration of its members into the great American mosaic. But, there comes a time when even its most integrated members cannot abide the injustices visited upon their own people. Above, we read precisely of such a case that is responded to by a transgressive act from below, a willful gesture of resilience and resistance, using an alternative transcript of the dominated. The juxtaposition of the notions of torture and justice is brilliantly posited to highlight the hypocrisy, absurdity and suffering of the moment. A riposte so full of subversive meaning that for a few brief minutes the status quo is ruptured and the world is turned the right way up. No longer tolerant of the abstract rationalisms of class-based legal coda, no longer accepting of the given tropes of this "correctional" social drama, the young woman underscores all the irony of proceedings that needlessly rip apart the social fabric of her vulnerable family. Her consciousness has changed. She will never be the same.

Lost in Translation— An Incomprehensible Moment

Judge (he is projected into the court room on a large screen since he was recently the victim of a physical attack in this deportation appeals court room):

"Do you understand what I am saying Mr. Suarez? Translator, are you getting across to him what I am saying?"

Translator: "Usted entiende lo que dice el juez Senor Suarez."

Suarez: "Si, yes, I do, but I'm just telling you what I did according to the charges."

Judge: "I don't care about the charges, Mr. Suarez, I just want the truth. On your presentencing docket it says that you were on the periphery of this drug transaction. You were a kind of middleman. The undercover officer asked your associate Papas for the drugs and Papas told you to go and get them. You got them from a third party and returned them to Papas who got the money. I don't know if he gave you any but that's what it says here. Now you're telling me something different. But now you're telling me the undercover officer asked you for the drugs and you went and got them and you took the money. That makes you the leader of this drug enterprise doesn't it? Do you understand Mr. Suarez? There is a big difference here and it makes a difference to the argument of your counsel who says that you do not meet the criteria of being a drug trafficker. Your crime, according to your attorney, cannot be called a "particularly serious crime" as described by the U.S. Attorney General in 2004. This change in your testimony Mr. Suarez has significant consequences. Do you understand?"

Translator: ... in Spanish ...

Suarez: (silence ...)

Judge: "I can't hear you Mr. Suarez. Can you hear me Mr. Suarez?"

Suarez: (looks at counsel and tries to ask him something)

Gov. Lawyer: "Judge, I object, Mr. Suarez cannot consult with his counsel."

Judge: "Yes, Mr. Suarez, you cannot ask someone else what to say. You just have to answer and speak the truth."

Suarez: (Looking puzzled and obviously uncomfortable) "Ok, Judge, what I have said is what happened."

Judge: "Mr. Suarez, do you understand what's at stake here? Do you understand that you are in deportation proceedings and that you could be permanently removed from this country based on your actions in the past? Based on what you are now telling me happened in the past?"

The Suarez family members sit and shake their heads. Suarez's mother is crying and tears stream down her cheeks as she receives the translation from the Dominican paralegal working for Suarez's counsel. Jessie, Suarez's lawyer, does his best to sport a poker face, trying not to give any hint of the profound disappointment he must be feeling.

Judge: I think that's enough for today. I will hear the expert witness the next time we meet....

Comment:

In the deportation judicial process the past can be endlessly reconstructed. The law says that the history of one's criminally transgressive actions can be revisited, redefined, reimagined, recategorized and repunished. It is hard to find such laws anywhere else in the world. Nonetheless, we still think of laws as understandable responses to the potential for deviant, though rational, actions; hence, we hear criminologists talk of the deterrence effect of certain punishments. But when a judge chooses to posit a recent reconstruction of the drug trafficker on the action of a young man some twenty years ago, something is clearly amiss. If we are looking for justice in the expulsion play, we will be disappointed. Rather, the play is saturated with the actions of the unjust with scripts premised on unethical considerations and motives. The result is nearly always that the actor has been prejudged. Despite this, we go through a ritualized process, a performance spectacle with the jousting of the lawyers, posing their questions, lodging their objections, and the judge playing his role as the final arbiter. But woe to the deportable subject who dares ask for legal advice—how dare this person enter the play!

In this case the judge interrogates the subject and conducts the appeal through a beamed-in image like the Wizard of Oz. Alas, there is no yellow brick road for this deportable non-citizen. His bipolar disability will not save him and his mother looks on powerlessly. As part of the audience she cannot remain detached from this dismal display of human interactions, she cannot stop the turn of events as her son is snatched from her by this judicial authority who seemingly has the power to make men and women disappear.

Conclusion

Artaud's work raises numerous questions, such as: Why are human beings so decentered in a society composed of so many centrifugal democratic structures and traditions? Why are so many human beings alienated, marginalized and excluded in a society that is supposed to be so empowering and characterized by individual choice and free will? Who or what provides the legitimacy for the hierarchies and their arrogation of power in so many forms when we are supposed to view freedom and justice as sacred corner stones of our socio-political life? And wherein lies the privilege of a language that banishes, humiliates and subjugates and yet is supposed to be the passage to selfhood and collective identity?

Artaud's sensibilities, which were often rooted in his own personal tragedies (one of his biographers called him the most extraordinary example of self-repair (Eshleman 1995)), have the potential of a rich application to the social and criminological dramas mentioned earlier. This is so clear as we encounter case after case of the brute rationalism of the state and the punishing practices of its agents draining the magic of life from its immigrant subjects.

I argue that the phenomenon of deportation with its courtroom tragedies and its manifold related social, political, economic and cultural dramas can be well served by an Artaudian-influenced analysis and representation. This is particularly so if we remember to include both the visible and invisible expressions of individual and collective social harm in the longue duree of the American democratic project. While the majority of criminological studies are fixated on the positivistic text, usually with the justification that some minutiae of criminological theory is being tested, the big picture of the everyday "suffering" (Bourdieu 2000) of human beings and their attendant agency is missed. In contrast, this exploratory dramaturgical analysis shows how injustice is carried out in our name and with our permission on some of most vulnerable members of our society. It is a feat and a task that I think the extraordinary Mr. Artaud would have welcomed.

Discussion Questions

1. What is meant by a Theater of Cruelty?
2. How does the Theater of Cruelty help make sense of the current immigration debate?
3. Do you agree with the statement that this analysis shows how injustice is carried out.... with our permission? Explain your answer.

References

Artaud, Antonin. 1958. *The Theatre and Its Double*, Trans. Mary Caroline Richards. New York: Grove Weidenfeld.

Artaud, Antonin. 1971. *Collected Works of Antonin Artaud*, Trans. Victor Corti. London: Calder and Boyars.

Bauman, Zygmunt. 2004. *Wasted Lives: Modernity and its Outcasts*. Cambridge, UK: Polity.

Bourdieu, Pierre. 2000. (Translated by Prescilla Parkhurst Ferguson). *The Weight of the World: Social Suffering in Contemporary Society*. Stanford University Press.

Brotherton, David. C. and Luis Barrios. 2011. *Banished to the Homeland: Dominican Deportees and Their Stories of Exile*. New York: Columbia University Press.

Chavkin, Sasha. 2012."NYC Lags in Granting Relief to Some Illegal Immigrants. Accessed 4/2/13 http://www.wnyc.org/articles/wnyc-news/2012/nov/26/nyc-lags-granting-relief-some-illegal-immigrants/.

Christie, Nils. 1993. *Crime Control as Industry. New York: Routledge.*

Cole, Christine. 2011. Performance, Transitional Justice and the Law: South Africa's Truth and Reconciliation Commission" in *Violence Performed: Local Roots and Global Routes of Conflict*. Edited by Patrick Anderson and Jisha Menon. London: Palgrave.

Coutin, Susan B. 2007. *Nations of Emigrants: Shifting Boundaries of Citizenship in El Salvador and the United States*. Ithaca, New York: Cornell University Press.

De Genova, Nichaols and Natalie Peutz. 2010. *The Deportation Regime: Sovereignty, Space and the Freedom of Movement*. Durham, NC: Duke University Press.

Douglas, Mary. 1966. Purity and Danger—an analysis of concepts of pollution and taboo. London: Routledge Classics.

Eshleman, Clayton. 1995. "Introduction" in *Watchfiends and Rack Screams: Works From the Final Period* by Antonin Artaud. Boston: Exact Exchange.

Feeley, Malcom and Jonathan Simon. 1992. The New Penology: Notes on the Emerging Strategy of Corrections and Its Implications. *Criminology* 30(4): 449-474.

Garland, D. 2002. *The Culture of Control: Crime and Social Order in Contemporary Society.* Chicago: The University of Chicago Press.

Golash-Boza, Tanya. 2013. "Obama's Unprecedented Number of Deportations." *Counterpunch.* January 25.

International Human Rights Law Clinic. 2010. *In the Child's Best Interest? The Consequences of Losing a Lawful Parent to Deportation.* Berkeley, CA.

Kanstroom, Daniel. 2013. *Aftermath: Deportation Law and the New American Diaspora.* New York: Oxford University Press.

Kanstroom, Daniel. 2007. *Deportation Nation: Outsiders in American History.* Cambridge, MA. Harvard University Press.

Simon, Jonathan. 2007. *Governing Through Crime: How the War on Crime Transformed American Democracy and Created a Culture of Fear.* New York: Oxford University Press.

Stumpf, Juliet. P. 2006. 'The Crimmigration Crisis: Immigrants, Crime, and Sovereign Power', *American University Law Review* 56: 368.

Urbina, Ian and Catherine Rentz. 2013. Immigrants Held in Solitary Cells, Often for Weeks. New York Times. March 29. A1.

Welch, Michael. 2002. *Detained: Immigration Laws and the Expanding I.N.S. Jail Complex.* Philadelphia: Temple University Press.

Young, Jock. 2011. *The Criminological Imagination.* London: Polity.

SECTION 2

State Laws

Chapter Four

Undocumented Immigration Policy in Arizona

Susanna Jones

The passage of Senate Bill 1070 in Arizona could arguably be the most poignant recent example of the criminalization of undocumented immigrants. Over the past several years Arizona has been a hotbed for issues relating to immigration, especially undocumented immigrants. With the introduction of Senate Bill 1070 (hereafter, SB 1070), also known as the "Support Our Law Enforcement and Safe Neighborhoods Act," Arizona wielded unprecedented political power and authority over immigration issues on a state-level. As a result, SB 1070 has generated reactions from as high as the U.S. Supreme Court to as local as Fuerza!, an Arizona campaign affiliated with a national movement against the prison industrial complex.

SB 1070 was and continues to be a pioneer bill in several ways. The trespassing provision was the first of its kind. The impact of this bill on policy, ideology, discourse, culture and practice regarding the criminalization of immigrants has been profound. Further, SB 1070 has been highly influential with multiple states—including but not limited to, Alabama, Indiana, South Carolina, Pennsylvania, Michigan, Illinois, Rhode Island and Minnesota—drafting copycat legislation.

To be clear, SB 1070 was not the first time that immigrants, especially undocumented immigrants, became targets. Immigrants have been suspect persons in Arizona pre-statehood (statehood was granted in 1912) (Santa Ana & Bustamante, 2012). Groundwork to criminalize undocumented immigrants on a state-level began with California's Proposition 187 (Save Our State) in 1994. California's act preceded the passage of the Illegal Immigration Reform and Immigration Responsibility Act of 1996, which further demonized and criminalized undocumented immigrants. Anti-immigrant legislation continued to build momentum and support on both a state and federal level. In 2007 for instance, the passage of 287g (a federal-level program that began in 1997) sanctioned Maricopa County Sheriff's Department to regularly enforce checking immigration status of people lawfully stopped. Arizona Sheriff Joe Arpaio is an architect of some of the most anti-immigrant law enforcement practices that include forcing a woman to give birth while shackled (Novoa, 2012) and for conducting "crime suppression sweeps" in Latino neighborhoods (Johnson, 2012). These actions lay bare the calculated move to criminalize undocumented immigrants.

What makes Arizona such an important case study when examining the process and practice of criminalizing immigrants? The answer to this question lies first and foremost in the passage of SB 1070 in 2010, which among many things, codified state-level law enforcement police practices that hinge on racial profiling. SB 1070 explicitly links race with criminality targeting the Latino population of Arizona (Santa Ana & Bustamante, 2012).

Second and less obvious is the longstanding racialized discourse of criminality in Arizona that has had profound negative impacts on undocumented immigrants—and other minorities—for a century. At the end of the U.S.-Mexican War of 1848 and the California Gold Rush of 1849, 50,000 Whites/anglos moved to Arizona. As a result, the number of Whites (80% of the state residents) substantially outnumbered the Mexican population (16%) for the first time in Arizona history. Since then Whites have seized economic and cultural dominance. The present day demographic shifts have resulted in Mexicans becoming a majority, including the electorate. The growing number, influence and power of Latino immigrants in Arizona pose a serious threat to white hegemony (Santa Ana & Bustamante, 2012). Coupled with the rise in number of immigrants are discursive and ideological battles about the place of immigrants in American society. Scholars such as Samuel Huntington (2004), for example, describe immigrants, particularly Latinos, as problematic for America's future because of their inability to culturally and linguistically assimilate thereby creating the "clash of civilizations." Huntington's view of immigrants—popularized by mass media and right wing politicians—helped set the context for policies like SB 1070.

Third, as a result of SB 1070, Arizona codified the introduction of corporate influence and power of the prison industry into immigration policy (Johnson, 2012). SB 1070 is an example of how immigration policies are largely motivated by the need for labor, powerful industries and corporate influence. The Bracero Program of 1942-1964, for instance, led to mass migration. It was a time when the agricultural and railroad industries needed low-wage labor power and Mexican nationals filled that need. The agricultural and agribusiness industries lobbied for less restrictionist policies to advance their need for a steady supply of low-wage labor. Yet, the treatment of immigrants and other minorities was no less harsh. Today, by contrast, the prison industry is a powerful lobby that benefits handsomely from restrictionist policies, which take the form of criminalizing undocumented immigrants through the expansion of law enforcement and incarceration. The total cost of incarcerating immigrants in the state of Arizona in 2004 was $91 million, $89.1 million of which was spent on incarcerating non-citizens. Of the 6,496 immigrant inmates in Arizona in 2004, 98% (6,367) were non-citizens while the remaining 2% (129) were naturalized citizens (Gans, 2008). Latinos make up 40% of all federally-sentenced offenders, which is more than triple their share of the total U.S. population. Among the 40% of federal offenders, 29% are non-citizens, while 11% are U.S. citizens (Lopez & Light, 2009). During the past decade, the citizenship profile of people who are incarcerated has shifted to a growing number of non-citizens. Among the population of Latinos offenders, 72% were non-citizens in 2007, up from 61% in 1991 (Lopez & Light, 2009). Furthermore, roughly half of all immigrants detained are held in private detention centers (Johnson, 2012); private prison industry profits are $5 billion a year (Johnson, 2012). Immigrants make up a disproportionate and growing number of the Arizona prison population and the costs of incarceration are growing as state budget expenditures. The Arizona Department of Corrections has an operating budget of $644 million dollars (Gans, 2008). Fourteen percent of that budget is spent incarcerating non-citizens. In 2004 there were 6,367 non-citizen inmates (compared to 129 naturalized citizens) who spent on average 249 days incarcerated (compared to 260 days for naturalized citizens). The budget cost to incarcerate non-citizens was $89 million for 2004, while that same cost for naturalized citizens was $1.9 million. The average cost of incarceration per day is $56.19. It is evident, therefore, that the cost of incarcerating immigrants translates into a financial gain for the prison industry.

Predecessors to SB 1070

Arizona has a past tainted with anti-immigrant sentiment and racial tension. Jim Crow racial segregation was the norm for most of Arizona's state history. Interracial marriage, for instance, was banned as were voting rights to Indigenous peoples, even those who worked outside of the reservation and paid taxes. African Americans were banned from attending public schools with white children (Santa Ana & Bustamante, 2012). This section tracks significant laws and policies in Arizona that inaugurated and reinforce the criminal-ization of immigrants. This historical timeline is not exhaustive but rather sug-gestive of the anti-immigrant roots from Arizona's inception (Santa Ana & Bustamante, 2012).

Just two years after being granted statehood in, 1914, Arizona passed a law that prohibited immigrants from taking jobs from native-born citizens. The law stated that any employer who had more than 5 employees had to reserve 80% of the jobs for native-born citizens. In 1915, this law was deemed un-constitutional by the U.S. Supreme Court (Santa Ana & Bustamante, 2012).

- 1930 Great Depression Repatriations taking place where 1 million Mex-icans and Mexican-Americans were deported.
- 1934 Arizona tried to pass a law that prohibited Asians from purchasing land. This law never passed but had an impact on shaping discourse and future legislation.
- 1942 Bracero Program was a temporary guest worker program that allowed immigrants to come and fill the labor market needs of war time pro-duction. Seventy percent of the workers during this period came from Mex-ico.
- 1954 "Operation Wetback" deported those who did not voluntarily return home from the Bracero program.
- 1960s Arizona attempted to legislate the denial of public benefits to law-fully resident non-citizens. This attempt was ruled unconstitutional by the U.S. Supreme Court in 1971.
- 1988 Arizona passed a law making English the official state language (Proposition 106). That law was repealed by the state Supreme Court in 1998 as a violation of the First Amendment.
- 1996 Arizona Supreme Court ruled that law enforcement could justifi-ably use race to enforce immigration laws.
- 2000 Arizona passed Proposition 203, prohibiting bilingual education for English Language Learners.
- 2004 Arizona passed Proposition 200 requiring proof of citizenship for voter registration and the acquisition of public benefits.
- 2006 Arizona passed Proposition 300 prohibiting students from receiv-ing state financial aid or paying in-state tuition without legal proof of residence.
- 2006 Arizona passed Proposition 100 which denied bail to undocumented citizens who committed serious crimes.
- 2007 Arizona passed a law, Legal Arizona Workers Act (referred to as E-verify), which mandates all employers use a federal electronic verification

system to avoid hiring undocumented workers. In 2011 the US Supreme Court upheld this Arizona law.

- 2008 Targeted attack of English Language Learners (ELLs) in K-12 to restrict their educational options.
- 2010 alongside SB 1070, the Arizona legislature drafted additional anti-immigrant bills targeted at Mexican immigrants. For example, the State Superintendent of Public Instruction, Tom Horne, audited Arizona teachers trying to rid the system of those who spoke with an accent; Proposition 107 restricted state governments, including colleges and universities, from using race, ethnicity or gender in hiring decisions.
- 2010 House Bill (HB) 2281 gave the Superintendent of Public Instruction in Arizona the legislative power to punish schools that taught ethnic studies or programs that taught about ethnic solidarity.
- 2011 the U.S. Supreme Court upheld an employer sanction bill in Arizona penalizing employers who hire undocumented immigrants.

Many other attempts to penalize and further criminalize undocumented immigrants have been proposed in the Arizona state legislature. In 2011, Russell Pearce (sponsor of SB 1070) sought to clarify citizenship qualifications (Fourteenth Amendment) that children born on US soil to undocumented immigrants be granted a unique birth certificate in an effort to punish undocumented immigrants who have "anchor babies" and according to Pearce abuse the system (Santa Ana & Bustamante, 2012). Furthermore, Senator Pearce proposed an omnibus bill that not only criminalized undocumented immigrants but their children too. The bill " … would have barred undocumented children from attending school, prohibited unauthorized immigrants from driving or purchasing a vehicle, and would have denied the ability of undocumented immigrants to obtain a marriage license in the state. The bill died in the legislature after pressure from the state's business industry" (Santa Ana & Bustamante, 2012, p. 46).

The criminalization of undocumented immigrants extends beyond the patchwork state legislation, dovetailing with federal policy such as the 287g and Secure Communities (SCOM) Programs. Both 287g and SCOM support racial profiling in that the former gives local law enforcement authority to check immigration status during a lawful stop and detain the individual if they are undocumented, the latter checks the immigration status of those inside local jails. Several counties and cities in Arizona have implemented 287g. Secure Communities operates in local jails throughout Arizona (Wessler, 2012b).

SB 1070

On April 19, 2010, the Arizona Legislature approved SB 1070. On April 23, 2010, Arizona's governor, Jan Brewer, signed SB 1070 into law. Russell Pearce (R-Sen.) was the main sponsor of the bill. As written, the law covers six areas. First, SB 1070 expands the enforcement of immigration issues from federal-only authorities (ICE) to state and local authorities. Law enforcement plays a larger role in investigating immigration status, reporting status to the federal government, arresting non-citizens and facilitating the removal of non-citizens into the hands of federal authorities. Local law enforcement has been granted the power to determine the status of an individual who is lawfully stopped, arrested, or detained.

Second, SB 1070 requires that all state residents 18 years of age and older carry specific forms of identification. The following forms of identification have been deemed legitimate: a valid Arizona driver's license, a valid Arizona non-operating identification license, a tribal enrollment card or tribal identification card, and a valid federal, state or local government-issued identification that required proof of legal status before being issued. Failure to comply will result in fines and/or imprisonment.

The third component of SB 1070 criminalizes the act of picking up passengers for work. This section seeks penalties for both those hiring and/or transporting a worker. SB 1070 made it a crime to impede traffic as a result of securing or applying for work and further, it is now a criminal act to impede traffic to hire an individual for work. Any undocumented worker who seeks to gain employment in a public space is violating SB 1070.

Unlawfully transporting or harboring unlawful aliens is a fourth component of SB 1070. Employer sanctions is fifth and lastly, the power to arrest without a warrant, which was previously permissible for law enforcement, has been extended to Peace Officers (National Conference of State Legislatures [NCSL], 2012).

By all accounts Arizona's law has been the harshest measure enacted toward immigrants to date. Until SB 1070, no state had been able to pass a law penalizing immigrants for entering a state boundary. Several states, Texas 2009, Colorado 2008, and California 2007, had attempted to criminalize state trespassing, yet no measures passed.

One change to SB 1070 was enacted on April 29, 2010 in the form of an amendment introduced by the Arizona House, HB 2162. HB 2162 specifically addressed concerns related to racial profiling. HB 2162 specifies that law enforcement cannot consider race, color or national origin when implementing provisions of SB 1070 except to the extent permitted in the U.S. or Arizona Constitution. Additionally, HB 2162 delineated what is meant by "reasonable suspicion" and clarified the meaning of "lawful contact." However, (as discussed later in this chapter) the Supreme Court ruled race could be used, essentially undermining HB 2162.

Later, On June 25, 2012 the U.S. Supreme Court ruled in Arizona v. United States. The court challenge, filed by the U.S. Department of Justice, argued that federal law preempts state law in four provisions of SB 1070. The first provision was section 2B, often referred to as the "Show me your papers" provision. This section requires law enforcement to determine an individual's legal status while lawfully stopped. The Supreme Court upheld this provision. The second ruling by the Supreme Court dealt with Section 3, which makes the failure to apply for or carry federally-issued alien registration papers a state crime. This provision was struck down. Third, section 5 of SB 1070, which makes it unlawful for an unauthorized immigrant to "solicit, apply for or perform work" was also struck down. Lastly, section 6, "Authorizing the warrantless arrest of a person where there is probable cause to believe the person to have committed a public offense that makes the person removable from the United States" was struck down (NCSL, 2012; Wessler, 2012a).

On September 5, 2012 Judge Susan Bolton, U.S. District Court in Phoenix, Arizona ruled that it was legal for authorities to verify the status of people they lawfully stop and suspect are in the state illegally. This decision was consistent with the earlier ruling by the Supreme Court (June 25, 2012). Judge Bolton went further, ordering the state to stop enforcing another provision of SB 1070 which makes it illegal to transport, harbor or shield an illegal immigrant (Santos, 2012).

Concerns about Constitutionality

Several elements of SB 1070 raise serious consideration regarding constitutionality and implementation. The sanction to racially profile has been one of the most controversial aspects SB 1070. Racial profiling, however, has long been established as a modus operandi in dealing with immigration matters. For example, in 1996 the Arizona Supreme Court affirmed the consideration of race and ethnic factors in immigration matters. The court said, "Mexican ancestry alone, that is, Latino appearance, is not enough to establish reasonable cause, but if the occupants' dress or hair style are associated with people currently living in Mexico, such characteristics may be sufficient" (Santa Ana

& Bustamante, 2012, p. 82). Moreover, in 1975 the U.S. Supreme Court ruled in United States v. Brignoni-Ponce that the U.S. Constitution allows race to be considered when dealing with immigration cases (Santa Ana & Bustamante, 2012). Additional constitutional concerns include:

> costs to the state for enforcing federal immigration law, particularly in tight budget times; how 'reasonable suspicion of immigrant status' will be interpreted; and the narrow list of documents eligible to demonstrate lawful presence. Court challenges have raised constitutional issues including due process, equal protection under the 14th amendment, the prohibition on reasonable search and seizure under the 4th amendment, and preemption under the Supremacy Clause of the U.S. Constitution (NCSL, 2011).

Impacts and Consequences

The consequences of SB 1070 have been significant not only for immigrants but for other state citizens. For example, in Maricopa County after the passage of SB 1070 local law enforcement arrived late to emergency 911 calls two-thirds of the time. This is because resources for local enforcement were diverted away from more pressing public safety problems to harassing and arresting immigrants (Branche, n.d.). As one observer stated, "Local immigration enforcement is counterproductive to public safety" (Branche, n.d., p. 1).

If allowed to proceed unbridled, mass removal of undocumented immigrants in Arizona would have serious negative economic impacts. Gans (2008) conducted an economic analysis that compared the fiscal costs and fiscal gains of immigrants in Arizona. She found the costs of immigrants throughout that state in 2004 were estimated at $1.4 billion dollars. The fiscal gains were approximately $2.4 billion, thereby resulting in an overall fiscal gain of $940 million dollars that immigrants generate in Arizona. These gains would be erased if Arizona's anti-immigrant policies go unchecked.

The criminalization of immigrants affects everyone. The policies and practices embedded in these anti-immigrant measures affect mixed families whose members often hold different legal status: legal, authorized or undocumented. All minorities are affected by de facto stop and frisk policies. Citizens alike are affected by criminalization vis-à-vis a general decrease in civil liberties and civil rights. Finally, the persistent trend toward criminalization has a negative impact on labor markets, labor standards, tax revenue, housing and beyond.

Advocacy and Activist Responses

This chapter would be incomplete without reference to the numerous grass-roots activist groups in Arizona, and throughout the nation, who have challenged the legitimacy and consequences of SB 1070. After the passage of SB 1070 mass demonstrations, direct actions and non-violent blockades drew national and international attention to the grassroots movements emerging as a result of the racist and anti-immigrant provisions of SB 1070. Groups like Puente Arizona—a movement for migrant justice and human rights—and the Black Alliance for Just Immigration (BAJI) are still busy organizing. BAJI is an education and advocacy group that started in 2006 that links racial oppression of blacks to all immigrant groups and finds solidarity among all disenfranchised people. In 2011 a BAJI chapter was formed in Arizona. Opal Tometi, from BAJI, says, "Drafters of anti-immigrant legislation meant to destroy our communities, however these types of laws have only emboldened our communities to fight harder together. We are working more collaboratively, fearlessly and deliberately between communities of African descent and Latino communities. We've built multicultural coalitions in the past to fight for our rights and we'll continue to do so" (Novoa, 2012). The efforts to fight back highlight the complexity of immigrant lives as a result of SB 1070. Similarly, "We Belong Together" is a national campaign led by women and children whose purpose is to expose the gripping consequences that anti-immigrant sentiment and legislation has on families. Moreover, the campaign supports the development of a "healthy multiracial democracy." Rep. Lucille Roybal-Allard (D-California), member of the Congressional Hispanic Caucus, is demanding that immigration reform focus on family unity. Not all law enforcement personnel were supportive of SB 1070, in particular the "show me your papers" component. The Phoenix and Tucson Police Departments along with the Pima County Sheriff's office were initially critical of this law (Billeaud & Riccardi, 2012).

Conclusion

Arizona has always been and continues to be contested terrain, beginning with the Treaty of Guadalupe Hidalgo in 1848 and later the signing of the Gadsden Purchase of 1853. In 1848 Mexico lost half of its land to the U.S. The lost land included Arizona north of the Gila River. In 1853 the southern half of Arizona (south of the Gila River) became U.S. territory as well. From statehood to present Arizona has had to grapple with the immigrant question. The overwhelming response has been punitive and has resulted in the scapegoating of an entire population of people who are an intrinsic part of our American past, present and future. Immigrants make up 14% of Arizona's labor force. Without the immigrant workers in Arizona what would become of the state's economy? Immigrants most commonly work in agriculture, construction and manufacturing as well as in the service sector (leisure and hospitality sectors). Overall, immigrants (both naturalized and non-citizens) have a positive fiscal impact on the state of Arizona (Gans, 2008).

In conclusion, state-level immigration policy merely treats symptoms of immigration, it does not address or tackle the complex issues that underlie and drive immigration (i.e. globalization, transnational markets and labor force needs/demands). Harsh criminalization policies, on the other hand, address anxieties of dominant groups that feel threatened — key voting constituencies — which propelled politicians who stepped into the breach, most dramatically in the case of SB 1070.

Discussion Questions

1. What forces propel people to leave their homes and endure often difficult journeys to get to another land?
2. What does it mean to be a "global citizen?" Do you think of yourself and/or others as global citizens?
3. Should immigration be addressed on a local, national, or international/global level? Explain.
4. Latinos supported Obama over Romney (71 percent to 27 percent) in the 2012 Presidential election. What implications does this have for immigration reform?
5. Is amnesty the answer? Should we be thinking about pathways to citizenship? If so, for whom? Who gets to decide?

References

Billeaud, J., & Riccardi, N. (2012, September 6). Arizona immigration law a police minefield.Washington Times. Retrieved from http://www.washingtontimes.com/news/2012/sep/6/<\h>\d>arizona-immigration-law-a-police-minefield/.

Branche, A. (n.d.). The cost of failure: The burden of immigration enforcement in America's cities. Retrieved from Drum Major Institute for Public Policy website: http://uncoverthetruth.org/wp-content/uploads/2011/04/DMI-Cost-of-Failure.pdf.

Gans, J. (2008). Immigrants in Arizona: Fiscal and economic impacts. Retrieved from UdallCenter for Studies in Public Policy website: http://udall-center.arizona.edu/immigration/publications/impactofimmigrants08.pdf.

Huntington, S. P. (2004, March 1). The Hispanic challenge. Retrieved from Foreign Policy website: http://www.foreignpolicy.com/articles/2004/03/01/the_hispanic_challenge.

Johnson, M. (2012, August 15). Fuerza! The fight against SB 1070 and the prison industry in Arizona. Retrieved from http://nacla.org/blog/2012/8/14/fuerza-fights-against-sb-1070-and-prison-industry-arizona.

Lopez, M.H. & Light, L. (2009, February 18). A rising share: Hispanics and federal crime. Retrieved from Pew Research Hispanic Center website: http://www.pewhispanic.org/2009/02/18/a-rising-share-hispanics-and-federal-crime/.

National Conference of State Legislatures (2011, July). Arizona's immigration enforcement laws. Retrieved from http://www.ncsl.org/issues-research/immig/analysis-of-arizonas-immigration-law.aspx.

National Conference of State Legislatures (2012). Arizona's immigration enforcement laws. Retrieved from http://www.ncsl.org/issues-reserach/immig/analysis-of-arizonas-immigration-law.aspx.

National Conference of State Legislatures (2012, June 25). U.S. Supreme Court rules on Arizona's immigration enforcement law. Retrieved from http://www.ncsl.org/issues-research/immig/us-supreme-court-rules-on-arizona-immigration-laws.aspx.

Newton, L. (2005). It is not a question of being anti-immigration: Categories of deservedness in immigration policy making. A. Schneider and H. Ingram (Eds.) Deserving and Entitled: Social Constructions and Public Policy (SUNY Press).

Novoa, M. (2012, June 26). The people of Arizona won't comply with hate. ColorLines: News for Action. Retrieved from http://colorlines.com/archives/2012/06/arizona_we_cannot_comply_with_hate.html.

Santa Ana, O. & C. G. De Bustamante (Eds.). (2012). Arizona firestorm: Global immigration realities, national media and provincial politics. Maryland: Rowman & Littlefield.

Santos, F. (2012, September 6). Arizona immigration law survives ruling. The New York Times. Retrieved from http://www.nytimes.com/2012/09/07/us/key-element-of-arizona-immigration-law-survives-ruling.html.

U.S. Census Bureau (2011). American Community Survey 1-Year estimates. Selected social characteristics in the United States. Retrieved from http://factfinder2.census.gov/faces/tableservices/jsf/pages/productview.xhtml ?src=bkmk.

U.S. Census Bureau (2011). State and County Quick Facts, Arizona. Retrieved from http://quickfacts.census.gov/qfd/states/04000.html.

Wessler, S. F. (2012a, June 26). What's next for Arizona and 'Show me your papers' laws? ColorLines: News for Action. Retrieved from http://color-lines.com/archives/2012/06/what_supreme_court_arizona_sb1070_ruling_means.html.

Wessler, S.F. (2012b, June 28). Feds reveal their janus face on Arizona's racial profiling. Colorlines. Retrieved from http://colorlines.com/archives/2012/06/feds_reveal_their_janus-face_on_arizonas_sb_1070.html.

Chapter Five

Undocumented Immigrant Policy in Alabama

María Pabón López and Natasha Ann Lacoste

Introduction

The purpose of this chapter is to explore one aspect of the contexts and consequences of criminalization of immigration in the United States: the recent state laws in the state of Alabama which restrict the lives of undocumented persons in the state. These laws have been enacted with the aim to make undocumented persons leave the state based on the obstacles they encounter in residing in Alabama. Thus, both in their context and consequence, these state laws treat undocumented persons as criminals who must be expelled, not as human beings whose lives are disrupted in contravention of federal law as this chapter will show.

While it is axiomatic that it is the exclusive power of federal government to regulate immigration, states do retain some ability to regulate persons who are not United States citizens who reside within their borders. This is done under their state police powers. However, these state laws can only be considered properly enacted if they do not impinge on the federal government's exclusive right to regulate immigration. Thus, once enacted, state laws affecting those who are not United States citizens may be brought before the courts, challenging their validity under the United States Constitution.

This chapter analyses in detail Alabama's anti-immigrant legislative scheme and the federal constitutional litigation which affects the validity of these laws. In particular, this chapter focuses on Alabama legislation interfering with the education of undocumented students, both in K–12 schools and postsecondary institutions. State laws touching other aspects of the undocumented persons' lives, such as verification of citizenship, the ability to work, and conduct business are discussed as well, as they form part of a legislative scheme enacted in Alabama and set forth a clearly anti-immigrant agenda and a form of undocumented immigration policy in the state. These can all be seen methods of impinging on the lives of those who are not United States citizens and who have settled to live in the state of Alabama.

This chapter begins with an analysis of the law that embodies these policies and methods: the Beason-Hammon Alabama Taxpayer and Citizen Protection Act, commonly known as H.B. 56 (Alabama Code, 2011). Even the title of this law evinces the view that immigrants are criminals of whom the citizenry and taxpayers of Alabama need to be protected. Enacted in June of 2011 by the Alabama legislature, and signed into law by Governor Robert Bentley, H.B. 56 was passed the year after Arizona enacted its notorious immigration law, S.B. 1070 (Arizona Revised Statute, 2010). As with the law in Arizona, it is the case that these state legislative enactments not only send an exclusionary message to those within their state borders, but to the larger United States polity as well. The message is clear — that those who are not United States citizens and even those who look like they are not citizens (recall the Arizona "show me your papers" law) have to be scrutinized closely, and their lives examined in detail — as would be the case with criminals.

This chapter then briefly discusses the litigation surrounding the Alabama Beason-Hammon Act and analyzes in detail various sections of how H.B. 56 was enacted and what the courts ruled pertaining to their validity under current law. Interestingly enough, and in response to intense criticism, the Alabama legislature later amended H.B. 56 via a later law, H.B. 658 (Alabama Code, 2012). These new statutory provisions are discussed where relevant, as they reveal again the context and consequences of the criminalization of immigrants. In conclusion, this chapter examines H.B. 56's consequences on Latinos and immigrants in Alabama and offers a context for hope and the bettering the lives of these vulnerable populations.

Examination and Context of the Litigation Surrounding Alabama's Immigration Laws

Shortly after H.B. 56 was enacted, three federal lawsuits challenging its validity were filed by its opponents such as Alabama community groups and the federal government (HICA, 2011; United States v. Alabama, 2011; Parsley v. Bentley, 2011). The main challenge made in the courts regarding the validity of H.B. 56 was that it was preempted by federal law. Because immigration law is federal law, state laws touching on immigration matters may violate the Supremacy Clause. The Supremacy Clause of the U.S. Constitution states that the Constitution, federal laws, and treaties are the supreme law of the land (U.S. CONST. art. IV, cl. 2.). This means that federal law trumps state law. And when these laws conflict, or when Congress has heavily regulated a field or stated its intent to displace state law—the state law will be invalid.

In June 2012, the Supreme Court ruled on Arizona's immigration law (Arizona v. United States, 2012). The fact that the Arizona law is similar to the Alabama law required consideration of the ruling of the highest court in the Alabama context. Then in August 2012 the 11th Circuit ruled on the three federal cases (United States v. Alabama, 2012; HICA, 2012); upholding various sections of H.B. 56 and H.B. 658, and invalidating others.

Recently, Alabama asked the U.S. Supreme Court to review some of the 11th Circuit's decision in the above cases, and these are presently pending. In February of 2013, another lawsuit was filed challenging a provision of H.B. 658 that requires the state to publish a database of illegal immigrants who have had run-ins with the law (Chandler, 2013). This case is currently pending as well. Those challenging this database evidence resistance to the notion that all run-ins with the law are criminal actions which require entry of the affected immigrant's name into a database, without adjudication of guilt and other procedural safeguards in place for the regular criminal databases.

Alabama Law's Impact on the Education of Immigrant Youth

Primary Education

Several sections of the Alabama law have posed serious obstacles to the education of the children of immigrants and of immigrant youth themselves. Section 28 of H.B. requires that public elementary and secondary schools determine whether the student enrolling was born outside the jurisdiction of the United States or is the child of an alien not lawfully present in the United States. Section 28 is "particularly concerning since it contains extensive information-gathering requirements that may hinder school enrollment for undocumented children, and administrators use the information from these questions to prepare an annual document to the Alabama Department of Education" (López, Tsitouras, & Azuma, 2011, p. 234).

Once the validity of this section was challenged, the Eleventh Circuit United States Court of Appeals found that the law violated the Equal Protection Clause of the Fourteenth Amendment; thus, it was invalid (HICA, 2012). The court noted a heightened level of scrutiny was appropriate in this case (HICA, 2012). A higher level of scrutiny is used when a statute "significantly interferes with the exercise of a protected right" (HICA, 2012). In Plyler v. Doe the United States Supreme Court unequivocally asserted that "education has a fundamental role in maintaining the fabric of our society" (2012, p. 2397). The Eleventh Circuit determined that section 28 "operates in such a way that it "significantly interfere[ed] with the exercise of the right to an elementary public education as guaranteed by Plyler" (HICA, 2012, p. 1245). Interestingly, Alabama did not challenge this aspect of the injunction when it asked the U.S. Supreme Court to review the Eleventh Circuit's decision (Lawson, 2013).

Although this provision was ultimately deemed invalid, it was in effect for a period of time before being enjoined by the Eleventh Circuit and had dire consequences for the education of immigrant children in Alabama. The day after H.B. 56 went into effect, more than 2,200 of the 34,000 Latino students in Alabama state public schools failed to attend school (Baxter, 2012). This was double the normal absentee rate (Reves, 2012). Thus, approximately 7% of Alabama's Latino student population stayed home from school the day after the law went into effect (Jonsson, 2011). Also, "[a] hotline set up by the Southern Poverty Law Center for people to report issues under H.B. 56 saw more than 2,000 calls in the first week" (Baxter, 2012, p. 18); and months after the law was in effect, the hotline was used by more than 6,000 people (Gomez, 2012).

Postsecondary Education

Another section of the law has posed obstacles for immigrant youth seeking higher education in the state of Alabama. As enacted, section 8 of H.B. 56 proscribed unlawfully present aliens from enrolling or attending public postsecondary institutions; nor were they eligible for any postsecondary education benefits, including scholarships, grants, or financial aid (Alabama Code, 2011). When challenged in litigation, the lower federal court found this section was preempted because it made a "classification" of aliens in order to determine who could attend Alabama schools (HICA, 2011). Thus, the ban on noncitizens attending higher education was struck down, since only the federal government can make such classifications (HICA, 2011).

Subsequently, H.B. 658 removed the second sentence of section 8 which read "[a]n alien attending any public postsecondary institution in this state must either possess lawful permanent residence or an appropriate nonimmigrant visa under" federal law (Alabama Code, 2012). On appeal, the Eleventh Circuit found plaintiffs challenge to section 8 was moot due to the removal of the second sentence (HICA, 2012). Thus, section 8 as amended is valid law, and the legislation requires lawful status to attend postsecondary institutions in the state.

This means that if you are an undocumented high school student residing in Alabama, you either must leave the state to attend a college or university or you must forgo a college education. Considering that both South Carolina and Georgia have similar laws restricting access to institutions of higher education, access to postsecondary education is severely curtailed for undocumented youth in the South. Such result has serious consequences not only for the lives of the children of immigrants, but for the economic and educational achievement statistics of the state of Alabama. This is hardly a desirable societal result, to place obstacles to higher educational achievement, no matter what the immigration status of the person seeking education. It is also an undesirable fiscal result to leave uneducated students who have been the beneficiaries of a K–12 education under the United States Supreme court decision of Plyler v. Doe.

Miscellaneous Provisions of Alabama's Law Presenting Obstacles for Immigrants

Registration of Those Who Are Not United States Citizens (Aliens)

Section 10 of H.B. 56 criminalized an unlawfully present alien's willful failure to complete or carry federally required alien registration documents (Alabama Code, 2011). A similar provision was enacted in Arizona and was dubbed by the press as the "Show Your Papers" portion of the bill. The Supreme Court found this provision preempted in Arizona, and made it clear that federal law occupies the field of alien registration (United States v. Arizona, 2012). Thus, following the Supreme Court ruling, the Eleventh Circuit found this provision preempted (United States v. Alabama, 2012). Thus, even though this part of the law is no longer valid and does not affect the lives of Alabama immigrants at present, the time period that elapsed between the passage of the law and the determination of its invalidity was one where the immigrants in the state were under the intense scrutiny and vigilance usually reserved for criminals.

Residing, Harboring and Renting

Another section of the law which caused undocumented families in Alabama serious concern regarding their ability to reside in the state is Section 13 which made:

> it unlawful for a person to (1) conceal, harbor, or shield an alien unlawfully present in the United States, or attempt or conspire to do so; (2) encourage an unlawful alien to come to the State of Alabama; or (3) transport (or attempt or conspire to transport) an unlawful alien (United States v. Alabama, 2011, p. 415).

The Eleventh Circuit found this section preempted (United States v. Alabama, 2012). It noted there is a comprehensive federal framework that "penalize[s] the transportation, concealment, and inducement of unlawfully present aliens" (United States v. Alabama, 2012, p. 1285, quoting Georgia Latino, 2012, p. 1263). This framework occupies the field, and thus preempts section 13, which created analogous state crimes as well as legislation that conflicted with the main federal law, the Immigration and Nationality Act (INA) (United States v. Alabama, 2012). Thus, the state of Alabama is not able to legislate on this matter as the federal government had done so in the INA, a federal law that has been in force for many years. There was no need for Alabama to pass this legislation essentially duplicating the federal law other than to send a message of exclusion to the immigrants in the state.

Another provision which was originally contained in section 13 effectively required Alabama landlords to become immigration law specialists since it made it unlawful for a person to enter into a rental agreement with an alien if the person knows or recklessly disregards the fact that the individual is an unauthorized alien (Alabama Code, 2011). It is unclear how a layperson can tell the immigration status of another person without the benefit of the usual training that immigration agents, judges and lawyers receive in this very complicated area of the law. Fortunately, the Eleventh Circuit found this section preempted; and stated that this section "effectuate[d] an untenable expansion of the federal harboring provisions" (United States v. Alabama, 2012, p. 1288).

If the above provisions were found to be valid, then it would be a crime to give an unauthorized alien a ride or rent them a place to live. This is hardly the environment that all residents of Alabama should be encountering—one fraught with the fear of interacting with immigrants and being subject to potential legal liability for so doing. Activity such as riding in a car or finding an apartment are normal actions of daily life and curtailing these by fear are unfortunate reminders of the outsider status of immigrants in Alabama, of their perceived criminality. Thus, the courts' invalidating of these sections is not only appropriate under the law but also in terms of the societal and communitarian wellbeing.

Enforcing or Recognizing Contracts

Similarly, Section 27 of H.B. 56 provided a continuation of the disincentives for Alabama residents to interact with immigrants. This section of the law prohibited state courts from enforcing or recognizing almost all contracts between a party and an unlawfully present alien, if the party had direct or constructive knowledge that the alien is in the United States unlawfully (Alabama Code, 2011). The Eleventh Circuit held that section 27 was both field and conflict preempted (United States v. Alabama, 2012). In other words, there are two ways in which this court found that the state law violated the federal government's preferential competence over all matters pertaining to immigration.

First, the court noted the power to expel aliens is exclusively a federal power and this provision essentially sought "to make the lives of unlawfully present aliens so difficult as to force them to retreat from the state" (United States v. Alabama, 2012). Thus, the court recognized the exclusionary character of the law and its anti-immigrant aim to have the undocumented "self deport." The court then found that the law "conflicts with Congress's comprehensive statutory framework governing alien removal" (United States v. Alabama, 2012). Removal, of course, is the federal term for deportation. Therefore, at present, undocumented persons can enter into contracts in Alabama.

Discriminatory Practices

Another section of the law put Alabama employers in an untenable position regarding the hiring of immigrant workers. Section 17 provided a civil cause of action for recovery of compensatory damages as well as court costs and attorneys' fees for the prevailing party if an employer engages in the "discriminatory practice" of either firing or failing to hire an individual authorized to work in the United States while simultaneously employing an unauthorized alien (Alabama Code, 2011). This provision is preempted. Federal law preempts any state or local law that imposes a sanction on those who employ unauthorized aliens (8 U.S.C. §1324a(h)(2)). The Eleventh Circuit found section 17 imposed a "sanction" on those who employ unauthorized aliens (United States v. Alabama, 2012). Thus, this part of the state law is invalid and not enforced.

Data Collection and Privacy Concerns

A provision in H.B. 658 requires Alabama law enforcement agencies to report and compile data on "unlawfully present aliens" detained by law enforcement on suspicion of criminal activity (Alabama Code, 2012). Section 5 of the bill mandates "the quarterly reports to the Alabama Department of Homeland Security of any unlawfully present alien brought before a court for violating state law" (Alabama Code, 2012, §5). This agency would then publish that information on its website making it available to the general public (Alabama Code, 2012). In February of 2013, two men and two women who were arrested for allegedly fishing without a license and potentially face having their name on the list filed a lawsuit to challenge this provision (Chandler, 2013).

Their attorney indicates that the law: "is designed to permanently brand, humiliate and otherwise make life difficult for immigrants regardless of status. It conflicts with federal privacy requirements and burdens the already cash-strapped state court system" (Gray 2013). The sponsor of the law, State Representative Beason, has defended the data collection effort as follows: "We're trying to figure out what the costs are involved. How many illegal aliens we are dealing with when it comes to the judicial system? ... Are there people out there that are repeat criminals?" (Gray 2013).

At present, the case is pending and the state of Alabama has requested dismissal of the lawsuit on the grounds that it will not enforce the law (Gray 2013). The state indicates that it will not enforce the law "at the request of federal immigration officials who said it could result in Alabama losing access to federal databases and prosecution of those responsible for publishing the information" (Gray 2013). This is an area of the law which will require additional updating to assess its validity.

Conclusion: H.B. 56/658's Effect on the Latino and Immigrant Population in Alabama

Consequences: Crops, Safety, Foreign Investment, Revenue and Licenses

Alabama's immigration law has been labeled a draconian measure, and is "the nation's only immigration law that was more aggressive—and more blatantly designed to banish illegal immigrants—than Arizona's" (Editorial, 2012). H.B. 56/658 affects not only undocumented persons, but legal immigrants as well. The Latino community in Alabama is very "mixed"—that is comprised of un-documented persons, legal immigrants and U.S. citizens (Constable, 2012). Many residents of Alabama live in these "mixed" families (Constable, 2012). As a consequence of H.B. 56, many of these families have fled the state (Constable, 2012). This exodus of Latinos has caused labor shortages. Employers say "they have not been able to find enough legal residents to replace the seasoned Hispanic field pickers, drywall hangers, landscapers and poultry workers who fled the state" (Constable, 2012). Not only are Latinos fleeing the state, but they have also gone "underground." In other words, they have become vul-nerable to exploitation.

Furthermore, farmers who are dependent on seasonal labor have a difficult time hiring workers to replace Latinos (Baxter, 2012). They note that locals do not want to do this type of work and many of them lack the necessary ex-perience (Baxter, 2012). A spokesman for a poultry farm said it "had to re-place about 130 employees (of a 900-employee workforce)" (Trotta & Bassing, 2012) and "our turnover rate has gone through the roof" (Constable, 2012). "We can't say for sure that it was because of the Alabama law, but the inference certainly was there that we can assume the people left because of their con-cern about the law. It definitely had a chilling effect on the migrant commu-nity" (Trotta & Bassing, 2012). These labor shortages can lead to loss of crops and financial revenue.

The passage of this law has also resulted in other societal losses. The safety and security of the all communities of Alabama is at risk. One police chief in Alabama noted the Hispanic community has " 'gone underground,' refusing to report crimes out of fear that officers will arrest them or their family on im-migration charges" (Gomez, 2012). He said this law has "enhanced the issue of under-reporting" (Gomez, 2012). Understandably, under-reporting of crime is a serious concern for all who reside in Alabama, since perpetrators of crimes do not check citizenship papers to ensure they are only victimizing foreigners. A community should be safe for all, citizens and non-citizens.

H.B. 56 may also have a negative impact on foreign investment. It is likely that foreign companies will hesitate to settle in Alabama as a result of its restrictive immigration law (Baxter, 2012). Since the law has been in effect, two foreign workers have been arrested. A German employee of Mercedes Benz was arrested while driving without proper documentation (Beadle, 2012). Two weeks later a Japanese Honda employee was also arrested "even though he reportedly had his passport and international driver's license" (Beadle, 2012).

Aside from its potential impact on foreign investments, H.B. 56 may lead to decreased tax revenue. The Institute for Taxation and Economic Policy has estimated that unauthorized aliens in Alabama pay approximately $130 million in taxes per year (Unauthorized Immigrants Pay, 2011). Under current federal tax law, persons who are not United States citizens and do not have a Social Security Number are able to pay taxes using an Individual Taxpayer Identification Number ("ITIN").

Additionally, this Act is too broad in its scope, as it touches Alabama residents who do not have any contact with undocumented persons. Because the state must verify the immigration status of those applying for or renewing a license, long lines have been reported at DMVs, courthouses, and utility companies (Reves, 2012). Is it really necessary for your pedicurist to have her immigration status verified? These are the types of questions all Alabama residents must consider in deciding the necessity of such restrictive anti-immigrant legislation.

Bettering the Lives of These Vulnerable Populations and the Misery Strategy

As states such as Alabama interfere in the federal government's immigration prerogative, they engage in counterproductive policymaking, when collaboration with the federal government would likely yield better results for all parties involved. This strategy, where states enact laws so as to have immigrants leave their borders, really would only result in a reallocation of immigrants to other states, since even in these tough conditions, life in the United States is easier than in many of the countries from which the immigrants come. This state legislative "misery strategy" which aims to cause "the human tide to flow backward" will work "only if life for illegal immigrants in America could be made significantly more miserable than life in, say, rural Guatemala or the slums of Mexico City. That will take a lot of time and a lot of misery to pull that off in a country that has tolerated and profited from illegal labor for generations" (Editorial 2007). This strategy will also fail because "The American people cherish lawfulness but resist cruelty" and there are many aspects of the Alabama law which seem downright cruel.

Furthermore, there is a context for bettering the lives of these vulnerable populations in actions such as the recent visit of the main federal civil rights agency to Alabama. The United States Commission on Civil Rights held a public field briefing in Birmingham on Friday, August 17, 2012 on the effects of recently enacted state immigration enforcement laws on the civil rights of individuals in the wake of the U.S. Supreme Court decision in Arizona v. United States. In addition to state lawmakers, immigrants' rights group leaders, law enforcement and others, the commission heard from two undocumented students who testified regarding the effect of these laws on their civil rights. There is hope for the immigrant residents of Alabama since the federal government is bringing awareness of the actions in the state which daily make their lives difficult beyond just the litigation in court but also in the policy arena through this Commission.

Discussion Questions

1. What legislation has the state of Alabama enacted that affects the lives of undocumented persons in the state?
2. What have been the consequences of these actions?
3. How are undocumented persons, Latinos and immigrants' lives affected by the immigration policies of the state of Alabama?
4. Which of these policies concern you the most? Why?
5. Will the misery strategy work? Why or why not?

References

Ala. Code §§ 31-13-1—31-13-34 (2011) ("H.B. 56").

Ala. Code §§ 31-13-1—31-13-34 (2012) ("H.B. 658").

Ariz. Rev. Stat. § 13-1509) (2010).

Arizona v. United States, 132 S.Ct. 2492 (2012).

Baxter, T. (2012, February). Alabama's Immigration Disaster: The Harshest Law in the Land Harms the State's Economy and Society. Center for Amer-

ican Progress, 10–11. Retrieved from http://www.americanprogress.org/wp
-content/uploads/issues/2012/02/pdf/alabama_immigration_disaster.pdf.

Beadle, A. P. (2012, June 11). One Year after Governor Signed Nation's Worst
Immigration Law, Alabama Still has Not Learned from its Mistakes.
ThinkProgress. Retrieved from http://thinkprogress.org/justice/2012/06/
11/497193/alabama-immigration-law-one-year/?mobile=nc.

Chandler, K. (2013, February 7). New lawsuit challenges 'scarlet letter' provision of Alabama immigration law. AL.com. Retrieved from http://
blog.al.com/wire/2013/02/new_lawsuit_challenges_scarlet.html.

Constable, P. (2012, June 7). Alabama law drivers out illegal immigrants but
also has unexpected consequences. Washington Post. Retrieved from http://
www.washingtonpost.com/local/alabama-law-drives-out-illegal-immigrants-
but-also-has-unexpected-consequences/2012/06/17/gJQA3Rm0jV_story.html.

Editorial, (2007, August 9). The Misery Strategy. New York Times. Retrieved
from http://www.nytimes.com/2007/08/09/opinion/09thu1.html?_r=0.

Editorial, (2012, August 22). Alabama's harassment of immigrants receives a
setback. Washington Post. Retrieved from http://www.washingtonpost.com/
opinions/alabamas-harassment-of-undocumented-receives-a-setback/2012/
08/22/193055ae-ebbb-11e1-a80b-9f898562d010_story.html.

Gomez, A. (2012, July 7). Hispanics feel harassed under Alabama's immigration law. USA Today. Retrieved from http://usatoday30.usatoday.com/news/
nation/story/2012-07-21/arizona-immigration-law-alabama/56394360/1.

Gray, J. (2013, February 26). Alabama seeks to dismiss 'scarlet letter' suit arguing it will not enforce that provision of immigration law AL.com. Retrieved from http://blog.al.com/wire/2013/02/alabama_seeks_to_dismiss_
scarl.html.

Jonsson, P. (2011, October 6). Is Alabama immigration law creating a 'humanitarian crisis'?. Christian Science Monitor. Retrieved from http://
www.csmonitor.com/USA/2011/1006/Is-Alabama-immigration-law-creating-
a-humanitarian-crisis.

Hispanic Interest Coal. of Ala. v. Bentley (HICA), — F. Supp. 2d—, 2011 WL
5516953 (N.D. Ala. 2011).

Hispanic Interest Coal. of Ala. v. Governor of Alabama (HICA), 691 F.3d 1236
(11 Cir. 2012).

Lawson, B. (2013, February 25). Alabama will not challenge ban on collecting
immigration information from students. Huntsville Times. Retrieved from
http://blog.al.com/breaking/2013/02/alabama_will_not_ask_supreme_c.html.

López, M. P., Tsitouras, D. J. & Azuma, P. C. (2011). The Prospects and Chal
lenges of Educational Reform for Latino Undocumented Children: An

Essay Examining Alabama's H.B. 56 and Other State Immigration Measures. Florida International University Law Review, (6), 234.

Parsley v. Bentley, No. 11-2736 (N.D. Ala. Sept. 28, 2011).

Plyler v. Doe, 102 S.Ct. 2382, 2397 (1982).

Reves, P. (2012, March/April). "It's Just Not Right": The Failures of Alabama's Self-Deportation Experiment. Mother Jones. Retrieved from http://www.motherjones.com/politics/2012/03/alabama-anti-immigration-law-self-deportation-movement.

Trotta, D. & Bassing, T. (2012, May 30). In Alabama, strict immigration law sows discord. Reuters. Retrieved from http://www.reuters.com/article/2012/05/30/us-usa-immigration-alabama-idUSBRE84T16P20120530.

Unauthorized Immigrants Pay Taxes, Too. (2011, April 18). Immigration Policy Center.

Retrieved from http://www.immigrationpolicy.org/sites/default/files/docs/Tax_Contributions_by_Unauthorized_Immigrants_041811.pdf.

United States v. Alabama, 813 F. Supp. 2d 1282 (N.D. Ala. 2011).

United States v. Alabama, 443 Fed. Appx. 411, 415 (11 Cir. 2011) (citing ALA. CODE § 31-13–13).

United States v. Alabama, 691 F.3d 1269 (11 Cir. 2012).

United States v. Alabama, 691 F.3d 1269, 1285 (11 Cir. 2012) (quoting Georgia Latino Alliance for Human Rights v. Deal (GLAHR), 691 F.3d 1250, 1263 (11 Cir. 2012).

United States v. Arizona, 132 S.Ct. 2492 (2012).

United States Commission on Civil Rights, PERFORMANCE AND ACCOUNTABILITY REPORT (PAR) FOR FISCAL YEAR 2012, Retrieved from http://www.usccr.gov/congress/2012_PAR_Report.pdf.

U.S. CONST. art. IV, cl. 2.

Chapter Six

Crimmigration at the Crossroads of America or How Divisive Politics Tarnish the Heartland

Sujey Vega

I met Socorro on a crisp fall Sunday afternoon in 2012. As we watched orange and crimson leaves fly across an Indiana soy field outside her church, Socorro related a life story full of pain, struggle, and endurance. Socorro, like all the names in this piece, is a pseudonym. It roughly translates to a call for help; this was symbolic of her life as a woman who daily struggled to express her need for assistance while simultaneously exerting the strength to survive. The mother of four, Socorro recently fled an abusive relationship and terrible circumstances. From Mexico originally, Socorro first arrived to the United States via Georgia. Now in Indiana, all she and her children know are non-traditional settling locations where intimidation and fear undergird their experience. Critically, these two states have passed some of toughest legislative actions against undocumented immigrants. In a manner reflective of her renewed sense of faith, Socorro bore witness to enduring a terrifying experience at the hands of her ex-husband in Georgia. A citizen himself, her ex-husband used his status as a means to control and silence. Stripped of self-worth, Socorro recalled feeling petrified, frozen in fear. Even if she could escape the physical and emotional abuse at home, there always existed the equally unnerving gaze of state officials that could deport her at any moment. Imprisoned in her home and condemned as a criminal in public, Socorro lacked a semblance of safety everywhere she turned. Even after fleeing her husband and moving to Indiana, she still lived with bouts of anxiety over state policies that once more targeted her body and signaled potential danger.

Using what Patricia R. Pessar and Sarah J. Mahler (2003) note as "gendered geographies of power" (p. 815), we see how the intersections of gender, class, race, and immigration status surface in the lives of transnational individuals like Socorro who are positioned within multiple hierarchies of power. In particular, transnational women must confront gender patriarchy with state-powered systems of oppression that determine how their classed, raced, and gendered bodies can be read, or abused, across particular power structures. In Georgia and in Indiana, Socorro faced multiple vectors of structural inequality that criminalized her for being undocumented and threatened her family's well being. Importantly, stories like Socorro's of transnational migrants following geographic routes to inhospitable nontraditional settling sites, are increasingly commonplace. Even as legislators attempt to curtail their arrival, economic opportunities remain situated in these difficult spaces. Thus, understanding immigration today means not only recognizing migrants' transnational identities, but also allowing for trans-regional experiences that become forged by multiple encounters with "new" sites. In other words, the geographies of power include the very real multiple spaces of settlement that are far from isolated. The places that Socorro traversed illustrates her expanded network of support, but also reveals the political network of state legislators that wished to delegitimize people like her.

Back in Georgia, the scars of domestic violence eventually did catch the attention of state agents who took Socorro's children out of her home. Blaming Socorro for putting her children in danger, Child Protective Services (CPS) left her childless, alone with an abusive husband, and without the resources to escape this situation. With no one to protect her, CPS criminalized Socorro along with her husband as if they were one and the same. It was in fighting the state to get her children back that Socorro finally gained the courage to press charges against her husband. She simultaneously battled the state and her husband, but was determined to assert herself against both. Still, without legal status, the options for Socorro were limited. As a single mother of four, returning to Mexico was not a viable option. Indeed, most of her family networks were already scattered across the United States. Instead, she turned to a brother in Indiana and moved there shortly after being reunited with her children.

Freed from her husband and Georgia's child protective services, Socorro confronted other barriers to her survival. Though no longer in an abusive situation, the emotional reverberations of such an experience continued to haunt Socorro and her children as they grappled to redefine their notions of family at the Crossroads of America. Importantly, the state motto of Indiana is "The

Crossroads of America" because it was considered the transportation cross-roads of the United States, now we can view this region as also encompassing the crossroads of human experiences and immigrant complexities. Trauma-tized by domestic violence, Socorro's family suffered from multiple levels of pain manifested in their new surroundings. Emotionally, the time spent in "the system" left a lasting impact on the children. Her eldest daughter resented her mother and partially blamed her for the family's heartache. It did not help that their new home was in rural Indiana and felt unwelcoming to the Mexi-can American pre-teen. At least in Georgia families of color were not rare. The demography of Indiana meant that Socorro and her children were one of few non-White families in the area. Moreover, Socorro's daughter refused to see her mother as an authority figure. Old enough to remember the abuse and ca-pable of understanding how the courts created a case against Socorro as a weak mother incapable of protecting her children, the eldest daughter's relationship with her mother was severely damaged. In stepping in as they did, CPS and the court system in effect demeaned Socorro before empowering her. As first an accomplice to domestic violence and then victim of it, Socorro was disem-powered by a state that resented her presence to begin with.

Facing new challenges in an equally uninviting state, Socorro wished her daughter and she would bond as survivors of trauma. Instead, there remained distance. This detachment carried over to her other children. For example, Pablito was only an infant when he was taken and placed in an English-dominant household with White parents. In the time that it took to regain custody of her children, Pablito had grown attached to his foster family and spoke only English as a result of being raised with them. Socorro still struggled to com-municate with her son even a year after reunification. Indeed, all her children attended English dominant schools where Spanish or bilingual education was not an option in this area of Indiana. It was in referencing Pablito that So-corro's voice finally broke. So many encounters with police officers, lawyers, judges, social service workers, and guardian ad litum had somehow normal-ized the telling and retelling of her abusive situation as part of her scripted self. Domestic violence was who she was, not what she had lived. Internalizing the abuse as part and parcel of her identity, Socorro retold the details of her life in an almost robotic, disconnected manner. But, it was the emotional and lin-guistic separation from her children that drew an emotive response from So-corro. As she noted through emotional pauses, "Mi niña, my middle daughter has to [long pensive pause] talk to him for me." In the middle of this state-ment, Socorro took a long breath and struggled to control the tears. We embraced as I let her know that her strength is ultimately what her children will remember.

Though many of Socorro's issues began in Georgia, moving to Indiana exacerbated her situation both with her children and in her search for autonomy. As an undocumented single mother, she still confronted daily struggles related to her class position, immigration status, and her gendered expectations that denied her opportunities, like day-laborer jobs, to support her family. Additionally, Indiana legislators had just made it more difficult for people like her to live. As Socorro related, she could not work because she could be flagged with E-verify, she could not drive due to fear of being caught without a driver's license and deported. Even though in Indiana Socorro learned she qualified for a U-visa, an option made available through the Violence Against Women Act that allowed victims of crimes temporary legal-status, the process for approval would take time and in the interim she was still deemed worthy of deportation according to state sanctions. Under Indiana's immigration bill, even immigrants who were in the process of seeking asylum or in queue for adjusting their status could be criminally charged for being undocumented and thus ruin their petitions for legal residency. The possibility of being picked up in Indiana further debilitated survival for the family and once again marked Socorro as a juridical threat worthy of policing.

Caught at the ideological crossroads of belonging, anyone imagined as possibly undocumented in Indiana struggled against intersecting sources of oppression. Racism, classism, gender expectations, and state-based attempts to control their every move created an inhospitable atmosphere. Living in Indiana under these circumstances meant Socorro still felt uneasy and incredibly debilitated by the continued lack of control over her own future. For instance, every time she saw a patrol car on the road or a police officer at the mall her heart raced for fear that they still had the right to deport her and once again sever her from her children. Rather than trust law enforcement, residents like Socorro feared them. As Zatz and Smith (2012) explore, the criminalization of immigrants creates more dangerous situations for undocumented populations whose fear of detection leaves them much more vulnerable to other, more damaging, threats from those willing to take advantage of their situation. In Socorro's case, the daily abuse of a terrifying husband was heightened by the threats of deportation. Critically, immigration status can play a devastating role in domestic violence because it heightens the power differential between partners (Menjívar & Salcido, 2002; Rieser-Murphy & DeMarco, 2012). Both in Georgia and Indiana, Socorro's undocumented status meant she was perceived as a criminal and that perception limited her wage-labor as well as her personal safety.

Indeed, male and female migrants confronted daily the devastating mechanisms of control that criminalized their very presence.

Justified as a fight for sovereignty against undocumented residents, the first decade of the twenty-first century reigned in multiple legislative attempts at local, state, and national arenas that de-humanized individuals and marked them as criminal threats. In a post-September 11th atmosphere, the fear of a dangerous outsider gathered steam in the American imaginary. Though those who attacked the Twin Towers in 2001 were all in the country with valid visas, it was undocumented immigrants whose bodies were found suspect. For undocumented immigrants their mere presence, or suspected undocumented presence, created a state of exception that warranted unconstitutional searches and violations of their rights (Rosas, 2006; Sanchez, 2011). Indeed, because they were deemed without rights, undocumented populations often found themselves the target of politicians and law officials. In late 2005, Wisconsin Representative F. James Sensenbrenner introduced HR 4437 or the "Border Protection, Antiterrorism, and Illegal Immigration Control Act of 2005." Nationally, this moment marked the regional leap to "new" immigration settling locations. What followed was months of deep national debate about what to do about the country's estimated 12 million undocumented immigrants. In ethnographic fieldwork I conducted in Indiana during the 2006 national immigration debate, I came to understand how the "xenophobia narrative" impacted interactions between people (Sanchez, 2011, p. 127). Neighbors, co-workers, classmates, and parishioners of the same church were suddenly demeaned as possible threats in the political debate. In Indiana, children were being accosted at school and in public places. Indeed, a U.S.-born daughter of Mexican immigrants recalled being in her vehicle at a red light when a car of college-age men screamed for her to go back to where she came from. Mothers feared taking their children to school or even venturing to the grocery store, afraid of rumors that ICE could pick them up even in these otherwise banal places. Indeed, the fears and feelings of resentment was palpable in 2006. When the Senate failed to reach an agreement on a federal immigration bill it seemed all the animosity would die down. Instead, actors at the state-level were busy planning their own answers. Four years later, Arizona passed its now infamous S.B. 1070. The bill's "show me your papers" provisions dangerously tied identifiable markers with unlawful behavior. Relying on arbitrary features to determine who was worthy of stopping tied criminalization to already engrained notions of racialized and classed belonging. Indeed, the self-proclaimed "toughest Sheriff in America," Joe Arpaio, is under federal investigation for an over-representation of brown working-class bodies in his detention centers. Even with significant challenges against Arizona's draconian legislations, other states across the country followed suit with their own renditions.

On May 10th, 2011, governor Mitch Daniels of Indiana signed S.B. 590 into law and affirmed where the state positioned itself in this contentious battle. Challenged for its divisive tone and Arizona-style punitive measures, S.B. 590 raised concern statewide. The bill's sponsor, Mike Delph, had a history of trying and failing to raise enough support for similar bills in the past. In each previous attempt, bipartisan reasonable minds won out as they contested Delph's bill. However, changes in the in the 2010 midterm elections, a rise in Tea Party advocates, and the Arizona bill emboldened Mr. Delph to re-introduce his anti-immigrant bill. Legally, undocumented status only warranted a misdemeanor in our court systems. To change this, Delph and his supporters created criminal and punitive measures that targeted the daily behavior of undocumented residents. Under these new restrictions, a minor traffic infraction would now warrant an arrest rather than simply a fine. If a law officer had "reasonable suspicion," they could demand to see proof of immigration status, detain, and report them to immigration officials. Again, like Arizona, identifying how reasonable suspicion could be gleaned was left undefined and open to the discretion of police officers. Delph also included English-only stipulations for all state-related business. Importantly, this provision is unrelated to undocumented status and has everything to do with the "language subordination" of Indiana residents presumed to be undocumented (Menéndez Alarcón & Novak, 2010). Though clearly ethnocentric and indicative of the race-based assumptions of legislators, the English-only stipulation remained unchallenged in the final passing of the bill. Additionally, the bill threatened to revoke business licenses to those who knowingly employed undocumented workers, required the use of E-verify system, and criminalized day labor practices. Lastly, the bill included stipulations that criminalized the transporting, aiding, or shielding of undocumented immigrants from detection, outlawed sanctuary cities, denied consular IDs as valid forms of identification, and rescinded a previously approved policy that left open the possibility for in-state tuition for undocumented youth graduating from Indiana schools and barred them from any forms of financial aid. Indeed, the bill aimed to make life so incredibly difficult and unwelcoming that undocumented residents would leave the state immediately.

In Indiana, and throughout the United States, contemporary attempts to criminalize immigrants created a new era of crimmigration. Described by Juliet Stumpf (2006) as a troubling move toward "the criminalization of immigration law, or 'crimmigration law'" that creates an "undesirable result [of] an ever-expanding population of the excluded and alienated" (p. 378). Stumpf imagines a future where it is more and more acceptable to exclude membership to community based on notions of race and class. Indeed, rather than evolve from our previous inclinations of racism and privilege, Stumpf fears that the move toward crimmigration law might solidify and reinforce previously debased notions that joined difference with hierarchy. Indeed, her warnings are ever more realized in the political debates against immigration that utilized rhetoric to de-humanize the undocumented population. Attempting to debate the broken immigration system, some have turned to damning those caught in it. Here, the people who circumnavigate the system for survival are stripped of their human qualities, called aliens, or referred to as "illegals." By stripping individual human beings of their noun signifier and replacing it with an adjective that is supposed to describe their illegal entry, millions of human beings become transformed into hordes of threatening menaces. No longer human, "illegals" can be dismissed and castigated in the communal psyche.

It is important to recognize that Indiana's bill received immediate resistance from those in the state that recognized the damaging impact of such legislation. Religious leaders, community members, and business representatives all expressed concern over the lived and financial impact of state-sanctioned hostility against certain members of the population. Indeed, Hoosiers, the colloquial term used to reference people from Indiana, of all racial and ethnic backgrounds joined together to promote an alternative approach toward immigration. Modeled after similar efforts of resistance in Utah against Arizona-style legislation, the Indiana Compact effectively contested the criminalization of immigrants and their families, opposed the separation of families, emphasized the need for a welcoming and business friendly Indiana, and finally adopted a "spirit of inclusion" that promoted a "humane approach" toward undocumented immigrants. The signers of the Indiana Compact argued that all Hoosiers would feel the negative reverberations of businesses divesting from the state, boycotts from potential conventions, state funds used to defend the law against inevitable lawsuits, and heightened fears promulgated against particular populations. Even churches would be targeted if they were known to be transporting, shielding, or aiding undocumented immigrants. In addition to the Indiana Compact, major companies with locations in Indiana tried to make a fiscal argument against the bill as a deterrent for investing in further employment opportunities to the state. They argued that if passed, S.B. 590 would thwart expansion into the state because future employees and residents could protest living in such a caustic environment. The fear of detracting future residents to Indiana was a real one, especially as the governor Mitch Daniels recently promoted financial initiatives to stem the brain-drain in Indiana. The "Hoosier Hopes Scholarship" was intended to fund undergraduates of Indiana as long as they made a commitment to remain in the state after graduation. Daniels' initiative for the Hoosier Hopes Scholarship was initially introduced in 2007, just around the same time that Indiana's Sagamore Institute for Policy Research maintained that "Indiana is more dependent on immigration for total population growth than is most of the country" (Sagamore Institute, 2007, p. 7). In other words, the state's dependence on immigrant population increased as its already present population was steadily decreasing. Even with the damaging projections of population drain, the fear of immigrant dependency may have created more of an anxiety over who Indiana would consider a proper and accepted resident.

Placed at the proverbial intersections of the nation, Indiana was divided on how to engage the politics of immigration. Though a growing number of voices came out against S.B. 590, a louder institutional push from legislators created momentum to alter the bill slightly and pass it with a 31–18 vote. The new bill looked slightly different from the old, with the most obvious changes taking place in the stipulations against business that hired undocumented workers. Instead of revoking their business license, they were now placed in a probationary pattern. Additionally, the ability to ask for proof of citizenship or immigration status by law enforcement officers was no longer required, now such queries were simply allowed if the officer so deemed it necessary. Additionally, legislators added safeguards throughout the text of the now adopted State Enrolled Act (SEA) No. 590 that explicitly noted how the law "shall be enforced without regard to race, religion, gender, ethnicity, or national origin." Possibly added to protect the bill from accusations of racial profiling, SEA 590 mirrors its predecessor in Arizona by leaving open the notion of "reasonable suspicion" to the interpretation of law enforcement officials. By itself, this caveat was not deemed unconstitutional by the Supreme Court's 2012 ruling against Arizona; however, the Justices did warn against the possible manner in which such a stipulation could be enforced.

Immediately after SEA 590 was signed into law in Indiana, the state found itself in court fighting the ACLU on the validity of warrantless arrest and the potential to "criminalize commonly accepted forms of identification" issued by other nations (Stafford, 2012). Significantly, Indiana's own attorney general, Greg Zoeller, supported the Indiana Compact when the bill was being debated and resisted any appeal to the preliminary injunction once it was law. After the 2012 Supreme Court ruling on Arizona's S.B. 1070, Zoeller announced that he was no longer obligated to defend certain parts of Indiana's law that were deemed unconstitutional by the decision of Arizona et al v. The United States. This would seem a victory, except that the majority of SEA 590 remained active in the state of Indiana. Moreover, efforts by Mike Delph and two other Indiana senators continued to challenge Zoeller's authority on the issue. In September of 2012, with the aid of Kris Kobach from Kansas, three Indiana senators filed suit against their own state to force Zoeller into defending the entire law regardless of the Supreme Court decision.

When I returned to Indiana in October of 2012 and met with Socorro I was also exposed to other personal accounts from undocumented and multi-generational Latino whose life was impacted by the passage of 590. Importantly, these narratives revealed the disparity, and ultimately the legal problems, with implementing SEA 590. Indeed, it sounded as if some parts of the state resembled what Loewen (2005) historically explored as sun-down towns, or the regions of the United States people-of-color often avoided due to racial intimidation tactics. Since the passage of the law, Latinos in Indiana were weary of certain areas of the state feared to target brown-bodies at rates much higher than in other regions. Notably, the areas that Delph and his allies represented were jurisdictions to be avoided. Latino drivers, regardless of documented status, expressed how certain regions of Indiana were hostile toward the popularly referred to crime of "driving while Mexican." In particular, Latino Hoosiers related stories of encounters with the law that yielded drastically different experiences depending on where one was stopped. In some jurisdictions, law enforcement simply handed out citations to drivers for their traffic violation rather than criminally charge them and report them to immigration officials. For instance, when Efraín, an otherwise law-abiding undocumented pastor, was stopped for a minor traffic violation he was charged with a Class C misdemeanor for driving without a license, jailed for a few hours, and fined. Lucía related an almost identical encounter for her friend Sandra who was pulled over just a few miles away from where Efraín was stopped, asked for a driver's license, and upon responding with a Spanish accent asked to provide proof of residency. Because she had no proof, Sandra was deported and had to take her U.S.-born children back to a country they had never known. Importantly, Indiana Code 9-24-18-1 stipulates that driving without a driver's license is simply a Class C Misdemeanor unless the person has a prior offense, in which case it becomes a Class A misdemeanor. Lucía had no prior offense, but her status as an undocumented immigrant led her into deportation proceedings. At most, this kind of Class C Misdemeanor carries with it a stint in jail and a fine regardless of the status of the driver. These scenarios reveal how defining "reasonable suspicion" varies throughout the state and how some police officers continued to rely on ethnic markers to probe those they stopped. In Efraín's case, the town's law enforcement worked for years to develop a trustworthy relationship with the Latino community. Once 590 passed, they ensured Latino residents that their race, accented Spanish, or skin color will never be used as a marker of "reasonable suspicion." However, other jurisdictions have purposefully left unsaid what would warrant an officer's further probing of someone's status and this flexibility has led to drastically different modes of carrying out the letter of the law.

Laws, like that of SEA 590, serve to inflame tensions and reinforce prejudice for residents of states and localities where miscommunication is already rampant. Indeed, inciting a panic against immigration only leads to further unsubstantiated claims of criminality that become cemented in the local psyches. As Zatz and Smith (2012) noted, it is not immigration that makes neighborhoods less safe, it is "the moral panic about immigration and crime—and the resulting plethora of anti-immigrant laws and policies—[that] have made immigrants and their communities less safe" (p. 1.2). These laws, and their resulting criminalizing efforts, reinforced racial prejudice by tying criminal behavior to immigrant residents whose only infraction often was their extralegal passage into the United States. For instance, Zats and Smith (2012) relate data from other studies where "cities with the greatest concentrations of immigrants have lower homicide rates" (p. 1.4). That is, instead of immigrants posing potential threats to communities and neighborhoods, it is the punitive measures and misconceptions that pose the greater threat to immigrants themselves. Exploitation often results from the devaluation of rights and human worth. Thus, abusive partners, wage theft and horrendous housing conditions are but some of the potential dangers immigrants face as the result of punitive political measures.

Immigration bills, like Indiana's 590, rely on erasing the personal from the political and purging the human element from the politics of immigration. Hyperbolic speeches and rhetoric of impending hordes of undocumented immigrants, what Sanchez (2011) calls the spectre of Latino demographic growth, disaggregate the real human experience from the impact of these laws. Rather than solving the broken immigration system, these crimmigration attempts only serve to create further fissures in our society. To criminalize, round up, or otherwise shun these people for merely attempting to survive recreates divisions and ignores the failures of a broken immigration system. Importantly, these all too familiar tactics overlook one simple truism; you cannot simply wish away or legislate people and their circumstances out of existence. Socorro, her children, Efrain, and Lucía represent only a fraction of real flesh and blood people who struggled daily to make Indiana home. Legislating state-sanctioned intolerance impinged on the lives of undocumented immigrants, their citizen-children, and those who are likely to be targeted as unlawfully residing in states like Indiana. Rather than demonize families like Socorro's, society needs to recognize that there are human faces, human experiences, human beings beyond the caustic language often used to describe this population. In keeping stories like that of Socorro's silent, political rhetoric distorts the lives of these extra-legal residents and simultaneously increases their vulnerability in society. Driven further into the shadows, families like Socorro's must find ways to navigate state-based intimidation tactics to quite literally survive. For many, Kris Kobach's answer to "self-deport" is simply not a possibility. Indeed, collectives such as the Indiana Compact showcase how such a scenario is not even desirable for many leaders of communities. Instead of fleeing, immigrants hold strong in these inhospitable spaces and "affirm the right to have rights in the society in which they live" (Oboler, 2010, p. 150). Rather than criminals, undocumented residents strive to prove daily their worth to communities. In doing so, they contest attempts to mark their bodies as unacceptable and affirm their rights to reside and raise children in these spaces.

Discussion Questions

1. How could CPS handle cases like Socorro's differently in the future so as not to create the damage done to Socorro's eldest daughter and Pablito?
2. Locate other examples of Class C misdemeanors in your state and consider how everyone one of us can be deemed "illegal" at one point or another in our lives.
3. What are the outcomes of crimmigration tactics 5–10 years down the line? Will immigration be solved this way? What about the personal stories, should they impact how we crimanilize otherwise law-abiding residents— or is Socorro the same as a violent offender deserving of deportation?
4. What is the issues of giving police officers jurisdiction over determining "reasonable suspicion" and what would be the problems of defining how to determine reasonable suspicion based on look, accented Spanish, or working-class background?

References

Loewen, J. W. (2005). Sundown Towns: A Hidden Dimension of American Racism. New York: The New Press.

Menéndez Alarcón, A. V., & Novak, K. B. (2010). Latin American immigrants in Indianapolis: Perceptions of prejudice and discrimination. Latino Studies, 8, 93–120.

Menjívar, C., & Salcido, O. (2002). Immigrant Women and Domestic Violence: Common Experiences in Different Countries. Gender & Society, 16, 898–920.

Oboler, S. (2010). On race, racial profiling, and states of mind(lessness). Latino Studies, 8, p. 150.

Pessar, P. R., & Mahler, S. J. (2003). Transnational Migration: Bringing Gender In. International Migration Review, 37, 812–846.

Rieser-Murphy, E. R., & DeMarco, K. D. (2012). The Unintended Consequences of Alabama's Immigration Law on Domestic Violence Victims. University of Miami Law Review, 66, 1059–1088.

Rosas, G. (2006). The Thickening Borderlands: Diffused Exceptionality and "Immigrant" Social Struggles during the "War on Terror". Cultural Dynamics, 18.3, 335–349.

Sagamore Institute. (2007). Indiana Immigration and Workforce Patterns Policy Brief. Indianapolis, Indiana.

Sánchez, R. (2011). The Toxic Tonic: Narratives of Xenophobia. Latino Studies, 9, 126–144.

Stafford, D. (September 26, 2012). Zoeller, senators at odds over immigration law. Retrieved from http://www.theindianalawyer.com.

Stumpf, J. (2006). The Crimmigration Crisis: Immigrants, Crime, and Sovereign Power. American University Law Review, 56, 367–419.

Zatz, M. S., & Smith, H. (2012). Immigration, Crime, and Victimization: Rhetoric and Reality. The Annual Review of Law and Social Sciences, 8, 1.1–1.19.

Actors and Players:
The Socio-Political Context
of the Criminalization
# of Immigration

Chapter Seven

Laborers or Criminals? The Impact of Crimmigration on Labor Standards Enforcement

Kati L. Griffith

Soon after Alabama passed its crimmigration law in the Spring of 2011, an undocumented immigrant worker named Hortensia felt its impact. When she was not paid for her landscaping work, she attributed her employer's behavior to Alabama's crimmigration law. As she stated, the law "gives him the power ... You're listening on the TV and the radio, knowing how little we can defend ourselves as immigrants now.... [T]here is no one to defend me." She reported that it was not worth making a complaint about the failure to receive wages for the work she had performed. As she put it, "You can't fight with anyone if you aren't legal, and that's why he didn't pay us.... We haven't gone to the court because it's like we have no case because we're illegal. We're afraid to do it." (Southern Poverty Law Center, 2012, pp. 11–12)

As we examine the criminalization of immigration, commonly referred to as "crimmigration" (Stumpf, 2006), it is essential to consider its impact on other areas of law and policy that involve immigrants but are not traditionally thought of as formal elements of either criminal law or immigration law. Why? As Hortensia's story illustrates, crimmigration may unexpectedly affect protections and rights that relate to immigrants' experiences but come from other areas of law and policy. This chapter explores the impact of crimmigration on labor standards enforcement. By labor standards enforcement, the chapter refers mainly to the wage and hour, health and safety, anti-employment discrimination, and collective activity protections that emerge when an employee performs labor for an employer. At the federal level, the statutes that provide these rights include the National Labor Relations Act (1935), the Fair Labor Standards Act (1938), the Civil Rights Act (1964), the Occupation Safety and Health Act (1970) and the Migrant and Seasonal Agricultural Workers Protection Act (1983). Most of these federal protections have state counterparts that provide equal or greater protections. Thus, labor standards protections generally come from the labor and employment law regime and arise because of the existence of an employment relationship, regardless of immigration status. As this chapter will illustrate, the crimmigration dynamic threatens to negatively affect these longstanding and baseline workplace protections in a number of ways.

While crimmigration threatens the labor standards of immigrants and non-immigrants alike, the crimmigration threat is felt most acutely by those immigrant workers who labor in the United States without sufficient immigration authorization to do so ("undocumented workers"). Thus, the chapter will focus on crimmigration as it affects the significant number of undocumented workers in the United States. Hortensia is not alone. A recent study by the Pew Hispanic Center concluded that the number of undocumented immigrants in the United States labor force reached eight million in 2010 (Passel & Cohn, 2011, p. 17). Some analysts believe that this is a very conservative estimate and that the undocumented workforce is actually much larger (Feltman, 2008, p. 80). Undocumented workers are concentrated in low-wage jobs. Indeed, the percentage of undocumented workers is highest in the farming (25%), building, grounds-keeping and maintenance (19%), construction (17%) and food preparation and serving (12%) occupations (Passel & Cohn, 2009, p. 15). Some analysts estimate that undocumented workers constitute more than a quarter of the meatpacking and chicken processing industries in the United States (Ordoñez, Hall, & Alexander, 2010).

Undocumented workers merit special attention when examining crimmigration's effects on labor standards enforcement, not only because of their significant presence in low-wage industries. When compared to low-wage documented workers, undocumented workers experience violations of their labor standards protections at higher rates (Bernhardt et al., 2009). Some of the most widely-publicized and extreme forms of workplace law violations involving low-wage immigrant workers have come from the meatpacking and chicken processing industries. An immigration raid at Agriprocessor's Iowa meatpacking plant in May 2008, for example, exposed major violations of workplace protections. Among other things, the search warrant alleged extensive injuries, child labor violations, sexual harassment, employment discrimination and failure to pay proper wages (Preston, 2008). These working conditions are consistent with an earlier and widely-publicized Human Rights Watch report about working conditions in the meatpacking industry. The report characterized jobs in the meatpacking industry as the "most dangerous factory jobs in the country" (as cited in Compa & Fellner, 2005). Injuries in meat-packing plants, according to the report, commonly include "cuts, amputa-tions, skin disease, permanent arm and shoulder damage, and even death from the force of repeated hard cutting motions" (Compa, 2004, p. 29).

What Is Crimmigration in the Labor Context?

Many aspects of crimmigration have been aptly characterized by the other authors of this volume. Nonetheless, very few scholars and analysts have fo-cused on the labor-related aspects of crimmigration. This chapter first de-scribes several characteristics of the crimmigration phenomena that are unique to the labor context. In Part II, it then elaborates the underappreciated con-sequences of these aspects of crimmigration on undocumented workers' wage, health and safety, employment discrimination and collective activity protections (labor standards enforcement).

Both the federal government and subfederal governments (states, cities and other types of local governments) have brought crimmigration enforcement directly into the workplace in a number of ways. As a result, the nature of im-migration enforcement in the workplace has increasingly included norms, pro-cedures, enforcement tactics and sanctions from the criminal law context. In 1986, the federal government introduced crimmigration into the labor con-text for the first time. That year, the U.S. Congress passed the Immigration Reform and Control Act, commonly referred to by its initials, "IRCA" (1986). This long-debated federal legislation represented the first time that the federal government explicitly aimed to regulate immigration flows via the workplace, rather than solely at the borderlands and through other types of interior en-forcement measures.

While IRCA's sanctions primarily targeted employers' behavior, this federal immigration law created new criminal sanctions for both employees and em-ployers. The U.S. Congress did not make the act of working without immi-gration authorization an illegal act. Instead, through an amendment, it instituted criminal penalties for employees who knowingly use fraudulent documents to gain employment (IRCA, 1986, § 1324c(a); Hoffman Plastic Compounds, Inc. v. N.L.R.B., 2002, p. 149). Thus, employees who provide false identification documents to their employers are subject to sanctions. These penalties add to the myriad other ways that criminal law intertwines with immigration en-forcement measures against undocumented immigrant workers.

IRCA's verification requirements and sanctions, however, illustrate that employers are the primary focus of IRCA's enforcement measures. Before IRCA, employers did not have to check whether their employees had proper immigration authorization to work in the United States. Because of IRCA, employers must verify that each employee has proper immigration authorization to work through the use of an I-9 form or an electronic verification system (E-Verify). Employers also face potential civil and criminal sanctions for knowingly hiring an undocumented worker. Specifically, IRCA provides criminal sanctions for employers who have a pattern or practice of knowingly employing undocumented workers (§ 1324a(f), 1986). Employers who knowingly hire undocumented workers can be fined up to $3,000 for each undocumented worker and/or face imprisonment for up to six months (IRCA, § 1324a(f)(1), 1986). Along with these criminal penalties, employers can be charged with other kinds of crimes "such as document fraud or harboring unauthorized aliens, and [can be] subject to the relevant penalties for those violations" (Bruno, 2012, p. 5).

The federal government is not alone in its efforts to bring crimmigration enforcement into the workplace. Subfederal governments have also brought crimmigration into the labor context in recent years through a variety of immigration regulatory measures and workplace-based enforcement actions. The laws of a number of states, for example, contain criminal penalties for employers who employ undocumented immigrants. A few examples include Fla. Stat. Ann., § 448.09, 2010, Va. Code Ann., § 40.1-11.1, 2010, W. Va. Code Ann., § 21-1B-5, 2010, Colo. Rec. Stat. Ann., § 8-2-122(4), 2010, Idaho Code Ann., § 44-1005, 2012 and Iowa Code Ann., § 715A.2A 2010. In addition, some localities have entered into agreements with the federal government, often referred to as "287g agreements," which allow local law enforcement officers to enforce some elements of immigration law (Vazquez, 2011, p. 658; Illegal Immigration Reform and Immigrant Responsibility Act [IIRIRA], § 1357(g), 1996).

For both the federal and subfederal governments, crimmigration enforcement efforts in the workplace sometimes take the form of surprise raids of workplaces by law enforcement officers and civil or criminal arrests in the wake of those raids. After the large-scale immigration raid of Agriprocessor's meatpacking plant described above, several supervisors were arrested and almost 300 undocumented immigrant workers were convicted of both immigration and criminal charges. The majority of these workers were sentenced to five months in prison. Many of them were then deported from the United States upon the completion of their incarceration (Preston, 2008).

Immigration cases constitute a significant portion of the federal government's criminal prosecutions each year in the United States. In fact, just over thirty percent of all federal prosecutions involve immigration matters. This percentage is higher than the percentage for any other type of federal criminal prosecution. Not surprisingly, therefore, the Immigration and Customs Enforcement Agency (ICE) is now the most significant investigative branch of the U.S. Department of Homeland Security (Stumpf, 2008, p. 1589). As the chapter will elaborate upon in Part II, mounting crimmigration pressures on both employers and employees at the federal and subfederal levels threaten to affect labor standards enforcement in a number of ways. The potential consequences of crimmigration in the labor context are all-too-often underappreciated aspects of the crimmigration story.

What Are the Potential Consequences of Crimmigration in the Labor Context?

Crimmigration may affect labor standards enforcement because it alters the set of incentives of both employers and employees. Incentives and disincentives play an important role in the development and enforcement of laws in the United States. Indeed, laws largely intend to "regulate[] behavior by generating incentives" and thus do not rely exclusively on "the direct exertion of coercive force" (Cox, 2008, p. 387). Crimmigration creates incentives for bad apple employers to discriminate against job applicants that "look foreign." Crimmigration in the labor context also fosters employer incentives to reduce workers' collective action efforts and potential complaints about wages, health and safety, and employment discrimination through immigration enforcement threats. Similarly, it establishes disincentives for employees to come forward to government authorities to complain about their employers' violations of their workplace protections.

These incentives and disincentives are important to highlight because the fundamental rationale underlying workplace protections for wages, health and safety, anti-discrimination and collective activity is that the law should create disincentives for employers to fail to provide these protections and should create incentives for employees to come forward when their protections have been violated. Rather than relying on government inspectors to police workplaces, U.S. labor and employment law largely relies on the power of employer disincentives and on the workers themselves to act as "private attorneys general" who come forward to notify government officials about potential violations of their rights (Griffith, 2011, pp. 431–36).

Crimmigration and Employer Discrimination

Crimmigration pressures from both the federal and subfederal levels may encourage risk-averse employers to steer away from Latino and other minority job applicants. This practice would violate employees' civil rights protections. As long as potential employees have proper work authorization, both Title VII of the Civil Rights Act and IRCA prohibit employers from favoring one national origin over another (Civil Rights Act, §2000e-2, 1964; IRCA, §1324b(a)(1), 1986). It is reasonable to conclude that if an employer faces potential criminal liability for hiring an undocumented worker, he or she may be nervous about hiring "foreign-sounding" or "foreign-looking" applicants who have proper work authorization. Instead of risking criminal liability, risk-averse employers may prefer to hire white, or "non-foreign-seeming," workers. In this way, crimmigration may unintentionally promote employment discrimination against Latino applicants and other minorities by creating problematic incentives to avoid hiring foreign employees.

The creation of additional burdens on employers in the immigration enforcement context encourages employment discrimination. When Congress enacted IRCA, it acknowledged that too many burdens on employers could lead to unwanted employment discrimination. As a result, it included a number of safeguards against employment discrimination based on national origin and citizenship status (IRCA, §1324b(a)(1), 1986). It also created an Office of the Special Counsel for Immigration-Related Unfair Employment Practices to enforce IRCA's employment discrimination protections. As I have argued elsewhere based on a review of IRCA's legislative history, "Congress arguably kept burdens on employers minimal, at least in part, to reduce incentives for employers to discriminate." Thus, the combined federal and subfederal crimmigration activity "raises the stakes for employers," creating additional incentives to discriminate against employees based on race, national origin and citizenship status (Griffith, 2011, p. 423). These incentives are in tension with Title VII of the Civil Rights Act as well as IRCA's protections against employment discrimination.

Crimmigration and Employer Retaliation

Crimmigration may affect labor standards enforcement by emboldening some bad apple employers to use immigration threats to retaliate against undocumented immigrant employees who are organizing collectively with their co-workers, or who may complain to government officials about violations of their workplace rights. The labor standards protections discussed here explicitly forbid employers from retaliating against employees who make complaints about potential violations of their wage, health and safety, anti-discrimination and collective activity protections (Civil Rights Act, §2000e-3(a), 1964; Fair Labor Standards Act [FLSA], §215(a)(3), 1938; Occupational Safety and Health Act [OSHA], §660(c), 1970; National Labor Relations Act [NLRA], §158(a)(4), 1935). Employers who retaliate against their employees by actually calling federal or subfederal enforcement officers, or by threatening to call these officials, endanger these baseline workplace protections.

Workers faced with the potential consequence of not only deportation, but also criminal sanctions, are more disinclined to join their co-workers in collective efforts to improve working conditions and to complain to government officials when their workplace rights are violated. As a federal appeals court judge put it, as compared to their documented counterparts, "undocumented workers confront the harsher reality that, in addition to possible discharge, their employer will likely report them to the [immigration authorities] and they will be subjected to deportation proceedings or criminal prosecution" (Rivera v. NIBCO, Inc., 2004, p. 1064). As a result, these workers are less likely to fulfill their crucial roles as private attorneys' general in the labor standards enforcement scheme.

The recent crimmigration trend to involve subfederal law enforcement officers in immigration enforcement threatens to be particularly problematic. Professor Stephen Lee has recently uncovered the ways in which some employers may use local law enforcement officers to retaliate against their undocumented immigrant employees. According to Lee, "crafty employers can report incompliant workers to local law enforcement officers" who then report the workers to federal immigration authorities. Thus, crimmigration enforcement by local officers further bolsters "the strong incentives employers have to report unauthorized workers at the first sign of labor-oriented activity" and has "begun to undermine the assertion of workplace-related rights" (2011 p. 1132).

Lee's invocation of a recent example from Tennessee illustrates this new subfederal crimmigration dynamic well (2011, pp. 1132–36). A cheese factory hired a number of undocumented workers and subsequently failed to comply with wage laws to compensate these workers for their work. The workers engaged in collective activity at their workplace to try to pressure their employer to pay them for the work they performed. In response, the employer called in subfederal criminal law officers and reported that the workers were undocumented immigrants. The subfederal criminal law officers detained the workers and contacted federal immigration authorities.

While there are numerous anecdotal reports and examples in the case law of this practice by some bad apple employers (Lee, 2009, p. 1120; Rivera v. NIBCO, Inc., 2004, p. 1064), there is very little empirical data on the frequency of employer retaliation in the crimmigration context. A three-city survey conducted in 2009, however, illustrated that employers who retaliate in low-wage industries often retaliate by threatening to call immigration authorities when faced with collective activity in the workplace or potential workplace law complaints (Bernhardt et al., 2009, pp. 24–25). Moreover, according to the Human Rights Report about the meatpacking industry referenced above, employers too often take advantage of immigrants' "vulnerabilities," which include "limited English skills; uncertainty about their rights; alarm about their immigration status if they are undocumented workers" (as cited in Compa & Fellner, 2005).

Crimmigration and the Culture of Fear

Crimmigration may not only affect labor standards enforcement by creating problematic incentives for employers to engage in employment discrimination, by encouraging new forms of employer retaliation, or by bringing subfederal law enforcement officers into the mix. Crimmigration may also affect labor standard enforcement by further fostering a culture of fear in immigrant communities. In this way, crimmigration has a powerful symbolic effect even when it does not directly affect employers' behavior or specific immigration enforcement initiatives in the workplace. As Hortensia said in the opening paragraph, "because we're illegal ... [w]e're afraid to" complain about our employer's failure to pay us for the work that we completed. In her words, Alabama's crimmigration law "gives him [the employer] the power" to fail to pay his undocumented immigrant workers if he so desires (Southern Poverty Law Center, 2012, pp. 11–12). Undocumented immigrants' fear of coming forward and organizing collectively with fellow workers because of immigration consequences is noted extensively by scholars and worker advocates (Griffith, 2012, pp. 633–35).

Heightened fear among immigrants reduces their incentives to come forward when they experience even the most severe abuses of their workplace protections. It also affects their incentives to engage in collective activity and the overall bargaining power of workers vis-à-vis their employers. These trends further weaken organized labor's efforts in the workplace. Professor Hila Shamir's proposal to bring labor norms into anti-trafficking law has recently highlighted, in a different context, that the criminalization of immigrant workers increases fear among workers and weakens workers' bargaining power. As a response, she proposed an innovative and inclusive approach to trafficking law which "focuses attention on elements of the legal order that shape workers' bargaining power, such as labor and employment laws, national immigration regimes, criminal law, welfare law, and private law background rules" (2012, p. 94).

Discussion Questions

1. What are the specific ways that crimmigration law affects the labor context?
2. Are you convinced of this chapter's claim that crimmigration negatively affects labor standards enforcement? Why or why not?
3. Current comprehensive immigration reform proposals do not explicitly address immigration law's effects on the wages, working conditions and collective activity protections of immigrant workers. Should they? Why or why not?
4. Assume for the purposes of this final question that you believe that comprehensive immigration reform proposals need to address the problems raised in this chapter; what explicit proposals should be added to new legislation that could deal with the specific problems raised in this chapter?

References

Bernhardt, A., Milkman, R., Theodore, N., Heckathorn, D., Auer, M., DeFilippis, J.... Spiller, M. (2009). Broken Laws, Unprotected Workers: Violations of employment and labor laws in America's cities. Retrieved from http://www.nelp.org/page//brokenlaws/BrokenLawsReport2009.pdf.

Bruno, A. (2010, March). Immigration-Related Worksite Enforcement: Performance measures (CRS Report No. R40002). Retrieved from http://www.fas.org/sgp/crs/homesec/R40002.pdf.

Civil Rights Act of 1964, Pub. L. No. 88–352, 78 Stat. 241, 253-66 (codified as amended at 42 U.S.C. §§ 2000e–2000e-17 (2006)).

Colo. Rev. Stat. Ann. § 8-2-122(4) (West 2012).

Compa, L. & Fellner, J. (2005, August 3). Meatpacking's Human Toll. The Washington Post. Retrieved from http://www.washingtonpost.com/wpdyn/content/article/2005/08/02/AR2005080201936.html.

Cox, A. B. (2008). Immigration Law's Organizing Principles. University of Pennsylvania Law Review, 157, 341–394.

Fair Labor Standards Act of 1938, Pub. L. No. 75–718, 52 Stat. 1060 (codified as amended at 29 U.S.C. §§ 201–19 (2006)).

Feltman, R. (2008). Undocumented Workers in the United States: Legal, Political, and Social Effects. Richmond Journal of Global Law and Business, 7, 65–86.

Fla. Stat. Ann. § 448.09 (West Supp. 2010).

Griffith, K. L. (2011). Discovering "Immployment" Law: The constitutionality of subfederal immigration regulation at work. Yale Law and Policy Review, 29, 389–452.

Griffith, K. L. (2012). Undocumented Workers: Crossing the borders of immigration and workplace law. Cornell Journal of Law and Public Policy, 21, 611–640.

Hoffman Plastic Compounds, Inc. v. N.L.R.B., 535 U.S. 137, 149 (2002).

Human Rights Watch. (2004). Blood, Sweat, and Fear: Workers' rights in the U.S. meat and poultry plants. Retrieved from http://www.hrw.org/sites/default/files/reports/usa0105.pdf.

Idaho Code Ann. § 44-1005 (West 2012).

Illegal Immigration Reform and Immigrant Responsibility Act of 1996 (IIRIRA), Pub. L. 104-208, 110 Stat. 3009-546 (codified as amended in scattered sections of 8 U.S.C.).

Immigration Reform and Control Act of 1986 (IRCA), Pub. L. No. 99-603, 100 Stat. 3359 (codified as amended in scattered sections of 8 U.S.C.).

Iowa Code Ann. § 715A.2A (West Supp. 2010).

Lee, S. (2009). Private Immigration Screening in the Workplace. Stanford Law Review, 61, 1103–1146.

Lee, S. (2011). Monitoring Immigration Enforcement. Arizona Law Review, 53, 1089–1136.

Migrant and Seasonal Agricultural Protection Act of 1983, Pub. L. 97-470, 96 Stat. 2583 (codified at 29 U.S.C. §§ 1801–1872 (2012)).

National Labor Relations Act of 1935 (NLRA), Pub. L. No. 74–198, 49 Stat. 449 (codified as amended at 29 U.S.C. §§ 141–69 (2006)).

Occupational Safety and Health Act of 1970, Pub. L. No. 91–596, 84 Stat. 1590 (codified as amended at 29 U.S.C. §§ 651–78 (2006)).

Ordoñez, K. H. & Alexander, A. (2010, June 25). Misery on the Line: Some Managers Knew Workers Were Illegal, Former Employees Say. Charlotte Observer. Retrieved from http://www.charlotteobserver.com/595/story/223444.html.

Passel, J. S., & Cohn, D. (2009). A Portrait of Unauthorized Immigrants in the United States. Retrieved from http://pewhispanic.org/files/reports/107.pdf.

Passel, J. S., & Cohn, D. (2010). Unauthorized Immigrant Population: National and state trends. Retrieved from http://pewhispanic.org/files/reports/133.pdf.

Preston, J. (2008, July 27). After Iowa Raid, Immigrants Fuel Labor Inquiries. New York Times. Retrieved from http://www.nytimes.com/2008/07/27/us/27immig.html.

Rivera v. NIBCO, Inc., 364 F.3d 1057 (9th Cir. 2004).

Shamir, H. A Labor Paradigm for Human Trafficking. UCLA Law Review, 60, 76–137.

Southern Poverty Law Center. (2012). A Boss Flashes Gun, Refuses to Pay. In Alabama's Shame: HB 56 and the war on immigrants. Retrieved from http://cdna.splcenter.org/sites/default/files/downloads/publication/SPLC_HB56_AlabamasShame.pdf.

Stumpf, J.P. (2006). The Crimmigration Crisis: Immigrants, Crime, and Sovereign Power. American University Law Review, 50, 367.

Stumpf, J.P. (2008). States of Confusion: The Rise of State and Local Power over Immigration, North Carolina Law Review, 86, 1557.

United States v. Alabama, 691 F.3d 1269 (11th Cir. 2012).

Va. Code Ann. § 40.1-11.1 (Supp. 2010).

Vazquez, Y. (2011). Perpetuating the Marginalization of Latinos: A collateral consequence of the incorporation of immigration law into the criminal justice system. Howard Law Journal, 54, 639–674.

W. Va. Code Ann. § 21-1B-5 (LexisNexis Supp. 2010).

Chapter Eight

Privatizing Immigration Detention Centers

Alissa R. Ackerman, Rich Furman, Britt Judy & Jeff Cohen

Introduction

The detention of immigrants and non-citizen residents in the United States is nothing new, nor is the use of incarceration as the primary means of punishment for citizens. The United States currently incarcerates approximately 2.3 million individuals, more than any other country in the world. With an incarceration rate of 716 per 100,000 people (International Center for Prison Studies, 2012) and an ever-increasing cost to incarcerate, the prison industrial complex, as it has been called, has had to develop new practices and cost-cutting measures.

Criminalizing immigrants has always been a way of handling the immigrant "problem" in the United States (Ackerman & Furman, 2013). However, criminalizing and detaining immigrants became more popular after the creation of Miami's Krome Avenue Detention Center to detain and process the Mariel refugees from Cuba in the early 1980s (Bosworth & Kaurman, 2011). Since the events of September 11, 2001, a nativist sentiment has perpetuated the criminalization of immigration and has resulted in the increased use of detention and possible removal of the undocumented. Not surprisingly, as with the prison industrial complex, Immigration and Customs Enforcement (ICE), and its predecessor the Immigration and Naturalization Services (INS), has turned to the private prison industry for incarceration and detention of immigrants.

In addition, states, in response to frustration with the lack of progress in passing comprehensive immigration reform at the federal level, have begun passing legislation targeting and criminalizing key aspects of the lives of the un-documented. Several scholars note the numerous and significant challenges faced by immigrants as the move toward the criminalization of immigration continues (Aman & Rehrig, 2011; Furman et. al 2012; Welsh, 2000). In this chapter we provide detailed discussions of the stake that the private prison industry has in creating the very policies used to detain immigrants in their facilities, the effects this has on the undocumented and their families, and how successful this endeavor has proven to be despite the questionable nature of such practices.

The Private Prison and Its Profit Motive

The prison industrial complex refers to the accelerated use of incarceration and the exponential increase of the prison population over the last thirty years. Some scholars have attributed the rise of the prison industrial complex to the profit motive of the private prison industry and ancillary businesses, small and large. The prison industrial complex is said to be the intersection between government and private business, where conflicting interests meet and combine. One potential consequence of this public-private partnership is that incarceration becomes nothing more than a profit stream for private industry. Schlosser (1998) contends:

> The United States has developed a prison-industrial complex—a set of bureaucratic, political, and economic interests that encourage increased spending on imprisonment, regardless of the actual need ... It is a confluence of special interests that has given prison construction in the United States a seemingly unstoppable momentum ... It is also a state of mind. The lure of big money is corrupting the nation's criminal-justice system, replacing notions of public service with a drive for higher profits (para. 7).

Various government functions, including incarceration, have trended toward privatization over the last several decades (Kaseke, 1998). Privatization has been viewed by as a means of meeting key social obligations while decreasing costs and closing budget deficits (Dorwart & Epstein, 1993; Furman, 2005). This belief has influenced the use of private entities or public/private partnerships at different levels of state and federal government, from private defense contractors such as Blackwater and DynCorp (see Scahill, 2007), to child protective services, health care entities, and the prison industry.

While there certainly has been private sector involvement within the corrections industry dating back to the 1700s, Ackerman and Furman (in press) suggest that the effects of the expansion of privatisation have been more profound within the penal system than anywhere else. By the 1980s, the face of private enterprise and incarceration began to change from individual prison services, such as food and laundry, to private companies contracting with the government to operate correctional institutions (Jing, 2010).

While several private corrections and security firms currently operate in the U.S. and abroad, the two largest are The Corrections Corporation of America (CCA) and The GEO Group. Under the premise that private companies were better equipped to produce cost savings for government run correctional institutions through public-private partnerships, CCA and The GEO Group began operations in the early 1980s. CCA and The Geo Group claim to offer quality and cost-effective services while decreasing the burden on taxpayers (Corrections Corporation of America, 2012; The Geo Group, 2012).

CCA alone incarcerates approximately 80,000 inmates in over 60 facilities across the U.S. The majority of these institutions are company owned, fewer than 20 are operated but not owned by CCA. To date, several federal agencies, including the Federal Bureau of Prisons (BOP), The U.S. Marshals Service, and ICE, as well as half of the U.S. states and several local municipalities have contracted with CCA (Corrections Corporation of America, 2012). The company continues to boast that it is the fifth largest corrections system in the U.S. The GEO Group owns or operates facilities in the U.S. and abroad. With 114 institutions worldwide, 65 of which are in the U.S., The GEO Group currently has an 80,000 bed capacity.

While the privately run correctional institution may be profitable, other possibilities for substantial profitability are found within subsidiary industries. CCA states that it specializes in the "design, construction, expansion and management of prisons, jails and detention facilities, as well as inmate transportation services ..." (Corrections Corporation of America, 2012). The GEO Group not only builds, designs, operates, and finances correctional institutions, detention centers, and residential treatment centers, they also provide services for secure inmate transport, pretrial and immigration custody services, correctional health care services and behavioral health and residential treatment services for both adults and juveniles (The GEO Group, 2012).

Over the last few years, state prison populations have decreased, but federal incarceration continues to increase. Despite the increase in federal inmates, the overall U.S. incarceration rate has decreased from 756 per 100,000 individuals just a few years ago to 716 per 100,000 in 2012 (International Centre for Prison Studies, 2012). Importantly, this is the first drop in the state prison population since the 1970s (Justice Policy Institute, 2011; West, Sabol, & Greenman, 2010). Private prison companies obtain the most revenue from state prison contracts and it stands to reason that as state prison populations decrease, so too will profits.

The Justice Policy Institute (2011) argues that private prison companies are concerned with profits above all else. Given this argument, it is essential to examine the profitability of both CCA and The GEO Group. In 2011, CCA had an estimated net worth of $1.4 billion and a net income of $162 million. The company's net income rose 1% and 3% in the 2009 and 2010 fiscal years, respectively. In fiscal year 2011, The GEO Group was estimated to have a net worth of $1.2 billion and a net income of $78 million. Given the decrease in state prison populations and the potential for decreases in profit, CCA and The GEO Group have entered into strategies to ensure future growth in revenue (Justice Policy Institute. 2011). The most obvious strategy is to ensure the acquisition of additional inmates from both federal and state institutions. Several opportunities exist to achieve this endeavor. Liptak (2011) describes one such opportunity when he discusses the recent order by the United States Supreme Court for the state of California to decrease its prison population by 46,000 individuals. The Supreme Court did not provide direction as to how this was to be accomplished; it is possible that instead of inmates being released, they may end up in private prisons.

Then Governor Arnold Schwarzenegger suggested that the state could cut costs and alleviate the problems associated with overcrowded prisons with a private venture to build prisons in Mexico. "Schwarzenegger said California could save about $1 billion a year if it built prisons in Mexico and then shipped those serving time in state prisons who are undocumented felons to Mexico to finish out their sentences. Nearly 20,000 of the state's 171,000 prisoners are illegal immigrants" (Brinkerhoff, 2010, para. 2). Though this was never a viable solution—some speculate that Schwarzenegger never spoke with any advisers about this—it points to the notion that, instead of releasing offenders, many will end up in privately run facilities. With government officials looking for cost cutting measures and for-profit prison companies looking to increase profits, many speculate that private prison corporations are focusing more on generating revenue above all else. This makes for the perfect union until one party can no longer fill the demands of the other. For example, Kirkham (2012a) recently reported that the CCA has sent letters to 48 states with offers to buy their prisons to remedy "challenging corrections budgets." In return, CCA is asking for a 20 year management contract and a promise that the prisons will be filled to at least ninety percent capacity. For some, this may represent an opportunity for states to reduce overcrowding in ways that maintain perceived safety and security. For others, the transfer of state inmates and institutions to private entities reduces the motivation to rethink and reform current, more punitive correctional policies that have resulted in overcrowding and increased costs.

Several entities, such as the Justice Policy Institute, suggest that the industry lobbies to influence criminal justice policies in their favor. Private prison corporations emphatically deny being in the business of lobbying for changes in criminal justice policy to positively impact their profit margins; however, reports have found evidence to the contrary. In an extensive report, the Justice Policy Institute (2011) discovered and analyzed a three stage strategy utilized by the private prison industry to increase revenue. The strategy includes 1) campaign contributions to state and federal lawmakers, 2) lobbying efforts within the U.S. Congress and various state legislatures, and 3) building and maintaining relationships with specific organizations, such as the American Legislative Exchange Council (ALEC). Since the beginning of the 21st century, CCA, The GEO Group, and Cornell Companies, which was recently bought by The GEO Group, have contributed almost a million dollars to federal lawmakers and an additional six million dollars to state politicians (Center for Responsible Politics, 2011 as cited in Justice Policy Institute, 2011). These companies are competent strategizers with regard to where they focus their campaign contributions. For example, CCA and The Geo Group both place the majority of their contributions in California and Florida, the states with the highest and second highest prison populations in the U.S. Florida also recently passed a mandate that several prisons be privatized (Justice Policy Institute, 2011; West, Sabol & Greenman, 2009; James, 2005).

In addition to various campaign contributions, active lobbying of state and federal lawmakers is a key strategic move (Justice Policy Institute, 2011). Lobbying efforts are focused almost exclusively on legislation related to correctional policy and law enforcement. Buffy McFayden, a Colorado state representative, gave an interview for a PBS documentary in 2008 in which she explained the lobbying strategies of the private prison industry. She stated that the lobbyists may not be sitting in the room when bills are voted on, but they are very much involved in insuring that any bill related to decreasing the prison population will fail (Brancaccio, 2008).

Since 2003, CCA has spent approximately $9 million on lobbying efforts (Center for Responsible Politics, 2011). In Florida alone, almost 30 individuals who work for the private prison industry lobby for contracts with private prisons and policies that promote their own existence (National Institute on Money in State Politics, 2001, as cited in Justice Policy Institute, 2011). It has been reported that The GEO Group was a driving force behind the Florida state legislature voting in favor of a budget deal that would privatize all South Florida prisons (Brown, 2011). Despite these and other examples, private prison companies maintain that they are not in the business of influencing criminal justice legislation. In fact, spokespeople for the industry emphatically deny taking part in any such practice (Brancaccio, 2008).

Finally, the private prison industry influences legislation, and therefore their own revenue stream, through relationships with organizations like ALEC, whose mission is to "advance the Jeffersonian principles of free markets, limited government, federalism, and individual liberty, through a nonpartisan public-private partnership of America's state legislators, members of the private sector, the federal government, and general public" (American Legislative Exchange Council, 2012). ALEC works to create "model" legislation that is often adopted by various state legislatures. The legislation drafted by ALEC is written by relevant stakeholders, including lobbyists from the private sector, business people, and lawmakers. Prison policy is only one area of possible legislation for ALEC. In fact, ALEC is responsible for legislation in the areas of civil justice, economic development, communications and technology, and health and human services, to name a few. According to Sullivan (2010b), private corporations, including CCA and The GEO Group pay millions of dollars a year to be members of ALEC. Both companies are currently active members. CCA contributes extra fees to sit on the Public Safety Task Force, even serving as its co-chair (Biewen, 2002, as cited in Justice Policy Institute, 2011).

State prison populations are decreasing and the private prison industry is examining new ways to generate revenue in an era where the public is becoming weary of mass incarceration. However, some of those who are weary of mass incarceration are also fearful and angry about immigration and want to see action taken by state and federal officials. Several authors in this volume have highlighted the various state laws aimed at criminalizing the immigrant population. The private prison industry and ALEC have been directly involved in the "model" legislation in this arena. As private prison companies continue their efforts to generate revenue, the next domain to increase market shares is immigrant detention. In fact, as recently as 2010, it was reported that the CEO of The GEO Group, during a call to investors, stated that " ... those people coming across the border and getting caught are going to have to be detained and that for me, at least I think, there's going to be enhanced opportunities for what we do" (last para.). As the CEO of The GEO Group candidly implied during this alleged call, immigrant detention is as good a venture as any. Indeed, 12%, or just under 23,000 individuals, of the federal prison population is currently comprised of individuals convicted of or awaiting trial for immigration offenses (Federal Bureau of Prisons, 2012). In addition to those in federal prisons, ICE currently detains, on average, 33,000 individuals, of which 17% are housed in contract facilities (Immigration, Customs, and Enforcement, 2012). These numbers will continue to increase as state level immigration laws become more ubiquitous and strict.

Despite continued efforts to disavow their stake in creating anti-immigrant legislation, a 2010 NPR investigation found that CCA publicly acknowledged that immigrant detention would increase company revenue (Sullivan, 2010b). During this investigation, Sullivan found that members of ALEC, state representatives, and individuals from the private prison industry met and drafted model legislation on immigrant detention. Soon after this meeting, Arizona's SB 1070 was introduced. In states that have enacted or have considered adopting Arizona-like immigration legislation, many of their lawmakers are members of ALEC. In fact five lawmakers from these states were in the room when the original model legislation was drafted (Sullivan, 2010b). It is without a doubt, according to Sullivan (2010), that both CCA and ALEC played key roles in the drafting of SB 1070. Referring back to the industry's three-pronged approach to increasing revenue, this example shows the plan in action. SB 1070 was co-sponsored by thirty-six Arizona state legislators, of which 30 had received donations or campaign contributions from the private prison industry and 24 were members of ALEC (Sullivan, 2010). The model legislation drafted by the parties noted above became what is essentially SB 1070.

The relationship between private prison corporations and government officials is more complicated than one would think. In fact, the relationship goes far beyond public-private partnerships or even the drafting of legislation. Government officials, themselves, are allegedly fostering and nurturing this already complex relationship. After serving as the director of the Federal Bureau of Prisons, J. Michael Quinlan became the head of Strategic Planning at CCA. He has also served as the Chief Operating Officer and Executive Vice President of the company. He now serves as Senior Vice President (CCA, 2012). Jan Brewer, governor of Arizona has ties to the private prison corporation as well. Though she is not and has not been employed by the industry, it has been reported that two of her most trusted top advisers were former lobbyists for the industry. That government officials are guilty of fostering these relationships should not be understated. Not unlike other industries (e.g., the financial sector), the blurring of the line between public and private interests has implications not only for the increased use of private prisons and detention centers but also the strength of government regulation and oversight. This increased reliance on the private sector is not without risk and consequence, including an amplification of the psychosocial risks associated with incarceration.

Immigrant Detention: Health, Safety, and Psychosocial Risk

The recent increase in anti-immigrant legislation and immigration related bills being brought before state lawmakers makes the discourse around the privately run detention center all the more pertinent. Despite the fact that illegal immigration, per se, is not an offense punishable by imprisonment, the onslaught of anti-immigrant legislation has turned immigration and the undocumented person into criminal justice issues. It is well known in the literature that incapacitation carries health and safety risk. This is even more pronounced for immigrants, especially those who are undocumented. Our criminal justice system has moved away from the former "catch and release" method, which allowed U.S. officials to escort undocumented immigrants back to their country of origin. Instead, we have moved toward mandatory detention, and later deportation, which has subsequently criminalized their very existence (Bosworth & Kaufman, 2011). This incarceration increases their risk of substance abuse and mental health issues, among other concerns.

In addition, many immigrants who come to the United States do so from collectivist cultures that place the family system at the center of life. As such, it is crucial that the family system be integrated into services for those detained in immigrant detention centers. Transnationally oriented services, despite their importance for migrants who frequently cross borders are not typically provided in U.S. institutions (Furman, Negi, Schatz & Jones, 2008). Such services provide connections between family members across nation state boundaries and integrate the family into service planning. While we note the difficulties in making connections across national boundaries, it is even more important to discuss how state and jurisdictional boundaries thwart the well-being and reintegration of immigrant families. Prisons and detention centers that are privately owned or operated are often located outside the jurisdiction from which their inmates come. As such, when immigrants are detained they are often sent hundreds, if not thousands, of miles from their families and support networks.

The inability to maintain regular contact with family and community while incarcerated has been linked to negative psychosocial experiences and serves as an additional barrier to successful reintegration. For instance, Martin's (2002) mixed-methods research with jailed fathers indicates that those who were living with their children prior to incarceration "experienced anguish as a result of their separation from their children" (p. 107). These fathers also report that their incarceration results in negative effects for their children, including financial strain as well as emotional and behavioral maladjustment. The incarceration of mothers has also been linked to negative psychosocial experiences for them and their children (Mallicoat, 2012). In this sense, the increased use of detention for undocumented persons results in significant collateral damage.

Not all detention centers are privately run, and no two privately run prisons or detention centers are the same. Those that are private face an inevitable paradox—providing safety while cutting costs. It is possible that cost control comes before safety and quality. Blakely and Bumphus (2004) highlight that private prisons are staffed by officers who receive less training and lower wages than officers who staff public facilities. Those housed in private facilities often face more violence (Blakely & Bumphus, 2004; Camp & Gaes, 2001; Lundahl, et al., 2009) and may receive inadequate health care (Mason, 2012). The drive towards cost cutting attributed to the private prison industry may contribute to these issues.

Across the U.S. there have been recent uprisings by immigrant detainees housed in privately run detention centers. It appears that these uprisings have primarily been the result of inadequate medical care, mental health care, and poor living conditions (Kirkham, 2012b). At one of the largest privately run immigration detention facilities in the United States, Reeves County Detention Center, located in Pecos, Texas, more than 1200 inmates engaged in a riot in December of 2008. After the detention center regained control, negotiations began and the prisoners "explained that the uprising had erupted from widespread dissatisfaction with almost every aspect of the prison: inedible food, a dearth of legal resources, the use of solitary confinement to punish people who complained about their medical treatment, overcrowding and, above all, poor health care," (Wilder, 2009, para. 10). This was not the first allegation brought against the private prison industry and it is sure to not be the last as budgets are tightened and government spending is decreased. These cost-cutting strategies combined with a push for increased use of detention in response to undocumented immigrants may very well be a recipe for disaster.

Conclusion

Since the 1970s, the U.S. has witnessed exponential growth in the US prison population. Concurrently, criminalizing immigration has rapidly accelerated, mostly since the events of September 11, 2001. As more recent trends towards decreased rates of incarceration among the general population continue, however, for-profit companies are experiencing a threat to their potential client base. As profit streams are stymied by decreased prison populations, for-profit immigrant detention centers have created a new source of revenue. The private prison industry is certainly not the only party involved in expanding the prison industrial complex, for-profit prisons and immigrant detention centers. Some argue that the U.S. government and several state governments are partners in privatizing the corrections industry.

Over the last several years, the Immigration Policy Center and the National Immigrant Justice Center have done extensive work in showcasing the human costs of immigrant detention, as well as the ways in which immigration policies are construed. During the same time period, National Public Radio has featured an investigative report on state legislators, lobbyists from the private prison industry, and ALEC and their creation and adoption of anti-immigrant legislation. This specific type of legislation aims to criminalize many aspects of an individual's life, and is directly related to immigrant detention.

This increased awareness of the business practices of the private prison industry does not seem to have stopped the companies from attempting to augment cash flow. The weakening of the prison industrial complex, as evidenced by recent decreases in prison populations, has pushed various stakeholders to find new client bases, including offering cash to states to buy their prisons and entering the immigrant detention business. Immigrant detention is of particular concern, given the onslaught of anti-immigrant legislation which has effectively criminalized various aspects of the lives of the undocumented. Once detained, these individuals are often sent far away from their loved ones and, when housed in private facilities, face alleged inadequate healthcare and increased levels of violence. The psychosocial risk factors associated with immigrant detention are vast, but the private prison industry continues to profit. Paraphrasing Buffy McFayden, a Colorado lawmaker, it is unconscionable to put a price on a human life in a prison cell. Hopefully with more attention focused on the private prison industry, the criminalization of immigration and proposed comprehensive immigration reform, changes for the better will begin to occur.

Discussion Questions

1. What are some implications of public-private partnerships for the criminalization of immigration and immigrants?

2. What are the ethical and moral implications of privatizing punishment?

3. How do cultural beliefs regarding immigrants influence the increased use of private detention for the undocumented?

4. In this chapter, several psychosocial risks associated with incarceration are discussed. What additional risks might merit consideration in the context of the detention of undocumented immigrants in private institutions?

5. If current trends towards decreased prison populations continue, what additional revenue streams might private prison corporations pursue?

6. What do you see as the primary costs and benefits of the use of private immigration detention centers?

7. What are the social justice implications of the private prison industry and its relationship to the political process?

References

Ackerman, A.R. & Furman, R. (2013). The Immigration Detention Center as a "Natural" Culmination of the Criminalization of Immigration: Implications for Justice. Contemporary Justice Review, 16, 251–263.

Aman, A. C., & Rehrig, G. (2011). The domestic face of globalization: Law's role in the integration of immigrants in the United States. Legal Studies Research Paper, #196, Indiana University School of Law. Bloomington, Indiana: University of Indiana.

American Legislative Exchange Council (2012). About ALEC. Retrieved on April 14, 2012 from http://www.alec.org/about-alec/.

Blakely, C.R. & Bumphus, V.W. (2004). Private and public sector prisons—a comparison of selected characteristics. Federal Probation, 68, 27–33.

Bosworth, M., & Kaufman, E. (2011). Foreigners in a carceal age: Immigration and imprisonment in the U. S. Legal Research Paper Series, No. 34. Oxford University. Retrieved on April 2, 2012 at http://papers.ssrn.com/sol3/papers.cfm?abstract_id=1852196.

Brancaccio, D. (2008). Prisons for Profit. In P. Producer (Producer). New York, NY: Public Broadcasting Service. Retrieved on April 1, 2012 from http://www.pbs.org/now/shows/419/video.html.

Brinkerhoff, N. (2010). Schwarzenegger Suggests Outsourcing California Prisoners to Mexico. Retrieved on February 1, 2013 from http://www.allgov.com/news/us-and-the-world/schwarzenegger-suggests-outsourcing-california-prisoners-to-mexico?news=840263.

Brown, T. (2011). Private prison business eyes big Florida prize. Reuters, May 12, 2011. Retrieved on April 14, 2012 from http://www.reuters.com/article/2011/05/12/us-usa-prisons-florida-idUSTRE74B49B20110512.

Camp, S.D. & Gaes, G.G. (2001). Growth and quality of U.S. private prisons: Evidence from a national survey. Washington, DC: Federal Bureau of Prisons, Office of Research and Evaluation.

Corrections Corporation of America (2012). About CCA. Retrieved on April 14, 2012 from http://www.cca.com/about/.

Dorwart, R. A., & Epstein, S. S. (1993). Privatization and mental health Care: A Fragile Balance. Westport, Connecticut: Auburn House.

Furman, R. (2005). Understanding privatization through the lens of Dowart and Epstein's "Privatization and mental health services": A warning for Latin America and the developing world. Revista Internacional Interdisciplinar InterThesis,2(2), http://www.periodicos.ufsc.br/index.php/interthesis/article/view/725/10787.

Furman, R., Ackerman, A., Loya, M., Jones, S., & Negi, N. (2012). The criminalization of immigration: Value conflicts for the social work profession. Journal of Sociology and Social Welfare, 39(1), 169–185.

Furman, R., & Negi, N. (2007). Social work practice with transnational Latino populations. International Social Work, 50(1), 107–112.

Furman, R. Negi, N. Schatz, M. & Jones, S. (2008) Transnational social work: using a wraparound model. Global Networks 8(4), 496–503.

GEO Group, The (2012). Who we are. The Geo Group. Retrieved on April 14, 2012 from http://www.geogroup.com/about.html.

Immigration Policy Center (April, 2011). Q & A guide to state immigration laws: What you need to know if your state is considering Arizona SB 1070-type legislation. Special Report. Retrieved on April 16, 2012 http://www.immigrationpolicy.org/special-reports/qa-guide-state-immigration-laws.

James, J. (2005). Private prison contracts may get a pass. Saint Petersburg Times, May 5, 2005. Retrieved on April 16, 2012, from http://www.sptimes.com/2005/05/05/State/Private_prison_contra.shtml.

Jing, Y. (2010). Prison privatization: A perspective on core governmental functions. Crime, Law and Social Change, 54(3–4), 263–278.

Justice Policy Institute (2011). Gaming the System: How the Political Strategies of Private Prison companies Promote Ineffective Policies. Washington, DC: Justice Policy Institute.

Kaseke, E. (1998). Structural adjustment programmes and the problem of urban poverty: An African perspective. International Social Work, 41(3), 311–320.

Kirkham, C. (2012a). Private Prison Corporation Offers Cash In Exchange For State Prisons. Retrieved on February 14, 2013 from http://www.huffingtonpost.com/2012/02/14/private-prisons-buying-state-prisons_n_1272143.html.

Kirkham, C. (2012b). Private prisons: immigration convictions in record numbers fueling corporate profits. The huffington post. Retrieved from http://www.huffingtonpost.com/2012/09/27/private-prisons-immigration_n_1917636.html.

Liptak, A. (2011, May 23). Justices, 5–4, Tell California to Cut Prisoner Population. New York Times. Retrieved on April 14, 2012 from http://www.nytimes.com/2011/05/24/us/24scotus.html?pagewanted=all.

Lundahl, B., Kunz, C., Brownell, C., Harris, N., & Van Vleet, R. (2009). Prison privatization: A meta-analysis of cost effectiveness and quality of confinement indicators. Research on Social Work Practice, 19, 383–395.

Mallicoat, S.L. (2012). Women and crime: A text/reader. Thousand Oaks, CA: SAGE.

Martin, J. (2002). Jailed fathers: Paternal reactions to separation from children. In R.L. Gido & T. Alleman (eds.), Turnstile justice: Issues in American corrections (2nd ed.). Upper Saddle River, NJ: Prentice Hall.

Mason, C. (2012). Too Good to be True: Private Prisons in America. Washington, DC: The Sentencing Project.

Naser, R.L. & Visher, C.A. (2006). Family members' experiences with incarceration and Reentry. Western Criminology Review, 7(2), 20–31.

Provine, M. D., & Sanchez, G. (2011). Suspecting immigrants: Exploring links between racialist anxieties and expanded police power in Arizona. Policing & Society, 21(4), 468–479.

Scahill, J. (2007). Blackwater: The rise of the world's most powerful mercenary army. New York: Nation Books.

Schlosser, E. (December, 1998). The Prison Industrial Complex. Atlantic Magazine.

Sullivan, L. (2010, October 28). Prison Economics Help Drive Ariz. Immigration Law. National Public Radio. Retrieved on April 14, 2012 from http://www.npr.org/2010/10/28/130833741/prison-economics-help-drive-ariz-immigration-law.

Sullivan, L (2010b, October 29). Shaping State Laws With Little Scrutiny. National Public Radio. Retreived on April 14, 2012, from http://www.npr.org/2010/10/29/130891396/shaping-state-laws-with-little-scrutiny.

Welsh, M. (2000). The role of the immigration and naturalization service in the prison-industrial complex. Social Justice, 27(3), 73–88.

West, H.C., Sabol, W.J., & Greenman, S.J. (2010). Prisoners in 2009. Washington, DC: Bureau of]Justice Statistics.

Wilder, F. (2009, October 08). The pecos insurrection: how a private prison pushed immigrant inmates to the brink. Texas Observer. Retrieved from http://www.texasobserver.org/the-pecos-insurrection/.

Chapter Nine

The Right and Undocumented Immigration: A Transatlantic Perspective

Ariane Chebel d'Appollonia

Undocumented immigration has become a highly sensitive issue on both sides of the Atlantic for three main reasons. The first relates to the perception that immigrants pose a threat to economic prosperity. Supporters of restrictive immigration policies argue that illegal immigrants take jobs from native workers, reduce their wages, and consume social benefits. The belief that they pose a socio-economic threat has gained currency in the current context of economic and financial crisis in the United States and Europe. The second reason relates to concerns about national identity. Immigrants, especially those who have recently arrived, are increasingly suspected of being unable to integrate into their host societies, supposedly preferring to form ethnic enclaves. Having no opportunity—and sometimes no incentive—to assimilate, undocumented immigrants allegedly constitute a major ethno-cultural threat. This belief is enhanced by the fact that most of them are non-Europeans, Mexicans in the US and Africans and Asians in Europe.[1] The third reason is concern about public security. Western governments have historically drawn a link between immigration and higher levels of crime. This emerged as a result of the progressive criminalization of immigration, dating back to the late 19th century when hostility to foreigners led to the adoption of discriminatory meas-

---

1. Mexicans represented in 2012 about 59 percent of the estimated total illegal population (11.5 million) in the United States. In Europe, recent estimates of undocumented immigrants range from 2 to 4.5 million. According to Frontex, the EU agency for the management of external borders, the majority of detected illegal border-crossings in 2012 involved Afghan migrants (up to 20 percent of the total). The other top six groups were Bangladeshis, Syrians, Algerians, Albanians, and Somalis.

ures such as the Chinese Exclusion Act of 1888, the Immigration Act of 1891 (authorizing the deportation of illegal aliens), and the National Quota Laws (of 1921, 1924, 1929) in the United States. European governments adopted similar measures on the assumption that immigrants had higher crime rates than natives.

These three beliefs about the negative impact of undocumented immigration largely predated 9/11 and the terrorist attacks in Europe. Since then, the framing of immigration as a security issue had led to the conflation of the notion of "terrorists" and "immigrants" by policymakers on both sides of the Atlantic. The fight against undocumented immigration is thus a security priority on both the American and European agendas. Controversial restrictive measures targeting undocumented immigrants (such as racial profiling, and expedited deportation) are legitimized as part of the "war on terror" and the fight against crime.

In this context, restrictionism constitutes the dominant trend, both in discourse and practice. It raises important questions about the role of right-wing parties in the framing of immigration policy. One is how to explain the current influence of the Right on immigration policy, although it is worth noting that the supporters of nativism are not all rightists and that all the rightists do not express migrant phobia. A second is how to explain the persistence of the Right in advocating the continued criminalization of undocumented immigration, despite a wealth of evidence that this approach is mostly counterproductive. A final issue is why the rightist parties keep on focusing on illegal immigration as their primary electoral theme when they make no progress in winning key elections.

The Right's Platform on Undocumented Immigration

The political substance of what constitutes the Right has varied over time and location due to different historical contexts. In Europe, liberals are today generally more conservative than ever because of the emergence of a plurality of leftist ideological families that have pushed them to the right of the political spectrum. The term conservative thus describes classical and neo-Liberals and liberal Democrats, as well as Christian Democrats. All these groups are conservative on cultural, social and moral issues. They strongly support traditional family values and public morality, as well as the preservation of national values and behavior. They only differ on the role of the government: Neo-Liberals, like the British Conservative party, advocate a minimal state, a free market economy, and a limited welfare state. Christian Democrats, by contrast, believe that public regulations are required in order to secure minimal levels of social justice and solidarity. Examples of Christian democratic parties include the German Christian Democratic Union (CDU), the Dutch Christian Democratic Appeal (CDA), the Christian Democratic People's Party in Switzerland, and the Italian Union of Christian and Center Democrats (UDC). Liberal Democrats, located at the center-right, also seek to balance free market policies with social liberalism, but their conservatism is based on secular values. At the European level, they form the Alliance of Liberals and Democrats for Europe (ALDE) with the participation of national parties such as the Italian Margherita, the French Mouvement Democrate, and the Bulgarian National Movement for Stability and Progress.

The US Republican Party (GOP) includes various groups, such as the social conservatives, Christian conservatives and free-market liberals. Like their European counterparts, they express strong nationalist sentiments, and a deep attachment to traditional values and social norms (as illustrated by the issues of the legalization of drugs, embryonic stem cell research, abortion, and same-sex marriage). These groups are largely divided between economic libertarians, moderates, and stringent social conservatives who support the Tea Party movement. They vary on how best to manage the economy. Yet most Republicans, despite the persistence of internal divisions, favor economic freedom, fiscal conservatism, a limited eligibility for welfare, and strong federalism with a large role reserved for individual American states.

In this context, legal immigration has been the subject of intense debate for the last two decades. Positions within this debate run across party lines rather than simply being identifiable by party. So conservatives, like other ideological families, have found themselves divided on both sides of the Atlantic. "Immigrationists," on the one hand, emphasized the positive contribution of immigrants to economic growth and advocate a rationalization of immigration controls designed to address specific labor shortages. They focused on the need to attract high-skilled workers, as well as "guest workers" needed in the agricultural and service sectors. Christian conservatives, such as the US Christian Coalition, emphasize the "importance of keeping families together" (Beck, cited in Ashbee, 1998, p. 74). "Restrictionists," on the other hand, asked for a moratorium on legal immigration in order to protect jobs for natives. The most radical of them referred to the negative impact of mass immigration on national identity, as illustrated by Peter Brimelow in his book, Alien Nation (1996), and Patrick J. Buchanan during his presidential primary campaigns. Similar anti-migration arguments were meanwhile endorsed by European conservatives who supported the "zero immigration" policy in their respective countries.

In France, for example, both the RPR (the Gaullist Rally for the Republic) and the UDF (Union for French Democracy—at the center right) supported restrictive measures such as the Pasqua Laws of 1993/94 which made family reunification more difficult.

Illegal immigration, by contrast, has always generated a broad consensus among both US and European rightist parties—all agreeing that more stringent measures should be taken against undocumented immigrants. Their main arguments generally refer to the rule of law and respect for authority—both violated by illegal immigrants in various ways: by crossing the border illegally, using false documents, overstaying their visa or a residence permit, or by staying in the country after being refused asylum. From this perspective, what is at stake is thus the enforcement of the law against people who violate it and who, subsequently, have neither rights nor standing in the community. The principle of equity before the law and the notion of fairness therefore justify exclusionary measures being taken against lawbreakers, as illustrated by the 2012 Republican platform, which stated that,

> In this country, the rule of law guarantees equal treatment to every individual, including more than one million immigrants to whom we grant permanent residence every year. That is why we oppose any form of amnesty for those who, by intentionally violating the law, disadvantage those who have obeyed it. Granting amnesty only rewards and encourages more law breaking (p. 15).

Furthermore, Conservatives argue that human rights are better protected when a strict law and order policy is implemented on immigration. According to British Prime Minister David Cameron (2011), "cracking down on illegal immigration is a question of fairness—yes to the British people—but also to those who have been shipped over here against their will, sometimes kept as slaves and forced to work horrendous hours." Among the major initiatives designed to fight human trafficking, the Right advocates tougher border controls in order to apprehend smugglers, as well as strict workplace enforcement and penalties for those who employ illegal workers. The GOP, for example, supports the mandatory nationwide use of the E-Verify program—an Internet-based system that verifies the employment authorization and identity of the employees. The GOP also supports the Systematic Alien Verification for Entitlements (S.A.V.E.) program—an Internet-based system that verifies the lawful presence of applicants prior to the granting of any federal benefits. In Europe, Conservatives advocate similar measures, both at the national and EU levels. They actively support European initiatives designed to improve the fight against trafficking in human beings and economic exploitation of illegal workers. These initiatives include, for example, the granting of new powers to Europol and Eurojust in their fight against trafficking and other serious forms of transnational crime. Right-wing governments have also implemented stiff penalties for those who smuggle illegal immigrants or sell fraudulent documents. European states also tend to widen domestic control by cooperating with public service providers (such as educational, social and health care institutions) that are required by law to inform authorities if they encounter individuals with an illegal status. Italy's conservative coalition led by Silvio Berlusconi went further in 2012 in adopting a series of legislative measures aiming at people who helped illegal immigrants living in the country. Renting or offering an accommodation to undocumented immigrants, for example, has become a criminal offense, carrying a jail term of up to three years.

For the Right, the reaffirmation of state sovereignty offers another justification for a tough border-enforcement approach, including the introduction of new technologies. The Bush administration, for example, adopted a series of measures such as the US-VISIT program, the 2002 Enhanced Border Security and Visa Entry Reform Act, and the 2005 Strategy for Protecting America. As a result, ICE (Immigration and Customs Enforcement) and Customs and Border Protection (CBP) budgets reached $8.8 billion in 2008 (including $6.6 billion for border security) This enlarged budget led to the introduction of new surveillance technologies (such as drones), in addition to new fencing, more weapons, and increased manpower. The effects on personnel have been palpable: CBP increased the number of Border Patrol agents by 21 percent in 2007 and by 11 percent in 2008.

Yet, despite the importance of federal budgets in this policy, US conservatives are divided over the role that states should play in the fight against illegal immigration relative to the US federal government. Most of them argue that local governments should be in charge, justifying their support for local initiatives, such as the Arizona's restrictive bill (SB 1070).[2] Others argue that the fight against illegal immigration should remain the preserve of the federal government—despite their preference for a "small government" in other areas. The Bush administration reconciled these two positions by implementing a

---

2. This legislative act requires all aliens over the age of 14 to carry registration documents at all times. Violation of this requirement is a federal criminal misdemeanor. It also requires that state law enforcement officers attempt to determine the legal status of immigrants during, for example, a "lawful stop, detention or arrest" when there is "reasonable suspicion" that individuals are illegal immigrants. The act imposes penalties on those sheltering, hiring or transporting undocumented immigrants. Similar legislation has been adopted in other states, such as the Alabama's HB 56.

partnership between the federal government and local authorities through collaborative enforcement agreements in section 287g of the Immigration and Nationality Act. A third smaller conservative group opposes harsh regulations at the local level. It works instead to manage the integration of undocumented immigrants through programs of bilingual education and access to some welfare benefits. Governor Rick Perry, for example, passed a law in Texas in 2001 granting in-state tuition rates to children of illegal immigrants—an initiative highly criticized by other conservatives during the 2012 Republican presidential primary.

Like their American counterparts, European rightists favor the militarization of border controls by using surveillance technologies and biometrics. They have lobbied the EU to adopt various system controls, such as Eurodac, ICOnet, and the Schengen information systems (SIS1 and SIS2). They also support Frontex's initiatives, such as thwarting illegal border crossing, hunting down smugglers and people who overstay their visas, and enforcing deportations. European rightists are, however, divided over the issue of where best to administratively tackle the issue. Supporters of the EU integration, such as the Christian Democrats, argue that common problems require common solutions. Hence, they believe that the fight against undocumented immigration should take place at the European level through a common visa and asylum policy, as well as the strict enforcement of the Schengen acquis by EU member states. They are referred to as "supranationalists." Other conservatives argue that the Europeanization of immigration policy poses a threat to national sovereignty and thus undermine the fight against illegal immigration. They advocate instead the restoration of national border controls. This perspective is illustrated by the comment made by then President of France, Nicolas Sarkozy, in March 2012. He threatened to withdraw France from Europe's open border zone unless other European countries did more to stop illegal immigration.

American and European Conservatives, by contrast, share a strong consensus about the need to address national and public security concerns. They collectively subscribe to the idea that illegal immigrants pose a major threat to social cohesion, as criminals, and national safety as potential terrorists. As the 2012 GOP platform stated,

In an age of terrorism, drug cartels, human trafficking, and criminal gangs, the presence of millions of unidentified persons in this country poses grave risks to the safety and the sovereignty of the United States. Our highest priority, therefore, is to secure the rule of law both at our borders and at ports of entry (p. 25).

Republicans therefore oppose any kind of "amnesty" for undocumented immigrants while encouraging their expedited deportation. Mitt Romney, during the 2012 presidential campaign, went further by introducing the notion of "self-deportation" by "which people decide they can do better by going home because they can't find work here." His main objective was to discourage illegal immigrants from staying in the US by making their life as difficult as possible. This includes the denial of access to social benefits for illegals (in the spirit of the former Californian proposition 187) or a path toward citizenship (as illustrated by the opposition of most Republicans to the DREAM act). European Conservatives also advocate the deportation of undocumented immigrants in the name of national and public security. Their main targets are minority groups, such as Roma, and varied Muslim immigrants—all suspected of being criminals or potential terrorists. In many countries, such as France, Italy, and Greece, illegal immigrants were deported at record rates when rightist governments were in power. They also support voluntary repatriation programs for illegal immigrants. Proponents of repatriation insist that the adoption of a firm stance is necessary to deter future immigrants. As in the United States, such a strategy includes a restrictive access to social benefits and none to citizenship. Conservative governments in many European countries have adopted such policies in order to fight against "birth tourism" (the European version of the US "anchor babies" issue). In Greece, for example, the center-right government led by the New Democracy coalition, voted in favor of new restrictions in 2012. This legislation banned the children of immigrants from becoming Greek citizens.

The Actual Influence of the Right on Immigration Policies

Restrictionism is not the preserve of right-wing parties. In the United States, the Clinton administration passed the reforms of 1996 criminalizing undocumented immigration. President Obama, during his first term, deported 1.4 million undocumented immigrants—at a faster monthly rate (1.5 times more on average) than the Bush administration. President Obama also expanded the Secure Communities Program aimed at checking the legal status of immigrants booked into local jails and deployed an additional 1,200 National Guard troops at the southern border. Similarly, restrictive policies have been designed and implemented by leftist governments in Europe. In the United Kingdom, for example, Tony Blair's Labour government adopted the Immigration, Asylum and Nationality Act in 2006. It sought to control and reduce undocumented immigration by limiting the right of appeal for dependents and students refused entry.

By contrast, conservative governments have adopted liberal measures. The Reagan administration, for example, gave amnesty to illegal immigrants in the United States in 1986. The Immigration Control and Reform Act thus legalized the status of about 3 million illegal immigrants who had been in the country for years. In 2006, President Bush and Senator McCain attempted to introduce measures that would provide a potential path to legal permanent residence for some categories of illegal aliens. The bipartisan "Hagel-Martinez compromise" (S 2611 and S 2612) included provisions requiring long-term undocumented immigrants to pass national security and criminal background checks, pay all federal and state income taxes owed, register for military selective service, and meet English and US civics learning requirements. Conservative governments in many southern European states (such as Greece and Spain) voted massive regularization programs during the 2000s, commonly known as "amnesties."

These puzzling variations raised questions about the effective impact of the Right on immigration policies. It seems, at first glance, that the Right dominates the policy agenda on both sides of the Atlantic. Their framing of immigration as a security issue put pressure on leftist governments. This is illustrated by the intensity of political debates in Spain, where the line through Ceuta, Melilla and the Strait of Gibraltar represents the southern border of the EU and one of the main routes for illegal immigration. In 2005, after more than two hundred immigrants tried to jump the fences separating Morocco from the cities of Ceuta and Melilla, the opposition conservative Popular Party (PP) accused the governing Socialist Party (PSOE) of weakness in controlling illegal immigration, a "lack of patriotism" in leaving the cities of Melilla and Ceuta defenseless, and of "cowardice" in its dealings with Moroccan authorities and terrorist networks. The government immediate response was to deploy additional armed troops to help the Guardia Civil strengthen the border. A second fence was built in 2005, followed by a third in 2006. That year, €1.5 million was invested in enhancing border controls (Barbero, 2012). In the United States, the securitization of immigration issues has created a similar trend, forcing Democrats to be as tough as Republicans (if not tougher) on the issue of border security. President Obama's response to the Arizona law, for example, was the deployment of a further 1,200 National Guard Troops, as well as an additional $500 million in funding for border security. This decision was clearly intended to deflect conservative criticism and to appease congressional Republicans who have consistently refused to support an immigration reform unless the White House boosts security first.

There is evidence, however, that the ideological dominance of the Right is diminished by several factors. First, most of the restrictionist measures advocated and/or implemented by rightists does not actually improve the fight against illegal immigration. Restrictive measures applied by the Bush administration did not significantly reduce the flows of illegal immigrants. For example, the unauthorized immigrant population increased by 37 percent between 2000 and 2008 according to the Department of Homeland Security (DHS). In adapting to these new measures, smugglers simply used different routes along the southern border. There was an upsurge in attempted entry by using false documents, as well as a dramatic increase in the number of people overstaying their visas, representing between an estimated 25 and 40 percent of the unauthorized immigrants (Passel, 2006). The shrinkage of the unauthorized population in 2010-11 was only partly due to the deterrence effect of tighter border controls. Other variables have played a more significant role in this smaller population, such as the economic crisis in the United States (the result of reduced job opportunities), economic growth in Mexico (providing more job opportunities there), and a decline in Mexico's population (thus reducing the pool of potential emigrants). In Europe, increasing numbers of illegal immigrants has also raised questions about the effectiveness of enhanced border security. The strengthening of border controls in Spain, for example, has diverted the flows of immigrants toward other routes along the EU southern border. This rechanneling effect was clearly illustrated by the upsurge of illegal entries in Greece and Italy in the wake of the Arab Spring. In Greece, there was an estimated 29 percent increase in illegal border crossings compared to the year before. Italy ranked second in the number of illegal border-crossings, despite the dramatic militarization of border controls implemented by Silvio Berlusconi (Frontex, 2012).

Second, conservatives (as well as leftists who subscribe to this securitization approach to immigration) still advocate measures against illegal immigrants that have consistently proved to be either inapplicable or counter-productive. New measures are simply overwhelmed by the daunting numbers. Despite attempts to deport as many criminal immigrants as possible, US authorities are simply unequipped with the resources to deport 11 millions illegal residents, comprising 5.2 percent of its labor force nationwide (and 10 percent in Nevada and California). Furthermore, a mass deportation campaign would cost an estimated $285 billion over five years. To put this figure in some perspective, the average cost of a deportation process (apprehension, detention, legal proceeding, and transportation) would be up to $23,480 per person according to 2010 figures (Fitz et al, 2010). Locating and deporting illegal immigrants in Europe is not inexpensive either. In 2006, the UK Home Office estimated that the average cost of deporting one individual was £11,000. In 2008, the French government spent €42 million for the deportation of twenty-six thousand illegal immigrants (based on an average cost of €2,186 per person). This French policy was not only expensive but also ineffective. For example, most of the ten thousand Romanian and Bulgarian Roma expelled in 2009 by Sarkozy's government returned to France (OFII, 2012).

Third, conservatives are often torn between competing ideological and policy options. Some of them support a flexible working migration policy in support of business interests but are fearful that a guest-worker program can bring terrorists across porous borders. Others advocate harsh measures against undocumented immigrants but they also manage or own businesses employing illegal workers who accept lower wages than natives and are willing to work at jobs that natives refuse. Some rightists resist immigration in the name of the protection of national values but in fact share social and economic values with a high proportion of immigrants. As Jennifer Hochschild notes (2009, p. 5), "rightists' views on gender and parental roles, homosexuality, and religiosity accord much more with the views of many immigrants than do leftists' views." The US Christian Coalition, for example, expresses strong concerns about immigration (both legal and illegal). Yet it praises the increasing number of evangelical Latinos in the country. These ideological conundrums sometimes make life complicated for party leaders, as illustrated by the failure in 2006 of the Bush administration to pass a comprehensive immigration reform. The bill adopted by the Republican-led Senate was rejected by the House (also led by Republicans) and was never voted on despite a myriad of amendments.

The Right's Political Dilemmas

Crosscutting political and ideological commitments affect both the Right and the Left. Yet, the issue of illegal immigration raises a series of questions that Conservatives must urgently address. In the United States, the main problem Republicans face is reconciling two opposite constituencies that require contrasting strategies. The first is their traditional core of white voters that favor a security oriented, restrictionist approach to immigration. The second is a large and growing Hispanic pool of potential voters who demand comprehensive reform. Hispanics accounted for 10 percent of the national electorate in 2012 and their share of the electorate will double by 2030. They voted overwhelmingly for President Obama over Republican nominee Mitt Romney (71 percent and 27 percent respectively) in 2012, and the percentage of Hispanics voting for the Democratic candidate has increased the past two presidential elections. There is today a sense of urgency among Republicans to improve their standing among Hispanics and other minorities. As one election analyst stated in the non-partisan Cook Political Report, "You cannot win a national election and lose Hispanics at a rate Mitt Romney did" (cited by Davis and Moore, 2013). The long-term strategy for Republicans is to reconcile their party's position on both border security and paths to citizenship that is acceptable to both its bedrock supporters and this critical new constituency. It also involves creating a more effective employment verification system and a greater integration of minorities (notably the children of undocumented immigrants). Senator Marco Rubio (R-Fla), a potential 2016 presidential candidate, recently advocated reforming the immigration system by offering a provisional legal status to immigrants who passed criminal background checks, paid fines, and passed English and civics tests. He also favors a faster track to citizenship for young undocumented immigrants who came in the United States as children.

Yet, there is a continued unease among traditional conservatives over the loosening of immigration restrictions. Some express concern that more flexible measures—particularly on undocumented immigrants—would do little to attract minority voters while upsetting the more conservative wing of the GOP. The party's white base (particularly in border states) tends to express strong nativist sentiments, particularly those that have experienced heavy waves of non-white immigration. Republican candidates "are faced with the choice of either following this populist appeal to immediate victory ... or gritting their teeth and opposing it, losing primaries to harder-line rivals" (Unz, 2011, p. 20). Conservatives, such as Senator Jeff Sessions of Alabama, have made it clear they will not support Senator Rubio's effort to reach a bipartisan agreement. Deep divisions about immigration policy may therefore contribute to a greater sense of factionalism within the conservative movement, unless the Republican leadership can convince its members to soften their rhetoric against illegal immigrants and support bipartisan legislation.

The electoral forces that drive the politics of immigration are quite different in Europe. Rightist parties have no incentive to view ethnic voters as a political resource. Despite the increasing number of immigrants in most countries, the actual pool of ethnic voters remains rather limited. This contrast is due to the effects of continued restrictive access to citizenship, combined with demographic factors. A large majority of French Muslims, for example, are under eighteen years of age and therefore cannot vote. Other contributory factors include the weak organization of immigrant groups, and heightened anti-migrant public opinion. Ethnic minorities are underrepresented at all levels of politics and government. They therefore have little influence on immigration policy.

By contrast, extreme-right wing parties (ERPs) play a key role in the politics of immigration and have a narrow but explicit electoral strategy. These parties have proliferated in many countries, such as France (Front National), Germany (People's Union Party), Italy (Northern League), and Belgium (Flemish Block). Their strong opposition to immigration (often tainted with racism) has secured an increasing electoral basis, thus posing a political threat to mainstream rightist parties. Conservatives have thus co-opted immigration-related issues in order to challenge the ERPs' electoral success and enhance their prospects of governing. In Italy and Austria, ERPs were invited by mainstream parties to form governmental coalitions. Yet, this strategy raises crucial current issues that European Conservatives need to urgently address. The tactic of being as tough as ERPs on immigration has indeed proved to be counterproductive. When established conservative political leaders endorse claims made by their extremist far-right competitors, anti-immigrant feelings become more acceptable which, in turn, enhances the ERPs' credibility. Furthermore, focusing on immigration issues almost exclusively in terms of security threat does not address the concerns of natives about other immigration issues (such as the effects on employment and wages). Mainstream rightist parties subsequently suffer from a growing political distrust—expressed either by ERPs voters (accusing them of being too soft) or by conservative voters (who accused them of being too extreme). In France, for example, Nicolas Sarkozy implemented restrictive immigration reforms during his first term (2007-2012) in order to reclaim the vote lost to the Front National (FN). Yet, he lost the 2012 presidential election while the FN achieved its largest electoral return in history. As a result, the conservative party (UMP) imploded, one faction advocating further FN's style measures, another denouncing the shift to extremism. Meanwhile, opportunities in France and other European countries to discuss a comprehensive immigration reform remain limited—a trend detrimental to illegal immigrants, and also to the Right. Conservative leaders face a catch-22 situation: either they stop demonizing immigrants and risk losing the support of large sections of their electorate or they further radicalize their agenda and risk strengthening the influence of their ERP competitors.

Discussion Questions

1. Discuss the reasons why immigration has become an issue on both sides of the Atlantic.
2. Compare and contrast the issues surrounding immigration reform in the U.S. and Europe.
3. How has the Conservative movement influenced immigration policy in both Europe and the U.S.?

References

Barbero, I. (2012). Legitimating Immigration Regimes in the European Union, November 8. Available at http://www.opendemocracy.net.

Cameron, D. (2011). Good Immigration, Not Mass Migration, Speech on April 14, 2001. Available at http://www.conservatives.com/News/Speeches.

Chebel d'Appollonia, A. (2012). Frontiers of Fear: Immigration and Insecurity in the United States and Europe. Ithaca: Cornell University Press.

Davis, S &Moore, M. (2013), Immigration Plan Could Be Long-Term Boon to GOP, USA Today, January 28. Available at http://www.usatoday.com.

Fitz, M & Martinez, G & Wijewardena, M. (2010). The Costs of Mass Deportation: Impractical, Expensive, and Ineffective, Report for the Center for American Progress. Available at http://www.americanprogress.org.

Frontex. EU Agency for the Management of Operational Cooperation at the External Borders of the Member States of the European Union (2012). Report, FRAN Quarterly, Issue 2, April-June, 1–70.

Hochshild, J. (2009). The Complexities of Immigration: Why Western Countries Struggle with Immigration Policies and Politics, In: Delivering Citizenship, edited by Bertelsmann Stiftung, European Policy Center, Migration Policy Institute. Berlin, Germany: Verlag Bertelsmann Stiftung. Available at http://scholar.harvard.edu.

Office Français de l'Immigration et de l'Intégration (OFII), (2012). Rapport d'activité 2011. Paris : La Documentation Française.

Passel, J. (2006). The Size and Characteristics of the Unauthorized Migrant Population in the US. Research Report, March 7, Pew Hispanic Center. Available at http://www.pewhispanic.org.

Chapter Ten

White Supremacist Stigma Management and Legitimation via Anti-Immigration Activism: The Case of the Keystone State Skinheads

Stanislav Vysotsky & Eric Madfis

The recent movement in opposition to immigration reform and immigrant rights has faced accusations of racism in response to its targeting of Latino, especially Mexican, immigrants to the United States. Movement leaders and spokespeople deny such accusations as ad hominem attacks by their opponents. However, activists, politicians, academics, and others have noted the consistent involvement of white supremacists in the anti-immigration movement. The fact is that white supremacists find common political ground with this movement, and they utilize it in attempts to publically legitimize their ideology and recruit new members. Comparatively mainstream opposition to immigration enables white supremacists to mobilize a number of stigma management strategies in order to portray themselves as legitimate political actors in this debate.

Even racist skinhead groups, often associated with criminality and violence (Simi & Futrell, 2009; Simi, Smith, & Reeser, 2008), have mobilized in the anti-immigration movement in order to present themselves as a political movement rather than a countercultural gang. Using a case study of the Keystone State Skinheads (KSS), a white supremacist organization based out of Pennsylvania, we outline the key strategies and actions employed by white supremacist groups to legitimize their ideology in public discourse. In order to build a holistic understanding of the way in which KSS has engaged with the immigration issue, we analyzed the organization's website (and websites of affiliated groups), materials produced by anti-racist watchdog groups and individual activists, as well as media coverage of the group. The data indicate the manner in which white supremacist group participation in the anti-immigrant movement demonstrates a number of stigma management strategies designed to garner legitimacy in a larger social climate that is hostile toward overt displays of racism and violent rhetoric.

White Supremacist Movement Sectors— Political, Religious, and Countercultural

In order to understand the legitimation processes employed by white supremacist groups, one must first comprehend the variety of organizations co-existing within the movement. The supremacist movement consists of three distinct sectors—political, religious, and countercultural groups—defined by the basis of each sector's ideology and forms of activism (Berlet & Vysotsky, 2006). Political organizations address social and political issues from a white supremacist analytic framework. They advocate neo-Nazi/fascist solutions based on racial hierarchy to rid the world of social problems (Berbrier, 1998a; Berbrier, 1998b; Berbrier, 1999; Daniels, 1997; Dobratz, 2000; Dobratz & Shanks-Meile, 2000; Ferber, 1999; Hamm, 1993; Ridgeway, 1995). In contrast, religious supremacist organizations often rely on a spiritual foundation for white superiority. Regardless of the specific type of white racist religion, there is a consistent theme that white dominance and control are the desire of god(s) or creator(s). This spiritual basis distinguishes religious supremacist organizations from their more secular, political counterparts and has at times been the cause of rifts in the movement (Dobratz, 2000). Countercultural groups, made up of predominantly teenage and young adult members, are less ideologically coherent than political or religious groups. While such non-normative youth-oriented groups share similar musical tastes, aesthetic styles, and argot (Clarke et al., 2006; Roberts, 1978; Smith, 1976), it is not uncommon to find a variety of ideals regarding the nature of white supremacy among members of countercultures. The skinhead scene incorporates members of neo-Nazi organizations, members of the Creativity movement, Odinists, and Christian Identity followers. In the Black Metal and industrial/Goth scenes, there exists a variety of both secular and religious beliefs. For example, some members of the National Socialist Black Metal scene reject religion entirely, while others embrace Satanism or neo-Pagan Odinism (Burghart, 1999). The prominence of one ideological stance over another among white supremacist countercultures is often the result of targeted recruitment and support on the part of other specifically political or religious supremacist organizations or influences (Berlet & Vysotsky, 2006).

While each sector represents a unique approach to ideology and action, organizations often overlap. This has been especially true in the case of the countercultural category. The association of white supremacy with skinheads and other countercultures has spread the ideology to a much wider and younger audience. Countercultures often represent the largest and fastest growing elements of the movement (Blazak, 2001; Burghart, 1999; Futrell & Simi, 2004). It is for this reason that many of the most successful political and religious organizations have courted countercultures as primary recruiting grounds for their membership (Burghart, 1999; Langer, 2003; Ridgeway, 1995). This, coupled with a number of high profile media representations, has led to a public association of white supremacy with the skinhead subculture. Such an association has greatly contributed to the growing stigma associated with open expressions of white supremacy.

Racist skinheads are often perceived as the most violent and stigmatized of all white supremacist groups. The subculture's comfort with nihilistic violence coupled with an ideological commitment to white supremacy creates a perception of the skinhead as a violent thug or "stormtrooper" in the race war (Blazak, 2001; Hamm, 1993; Sarabia & Shriver, 2004; Simi & Futrell, 2009; Simi et al., 2008; Wood, 1999). This stigmatized identity is further complicated by the skinheads' countercultural emphasis—they are largely focused on their status as outsiders from the mainstream and as subcultural participants instead of being primarily concerned with mainstream acceptance or legitimacy. Unlike political or religious groups which often seek to build a mass movement and gain widespread support through various "neutralization techniques" (Sykes & Matza, 1957) that rationalize violence or other deviant actions as what is best for the nation or as the will of God(s), racist skinheads seek status within their subculture or local "scene" and are largely unconcerned with the opinions of the general public (Blazak, 2001; Berlet & Vysotsky, 2006; Simi et al., 2008). By constructing subcultural identities as hooligans, thugs, or criminals, racist skinheads are significantly more subject to stigma (Simi & Futrell, 2009; Simi et al., 2008).

Stigma and Stigma Management of White Supremacist Identity

In an era where overt racism is largely taboo, active membership in a white supremacist organization is a highly stigmatized social identity. While scholars generally agree that racism persists as a structural and systemic force, public and even private expressions of such sentiments are generally considered unacceptable, and people tend to distance themselves from individuals who express such sentiments (Bonilla-Silva, 2006; Feagin & Vera, 1995). Berbrier (1999, p. 411) summarizes the attitude most people have towards white supremacists, stating that "[the] stigma of white supremacist racism evokes impressions of hatred, boorish irrationality, and violence or violent intent." This stigma is increased for racist skinheads who are often primarily identified with violence and criminality in addition to white supremacist stigma (Simi & Futrell, 2009; Simi et al., 2008; Sarabia & Shriver, 2004; Wood, 1999). To adapt to these stigmas, white supremacists have developed a number of strategies to minimize the stigma associated with their ideology.

Berbrier (1998a; 1998b; 1999) identified two key macro-level strategies used by white supremacists to reframe stigmatized identity: ethnic claims-making and intellectualization. The process of ethnic claims-making involves portraying white supremacist ideology as ethnic group representation, arguing, among other things, that the label "racist" is applied to them simply for having a healthy pride in their heritage and culture. Moreover, some argue that if, "according to the values of cultural pluralism and diversity, ethnic or racial pride is legitimate for (other) ethnic or racial minority groups ... then it is also legitimate for whites" (Berbrier, 1998b, p. 499, italics in original). With this logic, the average supremacist group member can feel comfortable in their racist ideas because they are no different from other American ethnic groups that express pride in their heritage. Conversely, there is a belief that minority groups who exhibit ethnic pride are equally as bigoted as members of their own organizations (Berbrier, 1998b). Berbrier's other macro-level stigma management strategy, intellectualization, involves legitimizing supremacist ideology through academic and scholarly sources. This is achieved through utilizing various empirical arguments to buttress racist worldviews. They point to the work of controversial educational psychologist Arthur Jensen, and more recently, Murray and Herrnstein (1996) in discussing correlations between IQ levels and race, specifically that African Americans score lower on IQ tests than whites (Dobratz & Shanks-Meile, 2000). As Dobratz & Shanks-Meile (2000, p. 95) point out, many white supremacists "discussed a number of scientists who support the 'new' scientific racist work, such as J. Philippe Rushton who maintained that whites and Asians were typically more family oriented and intelligent than blacks and anthropologist Roger Pearson who advanced the idea that the white race is threatened by inferior genetic stock." These strategies of ethnic claims-making and intellectualization allow white supremacists to position themselves as members of just another advocacy group in a pluralist political and social climate.

The micro-level strategies of stigma management deployed by white supremacists are more complex and varied than their macro-counterparts. Simi and Futrell (2009) outline a number of strategies which they believe allow white supremacists to maintain their ideology and movement affiliations in a society largely hostile to them. The first involves the physical distancing of supremacist political activity from other life activities. White supremacists create "free spaces" such as music events, parties, camping events, and intentional communities that allow them to openly express their beliefs and build the movement free of resistance (Futrell & Simi, 2004; Simi & Futrell, 2009). A second strategy involves strategic silencing, avoidance, or hiding of supremacist identity from family, friends, and coworkers. This process involves avoiding discussion or debate with others who may disagree, hiding racist symbols and markers from public display, and wearing clothing to cover racist and inflammatory tattoos. The processes of silence, avoidance, and hiding often inform the third strategy of civility/avoiding conflict. Simi and Futrell (2009) note that, in order to avoid conflict, white supremacists rarely engage in political discussions with people who do not share their beliefs. Surprisingly, they also found that supremacists often treat people of color with whom they work or interact in daily activities with civility, and at times, even respect. This strategy allows them to maintain employment and generally navigate through an increasingly multi-racial and multi-cultural world. The fourth strategy involves attempts at mainstreaming through the avoidance of the use of racial slurs and the presentation of their ideals in alignment with conservative positions. This often involves the framing processes discussed above wherein supremacists present their beliefs as legitimate political positions (Simi & Futrell, 2009). Finally, supremacists engage in passive expression of their belief through clothing and other symbolic displays. Simi and Futrell (2009) contend that this enables supremacists to enact their ideology without being directly confrontational. This often works effectively because such displays typically involve symbols recognizable only to other racists or individuals well versed in the ideology. Thus, the impetus for action falls upon those individuals able to recognize such symbols, rather than upon the supremacist (Vysotsky, 2009). Passive expression conveniently enables supremacists to interpret potential conflicts that arise via a victimization lens wherein they see themselves as victims of confrontations initiated by others. In the case study to follow, we address the manner in which the KSS use many of the aforementioned stigma management strategies in their attempt to gain legitimacy through the strategic adoption of anti-immigration political discourses and activism.

From the Keystone State Skinheads to Keystone United and the European American Action Coalition

The Keystone State Skinheads were reportedly founded in 2001 in response to a violent confrontation between white supremacists, primarily skinheads, and anti-racist, anarchist, and community protesters at a rally organized by the racist religious group, the Creativity Movement, in York, PA (ADL, 2009). The Southern Poverty Law Center (n.d.) identifies the KSS as one of the largest racist skinhead groups in the country with chapters in most major cities across Pennsylvania. Typical of countercultural groups, KSS activity was initially based around subcultural events such as music concerts and festivals, including Hammerskin Nation's annual Hammerfest and its own annual festival, "Uprise" (ADL, 2009; SPLC, n.d.). Like many skinhead groups, KSS strikes a precarious balance between operating as a political organization and criminal gang (Simi et al., 2008). While the group presents itself as "wish[ing] to break the stereotypes of skinheads being alcoholic thugs and violent drug-addicted criminals ... [by] offering education and guidance" (KSS website cited in SPLC, n.d.), the group's members and leadership have consistently been convicted of violent attacks against people of color and anti-racists (see ADL, 2009; SPLC, n.d.). With such an auspicious record, KSS struggles to present a more palatable public image by shifting its image from that of a countercultural to political group by focusing on political and social issues such as immigration.

As KSS attempts this transition, it faces the greater challenge of appealing to a broader population. To that end, the group officially promoted a name change to Keystone United and added leafleting, public protests, and media appearances to its action repertoire. A significant portion of this public campaign involved publicizing the group's opposition to immigration. KSS members staged anti-immigration leafleting campaigns with fliers headlining "American Jobs for American Workers" (Byrne & Sinclair, 2007) and others linking crime to changing racial demographics in Northeast Pennsylvania (Bello, 2008). Such campaigns are designed to not only educate the public on the group's positions, but also to present them as a political interest group, rather than a skinhead gang. KSS members have also participated in rallies at the state capital in Harrisburg demonstrating their opposition to "illegal-immigration" (Isis, 2007), in support of the acquittal of individuals accused of hate crime charges for the murder of a Mexican immigrant in Shenandoah (Bello, 2008; Holthouse, 2009), and in support of the introduction of a bill modeled on Arizona's S.B. 1070 in the Pennsylvania legislature (NoPawn, 2010).

These rallies put KSS in the same political context as more legitimate political actors, such as Ron Paul supporters and numerous elected officials (Denvir, 2012a; Isis, 2007).

In addition, KSS leader and spokesman Steve Smith formed the European American Action Coalition (EAAC) in 2011 as "an organization that advocates on behalf of White Americans" (EAAC, n.d.). The EAAC is designed as a strictly political organization advocating for "white people's rights" (Denvir, 2012b) rather than the countercultural, skinhead organization with which Smith has been previously affiliated. This repositioning allowed Smith to move into mainstream politics by being elected to the Luzerne County Republican Committee with one write in vote, likely his own (Denvir, 2012b). By distancing itself from the negative connotations and actions associated with skinheads, KSS has increasingly moved toward becoming a "political" white supremacist group.

The public attention created by such appearances and activities gives KSS leaders a unique opportunity to appear in media outlets to promote their organization. Steve Smith and fellow longtime member Keith Carney have become regulars in the Pennsylvania and national press as "Kinder, Gentler Skinheads" and "white people's rights activists" (e.g. Harte, 2009; Denvir, 2012b). Such appearances allow interested parties to seek out Keystone United or Smith's EAAC via their most public forums, their respective blogs and websites. These feature a number of "news" items that attempt to present a more mainstream version of supremacist ideology, including references to their immigration positions. The KSS blog features the transcript of an address by Mark Weber who directs the Institute for Historical Review, a think tank famous for producing "scholarly" evidence supporting the claims made by supremacists that the Holocaust was either a fabrication or a Jewish conspiracy (Lipstadt, 1994). Weber's address focuses primarily on the effects of Latin American immigration as understood by white supremacists—economic, intellectual, and political decline (keystonestate, 2011a). In a combination of the political and countercultural sectors, an interview with KSS member "Felix" features a question directly addressing the organization's position on immigration:

> The illegal immigration problem is out of control here. Not only do they have the same rights, they have MORE rights. Our people have been cast aside as second-class citizens to make way for this cheap, unchecked-capitalistic dream world, where all the laborers work for next to nothing, they don't want benefits of any kind, and there's lots of them! The business owners and farmers and politicians allow these invaders to enter our country and take all the jobs because it allows them to make a greater profit to be able to pay off one another ... (keystonestate, 2011b).

The EAAC's website presents an overlap between media appearances and blog posts with a collection of its members' letters to the editor. This includes a graph of predicted population demographics highlighting the increase in the Hispanic population and decline in the proportion of the white population. This seeks to prey on fears related to immigration and to bring individuals into the organization via this comparatively mainstream concern.

Immigration Concerns and Legitimation

The public debate on immigration provides a unique opportunity for white supremacists to participate in mainstream political discourse. The racialized rhetoric in opposition to immigration gives supremacists an opportunity to marshal stigma transformation strategies which present their movement as more legitimate. The KSS represent an ideal case study of the process utilized by many white supremacist groups. By engaging the immigration issue, KSS is able to mobilize both macro- and micro-level stigma management strategies in order to build relationships with more mainstream conservative actors and organizations.

With contemporary anti-immigration rhetoric focused on Latino immigrants, the racialization of the "illegal" immigrant serves to validate the ethnic claims-making strategies of white supremacists (Berbrier, 1998a; 1998b). Groups like the KSS can portray themselves not as racist bigots, but as advocates for a deindustrialized white working class. This was evident in the slogan used by KSS on their leaflet on immigration: "American Jobs for American Workers." By utilizing this slogan, KSS points away from its racism and instead claims to be advocating for "American" workers. Charges of racism can be deflected by noting that KSS supports native-born citizens as workers, while using a language that fellow racists understand as code for whiteness. Despite this patriotic or nationalist veneer, the racist politics of KSS and other white supremacists only genuinely recognize white Americans as true citizens with full rights. Further, by advocating against immigration, groups like KSS and EAAC construct themselves as ethnic advocacy organizations defending the interests of white American citizens against perceived threats of economic loss and increased criminal activity stereotypically associated with Latino immigration. They are able to claim a position of ethnic advocacy rather than overt white supremacy (e.g. KeystoneUnitedOfNEPA, 2010) and thus, such ethnic claims-making allows supremacists to deny allegations of racism.

Intellectualization processes further allow white supremacists like KSS to legitimize their opposition to immigration behind a rational facade of empirical evidence. The use of pseudo-scientific claims, such as the correlates of racial demographic changes with economic decline and increased crime noted above, imply empirical rationales to the reactionary emotionality of white supremacist discourse. The ideological position of racial exclusion in response to immigration taken by KSS and EAAC is portrayed not as the product of an emotional aversion to Latinos, but as a response to "legitimate" economic, social, and political concerns. Their citation of actual U.S. Census Bureau statistics regarding predicted demographic shifts in American society is also designed to legitimize supremacist claims about the loss of power experienced by whites. The predicted growth of the Latino population provides what white supremacists believe is clear empirical evidence for their political positions. By relying on empirical claims, KSS and EAAC are able to present their ideological and political positions as the products of intellectual engagement with the world rather than as the result of ignorance or emotion (Berbrier, 1999).

The strategy of distancing was the most evident micro-level product of ethnic claims-making and intellectualization for the KSS. As the group has attempted to transition from operating as a countercultural group to a political group, it has faced the obvious stigma associated with the skinhead subculture. This stigma has made it almost impossible for the group to engage in legitimate political discourse. Byrne and Sinclair's (2007) portrayal of KSS's anti-immigration leafleting campaign indicates that they received little support from the public with many individuals tearing apart the literature the group was distributing. In order to present itself as a more legitimate political actor KSS, officially changed its name to Keystone United in 2009 (SPLC, n.d.). Additionally, KSS leader and spokesman Steve Smith founded the European American Action Coalition (EAAC) in order to gain further distance from skinhead stigma and present himself as a legitimate actor in the anti-immigration debate (Denvir, 2012a; 2012b). By distancing themselves from the skinhead label and the countercultural stigma of criminality that comes with it, KSS has attempted to portray itself as a more legitimate organization (Berbrier, 1999; Simi & Futrell, 2009; Simi et al., 2008).

In order to properly distance itself from skinhead stigma, KSS has relied heavily on the strategy of avoidance, hiding, and mainstream displays (Simi & Futrell, 2009). This is primarily achieved through their public presentation. When engaging the public or media, KSS members avoid using overt racist and neo-Nazi symbolism or wearing traditional skinhead attire. At the leafleting event discussed above, KSS members dressed in jeans and hoodies—some with the KSS logo which itself is only an indirect racist symbol lacking any overt imagery (Byrne & Sinclair, 2007). This aesthetic allows them to portray themselves as "concerned" members of the working class, rather than as a group of countercultural racists. KSS members at the anti-immigration rally on the Pennsylvania capitol steps discussed above were only recognizable by the coded imagery on their clothing, such as the number 88 which stands for "heil Hitler," or the number 14, a reference to a central ideological slogan for the white supremacist movement,[1] in the url of the website featured on their picket signs (Isis, 2007). This is a conscious choice on the part of the supremacists at such protests because it allows them to participate as part of the broader anti-immigration movement without the stigma associated with their ideology. The average protester or citizen would not be able to readily identify these protesters as members of a racist skinhead group, thus allowing supremacists to blend in with other anti-immigration protesters and make connections with other activists in the movement.

Conclusion

The processes described above allow white supremacists to present themselves as legitimate political actors in the immigration debate. By engaging in macro-level strategies of ethnic claims-making and intellectualization, groups like KSS present their opposition to immigration as an advocacy position born of empirical data, instead of the product of a racist ideology. Utilizing micro-strategies of distancing, avoidance, hiding, and mainstream displays, groups like KSS attempt to portray themselves as "ordinary" citizens protesting a cause rather than as extreme racists, violent criminals, or countercultural deviants. By changing the organization's name and focusing on issues of public concern such as immigration, leaders such as Carney and Smith have removed many of the subcultural trappings of the skinhead identity when interacting with the general public. These strategies place white supremacists in greater contact with other types of activists on the right. In many of the cases outlined above, supremacists participate in the larger anti-immigration movement with little concern expressed by other participants. The danger of this is not that such a strategic dynamic will bring racists such as the KSS fully into the mainstream; it is that this type of relationship pulls anti-immigration groups further to the right towards more extreme and bigoted stances. Berlet and Lyons (2000) point out that the right-wing populist focus on issues such as immigration creates a link between supremacist groups and legitimate political actors on the right,

---

1. The 14-word slogan, "We must secure the existence of our people and a future for white children" is credited to David Lane, a member of the white supremacist terrorist group The Order (Dobratz & Shanks-Meile, 2000, p. 17).

such as elected officials. The participation of the KSS members in anti-immigration activism largely served as an embarrassment for other activists in the movement, as they tried to distance themselves from accusations of racism (Piggott, 2010). White supremacists like the KSS, however, benefit greatly from the increased media attention that campaigns such as the opposition to immigration provide. Such attention serves to reinforce many of their efforts at legitimation and stigma management, and therefore, these strategic tactics warrant serious concern and consideration.

In addition to legitimating and mainstreaming white supremacist activity, the participation of groups like KSS represents a shift to the right for the anti-immigration movement. Populist conservative social movements, such as the anti-immigration cause, provide a common ground where a variety of actors across the right of the political spectrum can interact with one another (Berlet & Lyons, 2000). By deploying legitimation and stigma management strategies, white supremacists are able to fully participate in such movements as legitimate actors and come in contact with other activists and political leaders on the right. Professional politicians and other political actors who would not typically associate with openly white supremacists for fear of a backlash from constituents, are able to espouse hard-right, even overtly racist positions because these become the norms in the movement. As the anti-immigration movement incorporates individuals and groups with overt white supremacist positions, conservative activists and politicians with more moderate immigration positions often find themselves losing the support of a base that is increasingly nativist (e.g. Denvir, 2012a).

What's more, the shift right-ward in the anti-immigration movement ultimately allows mainstream politicians and pundits to express overtly white supremacist and racist sentiments under the guise of opposition to immigration. As white supremacists engage with and support the anti-immigration movement, nationalist and nativist rhetorical framing has become increasingly infused with explicitly racist sentiment. Mainstream advocates against immigration can then use coded, and occasionally overt, racist statements while still distancing themselves from the more extreme positions taken by white supremacists. For example, prominent television hosts such as Lou Dobbs, Bill O'Reilly, and Glenn Beck have linked Latino immigration to crime, economic recession, loss of sovereignty, and even leprosy (Media Matters for America, 2008). Republican presidential candidate Mitt Romney's "joking" comments on the campaign trail that "had he [George Romney, Mitt's father] been born of Mexican parents, [Mitt would] have a better shot of winning this" evokes white supremacist sentiments of racial resentment, white victimhood, and loss of sovereignty (Fabian, 2012). Such claims mirror supremacist thinking about widespread anti-white discrimination and the evils of immigration, yet mainstream pundits and politicians can distance themselves from direct associations because supremacists are assumed to be virulent racists whose statements are limited to direct expressions of hate through the use of racial slurs and incitement to violence.

Likewise, white supremacists also use statements from mainstream actors as part of their strategies of distancing, mainstreaming, and intellectualization. They may more easily claim that their positions on immigration are not racist when these views are similar to those of widely known and popular television commentators and politicians. This dynamic creates a feedback loop where the reactionary and bigoted positions of white supremacists allow mainstream politicians to make racialized statements while still presenting themselves as less extreme by comparison, and white supremacists can claim not to be extremist racists because their positions on issues such as immigration are similar to mainstream politicians. Through this interplay, the ideology and rhetoric of the right becomes more extreme, overtly racist, and potentially violent.

Therefore, supremacist involvement in anti-immigration political activity has distinct and significant functions for their members. It allows them to engage in mainstream political conversations where they would otherwise be stigmatized and excluded. This enables them to adopt an image as political advocates rather than merely racial agitators, violent criminals, or domestic terrorists. Their participation in the larger anti-immigration movement pulls the acceptable discourse and goals of that movement further to the right and towards more extreme and bigoted positions. The adoption of more extremist stances on immigration occasionally serves to highlight the often implicit and covert biases of anti-immigration activists in general. However, such statements are frequently rebranded and reframed as conventional anti-immigration policy concerns, when in fact, the rightward shift reflects a strategic and deliberate advancement of the white supremacist agenda. Thus, we must understand and appreciate the significant role of white supremacist activists, and their hateful ideology more generally, if we wish to fully comprehend the state of the American immigration debate in the 21st century.

Discussion Questions

1. How does the activism and involvement of white supremacist groups in the anti-immigration movement impact the larger national debate about immigration?

2. What are the various stigma management strategies deployed by white supremacists in their engagement with the issue of immigration?

3. What are the differences between political supremacist groups and youth countercultural supremacist groups?

References

Anti-Defamation League (ADL). (2009). Racist skinhead project: Pennsylvania. Retrieved December 19, 2012, from http://www.adl.org/racist_skinheads/states/pennsylvania.asp.

Bello, M. (2008, October 21). White supremacists target middle America. The USA Today. Retrieved December 19, 2012, from http://usatoday30.usatoday.com/news/nation/2008-10-20-hategroups_N.htm.

Berbrier, M. (1998a). "Half the battle": Cultural resonance, framing process, and ethnic affectations in contemporary white separatist rhetoric. Social Problems, 45(4), 431–47.

———. (1998b). White supremacists and the (pan-)ethnic imperative: On "European Americans" and "White Student Unions." Sociological Inquiry, 68(4), 498–516.

———. (1999). Impression management for the thinking racist: A case study of intellectualization as stigma transformation in contemporary white supremacist discourse. Sociological Quarterly, 40, 411–433.

Berlet, C. (1992). Fascism. Retrieved December 15, 2012, from http://www.publiceye.org/fascist/berlet_fascism.html.

Berlet, C. & Lyons, M. (2000). Right-wing populism in America: Too close for comfort. New York, NY: The Guilford Press.

Berlet, C. & Vysotsky, S. (2006). Overview of U.S. white supremacist groups. Journal of Political and Military Sociology, 34, 11–48.

Blazak, R. (2001). White boys to terrorist men: Target recruitment of Nazi skinheads. American Behavioral Scientist, 44, 982–1000.

Bonilla-Silva, E. (2006). Racism without racists: Color-blind racism and the persistence of racial inequality in the United States. Lanham, MD: Rowman & Littlefield Publishers.

Burghart, D. (Ed.). (1999). Soundtracks to the white revolution: White supremacist assaults on youth music subcultures. Chicago, IL: Center for New Community.

Byrne, N., & Sinclair, M. (Writers). (2007). American skinheads [Television series episode]. In M. Sinclair (Producer), Inside. Washington, DC: National Geographic Society.

Clarke, J., Hall, S., Jefferson, T., & Roberts, B. (2006). Subcultures, cultures, and class. In S. Hall & T. Jefferson (Eds.), Resistance through rituals: Youth subcultures in post-war Britain (pp. 3–59). New York, NY: Routledge.

Daniels, J. (1997). White lies: Race, class, gender, and sexuality in white supremacist discourse. New York, NY: Routledge.

Denvir, D. (2012a, April 5). Right makes might: Meet Daryl Metcalfe, the gun-toting, gay-bashing, tea-partying state rep who's taking over Harrisburg. Philadelphia City Paper. Retrieved December 19, 2012, from http://www.citypaper.net/cover_story/2011-07-28-daryl-metcalfe-pennsylvania-state-representative.html?viewAll=y.

Denvir, D. (2012b, August 10). Daily News and Scranton Times-Tribune refer to white supremacists as white people's rights group. Philadelphia City Paper. Retrieved December 19, 2002, from http://www.citypaper.net/blogs/nakedcity/Daily-News-and-Scranton-Times-Tribune-refer-to-white-supremacists-as-white-peoples-rights-group.html.

Dobratz, B. (2000). The role of religion in the collective identity of the white racialist movement. Journal for the Scientific Study of Religion, 40(2), 57–75.

Dobratz, B., & Shanks-Meile, S. (2000). White power, white pride! The white separatist movement in the United States. Baltimore, MD: Johns Hopkins University Press.

European American Action Coalition. (N.d.) "European American Action Coalition." whiteadvocate.weebly.com. Retrieved December 29, 2012, from http://whiteadvocate.weebly.com/index.html.

Fabian, J. (2012, September 18). Romney secret video sums up his Latino problem." ABC News. Retrieved January 4, 2012, from http://abcnews.go.com/ABC_Univision/Politics/romney-secret-video-exposes-latino-problems/story?id=17263605#.UOdF2awqiSp.

Feagin, J. & Vera, H. (1995). White racism: The basics. New York: Routledge.

Ferber, A. (2000). White man falling: Race, gender, and white supremacy. Lanham, MD: Rowman & Littlefield Publishers.

Futrell, R. and Simi, P. (2004). Free spaces, collective identity, and the persistence of U.S. white power activism. Social Problems, 51:16–42.

Hamm, M. (1993). American skinheads: The criminology and control of hate crime. Westport, CT: Praeger.

Harte, J. (2009, October 14). Kinder, gentler skinheads: Inside Keystone United's "family-friendly" Leif Erikson Day celebration. Philadelphia City Paper. Retrieved December 19, 2012, from http://archives.citypaper.net/articles/2009/10/15/keystone-state-skinheads.

Holthouse, D. (2009). Acquittal in Pennsylvania killing sparks nativist rally. Retrieved December 18, 2012, from http://www.splcenter.org/blog/2009/05/26/acquittal-in-pennsylvania-killing-sparks-nativist-rally/.

Isis. (2007). Harrisburg PA immigration rally September 1 2007. Retrieved December 19, 2012, from http://www.flickr.com/photos/isisdc/sets/72157601846205354/detail/.

keystonestate. (2011a). America in decline: A society in denial. Retrieved December 19, 2012, from http://keystonestateskinheads.wordpress.com/2011/11/27/america-in-decline-a-society-in-denial/.

keystonestate. (2011b). Felix's interview with 28 Croatia." Retrieved December 19, 2012, from http://keystonestateskinheads.wordpress.com/2011/09/07/28croatiainterview/.

KeystoneUnitedOfNEPA. (2010). Keystone United TV interview from 2008 Part 1. Retrieved December 19, 2012, from http://www.youtube.com/watch?v=ZiU4_NEjTZY.

Langer, E. (2003). A hundred little Hitlers: The death of a black man, the trial of a white racist, and the rise of the neo-Nazi movement in America. New York, NY: Metropolitan Books.

Lipstadt, D. (1994). Denying the Holocaust: The growing assault on truth and memory. New York, NY: Plume Publishing.

Lyons, M. (1995). What is Fascism? In C. Berlet (Ed.), Eyes right! Challenging the right wing backlash (pp. 244–245). Boston, MA: South End Press.

Media Matters for America. (2008). Fear and loathing in prime time: Immigration myths and cable news. Retrieved January 4, 2012, from http://mediamattersaction.org/reports/fearandloathing/online_version).

Murray, C. and Herrnstein, R. (1996). The bell curve: Intelligence and class structure in American life (2nd ed.). New York, NY: The Free Press.

NoPawn. (2010). Neo-Nazis at anti-immigration rally as organizer plays dumb. Retrieved December 19, 2012, from http://www.youtube.com/watch?v=QqlYOmU7iew.

Piggott, S. (2010). ALIPAC cancels rally involvement over racist controversy. Retrieved December 21, 2012, from http://imagine2050.newcomm.org/2010/05/18/alipac-cancels-rally-involvement-over-racist-controversy/.

Ridgeway, J. (1995). Blood in the face: The Ku Klux Klan, Aryan Nations, Nazi skinheads, and the rise of a new white culture. New York, NY: Thunder's Mouth Press.

Roberts, K. (1978). Toward a Generic Concept of Counterculture. Sociological Focus, 11(2), 111–126.

Sarabia, D. & Shriver T. (2004). Maintaining collective identity in a hostile environment: confronting negative public perception and factional divisions within the skinhead subculture. Sociological Spectrum, 24, 267–294.

Simi, P. & Futrell, R. (2009). Negotiating white power activist stigma. Social Problems, 56 (1), 89–110.

Simi, P., Smith, L. & Reeser, A. (2008). "From punk kids to Public Enemy Number One. Deviant Behavior, 29, 753–774.

Smith, D. (1976). "The concept of youth culture: A reevaluation. Youth and Society, 7(4), 347–366.

Southern Poverty Law Center. (N.d.) Keystone United. Retrieved December 19, 2012, from http://www.splcenter.org/get-informed/intelligence-files/groups/keystone-state-skinheads.

Sykes, G., and Matza, D. (1957). Techniques of neutralization: A theory of delinquency. American Sociological Review, 22(6): 664–70.

Vysotsky, S. (2009). The Good Fight: Variations in Explanations of the Tactical Choices Made by Activists Who Confront Organized White Supremacists. (Doctoral Dissertation). Northeastern University, Boston, MA.

Wood, R. (1999). The indigenous, nonracist origins of the American skinhead subculture. Youth and Society, 31: 131–151.

Immigration, Transnational Migration, and International Context

Chapter Eleven

Human Rights and the War on Immigration

David Androff

Social policy in the United States, when directed at solving a large-scale and seemingly intractable social problem, has often been referred to as a "war." The 1960s Great Society social programs included the major anti-poverty initiative known as the "War on Poverty." Federal drug enforcement and prevention policies beginning in the 1980s and continuing today are referred to as the "War on Drugs." After the terrorist attacks on 9/11, the "War on Terror" was launched. These examples refer to concerted federal policy efforts; however the metaphor has been applied to attempts to influence policy across local, state, and federal levels such as the "War on Women," much discussed during the 2012 presidential campaign.

This chapter extends this metaphor to immigration policy. Immigration has long been the province of policy controls. However, the response to immigration in the United States has grown increasingly restrictive and punitive: criminalizing immigrants, militarizing the US-Mexico border, and resulting in human rights violations.

Despite current proposals for immigration reform, the federal policy response to migration in recent decades has been restrictive and punitive (Androff, Ayón, Becerra, Gurrola, Salas, Krysik, Gerdes, & Segal, 2011). In the absence of federal immigration policy reform, various states have enacted a flurry of laws controlling immigration, most famously Arizona's SB 1070 in 2010 (Androff & Tavassoli, 2012). The federal Secure Communities program initially included a provision, 287(g), for cooperation between federal and local law enforcement agencies in immigration control. These policy constrictions have been accompanied with increased immigration enforcement, apprehensions, detention, and deportation. Penalties and sanctions against immigrants have effectively criminalized migrants. Heightened security to prevent unauthorized immigration has been characterized as the militarization of the border (Androff & Tavassoli, 2012).

The War on Immigration refers to massive expenditures, large deployments of personnel, infrastructure and sophisticated technologies to deter immigration. On September 18, 2012, Janet Napolitano, U.S. Secretary of the Department of Homeland Security, said "there has been more money, manpower, infrastructure, technology invested in the border protection mission in the last three years than ever before" (National Immigration Forum (NIF), 2012, p. 1). This is despite the recent diminishing numbers of unauthorized border crossings. In the last decade border security, customs, and immigration enforcement spending has more than doubled from over $7.4 billion in 2002 to almost $17.2 billion in 2010. Since 1986, $219 billion has been spent on immigration enforcement (NIF, 2012).

An estimated 80,000 workers are employed in what has been called the "border industrial complex," a rampant spending coupled with increasingly sophisticated control technologies, including towers, camera, radar, infrared and motion sensors, lasers, thermal imaging systems, aerial drones, blimps and Blackhawk helicopters (NIF, 2012). The infrastructure includes, as of 2011, 142 border stations, 34 permanent checkpoints, 93 tactical checkpoints, and 2 remote forward operating bases—with plans for more (NIF, 2012). This infrastructure also includes a fleet of 16,875 vehicles, 269 aircraft, and 300 water craft. Then there is the fence itself, a border wall which the last 650 miles of construction costs $3 billion (NIF, 2012). The development of a virtual fence has been abandoned; however the physical fence has been shown to be ineffective, inaccurate (sometimes crossing into Mexico), to interrupt animal migration and to be disruptive to natural drainage patterns (NIF, 2012). The number of border patrol agents stationed along the southwest border has grown from 3,555 in 1992 to 17,415 in 2009 (NIF, 2012). As of 2012, there were 21,063 Border Patrol officers, 21,137 agents, 2,312 agricultural specialists, 1,576 canine enforcement teams, 334 equestrian patrols, and 1,229 air and marine agency. In May 2010, 1,200 National Guard troops were deployed to the southwest border.

The consequences of the War on Immigration are severe. The devotion of such resources to controlling mobility across boundaries is accompanied with a lack of resources devoted to protecting migrants' rights. Restrictions in immigration policy have been accompanied by anti-immigrant rhetoric and negative stereotyping. The resultant stigma and dehumanization facilitates human rights violations against migrants. The social exclusion processes that denigrate minorities, stigmatize vulnerable populations, and dehumanize 'outsiders' from society have been identified as common features of human rights violations around the globe.

Migrants' Rights Are Human Rights

Is immigration a human right? Human mobility is addressed in the 1948 Universal Declaration of Human Rights (UDHR). Article 13 specifies that the right to freedom of movement is a basic human right, and links this right to national sovereignty. International human rights law does recognize a migrant's human right to leave their home country, however this is not accompanied with a corresponding right to enter another country without permission (Grant, 2005).

Yet migrants do have human rights. They are humans; their rights derive from their humanity. The UDHR sets the foundation for all people to be equal, with dignity, and free from discrimination. Even when international human rights treaties do not specifically mention migrants, migrants are indeed covered because the human rights in these treaties are universal (Grant, 2005). The issue of human migration and the special vulnerabilities of migrants are addressed in several human rights conventions and covenants. These vulnerabilities include working in less favorable working conditions, being party to unfair competition among employers, and a lack of protection from exploitation and victimization. Several core international human rights treaties contain non-discrimination clauses—which apply to migrants regardless of their status. However there remains a distinct lack of multilateral cooperation on international migration. Many international human rights documents have been criticized as 'soft law,' without meaningful enforcement mechanisms (Cholewinski, 2005).

International Human Rights Law

International law on the human rights of migrants protects the rights of people working in countries other than their own and recognizes the vulnerability of migrant workers and their families. This section reviews and describes the relevant Covenants and Conventions that comprise international human rights law.

The 1966 International Covenant on Civil and Political Rights (ICCPR) protects the human right to life, freedom of religion, freedom of speech, and freedom of assembly for everyone within states' jurisdiction (Grant, 2005). This Covenant applies to the so-called "negative rights," including freedoms from killing, detention, torture, inhuman or degrading treatment or punishment. Other freedoms contained in this Covenant include the freedom of religion, freedom of speech, and the freedoms of association and assembly, freedoms to courts and tribunals, and to receive protections as minors. This Covenant distinguishes between nationals and non-nationals, but prohibits discrimination on any basis. The ICCPR entered into force in 1976 and has been ratified by 154 countries.

The 1966 International Covenant on Economic, Social, and Cultural Rights (ICESCR) mainly concerns the right to health, education, and an adequate standard of living, including the right to work (Grant, 2005). Everyone, including migrants, has labor rights and rights to working conditions that are "just and favorable," The Covenant states that protection and assistance should be accorded to the family, including migrant families. Migrants and their families are entitled to rights to highest attainable standards of physical and mental health, and education. The ICESCR entered into force in 1976 and has been ratified by 151 countries.

The 1965 International Convention on the Elimination of All Forms of Racial Discrimination (CERD) condemns "any distinction, exclusion, restriction, or preference based on race, colour, descent, or national or ethnic origin" (Grant, 2005). Although the Convention grants that distinctions and differential treatment with migrants is allowable, it also prohibits discrimination—such as distinctions of migrants which are unfair, unjustifiable, or arbitrary. It also maintains that non-citizens must be treated equally and their rights cannot be limited. The CERD entered into force in 1969 and has been ratified by 170 countries.

The 1979 Convention on the Elimination of All Forms of Discrimination against Women (CEDAW) has been described as an international bill of rights for women, and recognizes the gendered nature of many human rights violations (Grant, 2005). The Convention affirms that nation states must uphold the rights of women, including migrant women and their family members. The CEDAW was adopted in 1981 with 179 ratifying countries.

The 1989 Convention on the Rights of the Child (CRC) protects and specifies the rights of everyone under the age of 18. In addition to the universal rights of children to health and education, additional relevant provisions for migrants include the right to a name, nationality, and birth registration documentation. This Convention maintains that states must act in the best interests of the child and that whatever benefits a state gives to its citizen children must be given to all children. Migrant children and children without identity papers are among those particularly likely to be excluded from education. The CRC entered into force in 1990 and has 192 ratifying countries.

The 1960 Convention against Discrimination in Education, adopted by the United Nations Educational, Scientific, and Cultural Organization (UNESCO) combats discrimination and segregation in education. Although this Convention sets strong standards and has had an impact on other conventions and on raising awareness, it has been limited by a low rate of ratification and limited enforcement mechanisms. Just as UNESCO is the international body dedicated to education, the International Labor Organization focuses on labor issues. Both are important for migrant rights.

International Labor Organization (ILO) Instruments

The ILO was the first international organization to provide for the human rights of migrants, and has brought awareness to related issues of child migrants, the treatment of undocumented workers, forced labor, and human trafficking (Wexler, 2007).

The 1949 ILO Migration for Employment Convention (No. 97) calls for equal wages, social security, and unionization between national and migrant workers (Grant, 2005). State parties are required to submit information on their national policies, laws, regulations, and special provisions on migration for employment and migrants' work and livelihood conditions. This Convention applies to the whole migration process from entry to return, and even the conditions of the recruitment of migrants for work (Cholewinski, 2005). This entered into force in 1952 and has 42 ratifying countries.

The 1975 ILO Migrant Workers Convention (No. 143) goes further to protect the human rights of migrant workers in abusive conditions by promoting equality of opportunity and treatment with anti-smuggling and anti-trafficking measures (Cholewinski, 2005; Wexler, 2007). This entered into force in 1978 and has only 19 ratifying countries.

International Convention on the Rights of All Migrant Workers and Their Families

Building on these frameworks, the international community has recognized the increasing numbers of migrants around the globe and the need to foster respect and protection for migrants and their families. The United Nations' International Convention on the Rights of All Migrant Workers and Members of Their Families protects migrants against discrimination, dehumanization, and human rights violations (Cholewinski, 2005). The comprehensive Convention applies to all migrant workers and family members, and to the entire process of migration, including "preparation for migration, departure, transit, and the entire period of stay and remunerated activity in the State of employment as well as return" (UN, 1990). Specific provisions include non-discrimination with respect to rights, the human rights of all migrants, the rights of regular and irregular migrants, and the obligations of states to cooperate in promoting equitable and humane migration conditions.

Work related rights include the right to equal work and employment conditions with nationals, the right to freedom of association—specifically trade unions, and rights associated with past employment, such as social security (Wexler, 2007). Other rights include the right to emergency medical care, equal access to education with nationals, and to respect for migrants' cultural identity. The Convention holds that children of migrants cannot be refused primary education. For lawfully resident migrant workers and their families, rights include access to employment, family reunification, and equal access with nationals to housing, health, and social services. Migrants also have special rights including access to diplomatic authorities, to transfer remittances, to the protection of their identity and travel documents, and to access to the Convention with information about their rights.

This Convention was adopted by the General Assembly of the United Nations on December 18, 1990. This day has become International Migrants Day. The Convention entered into force on July 1, 2003. However signatories are few. There have been 46 countries who have ratified the Convention and an additional 16 that have signed, signaling their intent to ratify. These nations are mainly migrant sending countries, for example, Mexico, Philippines, and Indonesia. No major migrant destination countries have signed or ratified the Convention; the United States has not ratified or signed any of these international conventions.

Knowledge of this Convention is limited, and its length and complexity have been identified as obstacles to its ratification. Economic pressured tied to the globalization of labor markets contribute to the lack of political will preventing the adoption of these safeguards for irregular migrant workers. However this Convention would provide the legal foundation for international migration policy, promote social cohesion and human dignity, and prevent abuses, violations, and social injustice.

Some argue that the reason the United States does not ratify many international treaties is due to the U.S. Constitutional requirements requiring Congressional support, while others cite political conservatism and an attitude of American exceptionalism that views America as a distinct nation, which does not have the same human rights issues as the rest of the globe. However, public policies and discrimination in the United States deprive immigrants of many human rights, including health care, welfare, and economic opportunities.

Additional Tools for Migrant Rights

The Committee on Migrant Rights engages with states who are parties to the above international human rights treaties. Countries submit reports with input from NGOs and civil society organizations and participate in a dialogue the Committee, which makes comments and recommendations for implementation for human rights protections.

Individual complaint mechanisms enable people to raise awareness violations of human rights. Complaints can be initiated by any individual in a state which is party to a treaty, about an alleged violation of his/her rights. These complaints are made in writing, kept confidential, and undergo a semi-judicial procedure to assess the admissibility and the merits of the complaint. The Committee may initiate inquiry procedures if they have reliable information about a systematic violation of treaty rights by a state party.

The United Nations also has a Special Rapporteur on the Human Rights of Migrants (Wexler, 2007). The special rapporteur's responsibility is to report on the global state of the protection of migrants' human rights, and to respond to information from migrants and their families about human rights violations. They request information from countries and communicate with governments about specific cases. The special rapporteur also conducts fact finding missions to countries and submits an annual report to the United Nations Commission of Human Rights. Specific violations that the special rapporteur has addressed include sexual assault of domestic workers, mistreatment by manpower employment agencies, detention, mass expulsions, and lack of access to legal representation.

In recent years the connection between rights and economic and social development has become widely recognized. The human right to development is considered to be among the third generation of human rights. Reflecting this, the 2009 United Nations Development Program (UNDP) Report on Human Development highlighted human mobility (UNDP, 2009).

In addition to these international charters and treaties, nation states can emphasize the legal status of migrant workers in bilateral agreements, promoting employment contracts and working conditions equitable with nationals.

However these protection mechanisms are inadequate because of current trends in the globalization of migrant labor. These include the increasing presence of private agents and intermediaries involved in recruiting migrant labor that are less subject to state oversight or regulation (Cholewinski, 2005). Another factor is the feminization of migrant work—specifically female migrants engaged in sex work and domestic work. These categories of migrant labor are not specifically attended to in the Covenants and Conventions and are often beyond the reach of the law and ripe for exploitation and abuse (Cholewinski, 2005; Wexler, 2007).

Human Rights Violations against Migrants

Despite the protections identified in the previous section, the plight of migrants is perilous. Migrants, particularly in the United States are caught between a contradictory counter-play of historical, economic, social, and political tensions. Much of the national equivocation on immigrants and immigration policy rests upon the foundation of a colonial legacy consisting of waves of voluntary and forced migrations. The historic fluidity of the U.S.-Mexican border coupled with previous encouragements to Mexican laborers to immigrate, such as the Bracero program, contrasts sharply with many contemporary views. Many families in the Southwest trace their heritage from living in Mexico to the United States without having made a physical move due to the shifting border (Becerra, Ayón, Gurrola, Androff & Segal, in press).

Powerful economic demands for low-skilled and unskilled labor in agricultural and industrial sectors have conflicted with the national security and political demands to securitize borders. In the national security crisis following the 9/11 terrorist attacks, anti-terrorism efforts have furthered the criminalization of labor migrants (Androff et al., 2011). In this time of economic recession, budget reductions and austerity measures are coupled with xenophobia. On International Migrants Day, December 18th, 2012, the United National Secretary General said

> "As budgets tighten, we are seeing austerity measures that discriminate against migrant workers, xenophobic rhetoric that encourages violence against irregular migrants, and proposed immigration laws that allow the police to profile migrants with impunity" (UN, 2012).

Political exploitation of nativist fears, already exacerbated during the economic recession, contributes to a policy environment where human rights are not protected, or acknowledged. The incentive for politicians to gain popular support for anti-immigrant measures at the expense of human rights based policy is similar to the "tough on crime" dynamic that has contributed to the present hyper-incarceration and massive extension of the population in the criminal justice system — despite falling rates of crime. In the 1990s many politicians gained popular support for imposing harsh penalties and a strong anti-crime rhetoric at the expense of rational policy analysis. The potential for politicians to exploit nativist fear is heightened by the rapidly changing racial/ethnic demographics. As people of color begin to outnumber the historically white majority, the population becomes a minority majority nation. Surges in nativism or nationalism, especially in periods of economic downturn, have been linked to the dehumanization of vulnerable minority groups and to violations of their human rights.

The special rapporteur on the human rights of migrants has said that migrants face "a continuing deterioration in their human rights situation" (Wexler, 2007). Human rights violations in the U.S. against immigrants include hundreds of migrant deaths annually, the derogation of due process, physical abuse and deprivation in detention and inhumane deportation practices.

Violations of the Right to Life

Thousands of migrants have died preventable deaths trying to cross the Sonoran desert into the U.S. (Androff & Tavassoli, 2012). These deaths have been linked to the border enforcement strategy of "prevention through deterrence" which funneled migrants away from urban crossings and toward remote and dangerous sections of the border (Cornelius, 2001; U.S. Government Accounting Office (GAO), 2006; Rubio-Goldsmith, McCormick, Martinez & Duarte, 2007). Most migrant deaths in the desert result from dehydration, starvation, snakebites, becoming lost, or assault by criminal gangs (Androff & Tavassoli, 2012). Since the mid-1990s, estimates of migrant deaths range from 3,861 to over 5,607, with annual averages of 356 to 529, depending on various methodologies and data sources (Jimenez, 2009). The migrant mortality rate, per 10,000 apprehensions, has risen from less than 2 in 1997 to over 7 in 2009 (Haddal, 2010). The true numbers of migrants deaths will never be known; these estimates are based on only the bodies that are found (Bowen & Marshall, 2008; GAO, 2006; Rubio-Goldsmith et al., 2007; Sapkota et al., 2006; Whitaker, 2009). Estimates of migrant deaths, especially deaths of migrant women and children, also indicate that the deaths are rising despite the decrease in migrant crossings overall (Bowen & Marshall, 2008; Jimenez, 2009).

Violations in Court

Although immigration violations are technically a civil violation (Androff et al., 2011), federal courts criminally prosecute all people caught crossing the border without documentation (Williams, 2008). In order to more efficiently process the high number of apprehended migrants, Operation Streamline was developed in 2005 which combined all aspects of processing, including initial appearances, arraignments, pleas, and sentencing, into one "mass hearing."Hearings consist of sometimes up to 80 migrants being questioned and giving pleas in unison (Williams, 2008). The deprivation of due process restricts migrants' access to legal representation (Chacón, 2009; Jimenez, 2009; Lydgate, 2010; Williams, 2008). Most have only a few minutes with an attorney and cannot explore potential legal defenses, such as issues of competency due to illness, language, literacy, or intoxication. In such circumstances it is likely that at least some migrants do not understand or appreciate their charges, pleas, or rights. This policy has caused immigration cases in federal court to grow over 330% in the last decade, and has diverted judicial and prosecutorial resources from actual criminal cases such as human trafficking (Lydgate, 2010).

Violations in Detention

Immigrants comprise the federal prison population with the highest rate of growth. TheU.S. Immigration and Customs Enforcement (ICE) detained a record breaking 429,000 individuals in 2011. Over 33,400 immigrants are detained every day in over 250 facilities, many in privatized prisons (Department of Homeland Security (DHS), 2009). Violations of human rights have been documented in immigration detention, including over 110 deaths since

2003 (ICE, 2008), lack of medical care and legal counsel, and inhumane conditions, such as physical and verbal abuse (U.S. Department of Homeland Security (DHS), 2006; Phillips, Hagan, & Rodriguez, 2006; Southwest Institute for Research on Women, 2009). The nonprofit group No Más Muertos (NMM) has documented hundreds of violations of immigrants' human rights in detention including denial of food, water, and medical care; physical, sexual, and verbal abuse; and the separation of families, including parents and children; denial of bathroom facilities; extreme temperatures in cells; and refusals to provide blankets to women and children, even pregnant women and infants (NMM, 2008).

Violations Related to Deportation

In 2012 409,849 people were deported from the U.S., over three times more than the 116,464 removed in 2001 (ICE, 2008). People are often deliberately separated from family members during repatriation. Women and children, vulnerable to crime, are sometimes deported at night without identification, money, and clothes (Hagan, Eschbach, & Rodriguez, 2008; Williams, 2008). Violations of human rights have been reported during deportation, including physical and verbal abuse and denials of medical attention by Border Patrol agents. Many deported people had lived for years in the U.S., and may not speak Spanish or have any contacts in or familiarity with Mexico. Families separated by deportation suffer financially and experience housing and food insecurity (Chaudry et al., 2010). Children separated from their parents due to deportation are at risk for their physical safety, economic security, well-being, and long-term development (Androff et al, 2011).

Violations of the Right to an Adequate Standard of Living

Immigrants are much more likely to be poor and uneducated than native-born people (Becerra et al. in press). They suffer many socioeconomic disparities; they have a significantly lower median household income, they are more likely to have less education, and their poverty rate is greater. While many Latino immigrants live in urban centers, some live in isolated rural communities near the border called colonias. Colonias are among the poorest areas in the U.S., often lacking basic needs such as potable water, sewer systems, electricity, paved roads, and have limited access to health and social services. Immigrants are 2.5 times more likely to be without health insurance; Latino immigrants are the group with the highest rate of lack of health insurance (DeNavas-Walt, Proctor, & Smith, 2010).

Conclusions for Human Rights-Based Immigration Policy

While this chapter has focused primarily on immigration to the U.S., migration is a major global phenomenon. The United Nations (2008) estimates that there are 214 million migrants around the world, and that each year 5 million people migrate across international borders. If one includes internal migration, then the numbers are much higher. An increasing share of the world's population is migrating across political borders, primarily seeking improved economic opportunities (Bacon, 2008).

Unfortunately, violations of the rights of migrants are also a global phenomenon. Australian immigration restrictions have also been guided by a deterrence policy which has contributed to the deaths of migrants (Briskman, Latham & Goddard, 2008). However instead of dying in the American desert, migrants to Australia are dying at sea. Grave human rights violations have been identified in the mandatory immigrant detention program that has been in place since 1992.

Immigration pressures are also not a new phenomenon in Europe (Human Rights Watch (HRW), 2011). Migrants from Muslim backgrounds encounter significant nativist resistance and discrimination throughout Europe. It is estimated that between 1988 and 2010 around 15,000 migrants died trying to reach the European Union, the majority drowning. In 2011, a record 1,500 migrants died trying to reach the continent. The Arab Spring and ensuing instability has resulted in an increased number of migrants from North Africa and the Middle East, and an unfortunate concomitant increase in migrant deaths (HRW, 2011).

The reelection of President Obama and the Republican political defeat at the hands of an emerging Latino electorate has created a political opening for immigration reform. The question is whether immigration policy reform will be based on the principles of human rights and the international human rights law documents that protect the rights of migrants and their families. It may be unlikely given the reluctance of Congress in 2013 to afford women migrant protection from domestic violence in the opposition to reauthorizing the Violence Against Women Act (Graham, 2008).

Human mobility is about freedom; immigration policies which protect human rights enhance people's freedoms. Rights-based immigration policy reforms would ensure migrants access to equal wages, safe and healthy work conditions, health care and education, and protection from arbitrary detention or harassment. Strategies for promoting rights based immigration policy include working with employers, facilitating the inclusion and integration of migrants in destination communities, and fostering tolerance and empathy.

Current policy favors a law enforcement approach over a human rights approach; at present border security trumps human security. A rights based approach to migration would start with the migrant, and prioritize their human rights in relation with economic and security priorities.

Discussion Questions

1. What is the purpose of international human rights laws?
2. Describe some of the various humans right violations discussed in this chapter.
3. Discuss some of the protections that international human rights laws should encompass.

References

Androff, D., Ayón, C., Becerra, D., Gurrola, M., Salas, L., Krysik, J., Gerdes, K. & Segal, E. (2011). U.S. immigration policy and immigrant children's well-being: The impact of policy shifts. Journal of Sociology & Social Welfare, 38(1), 77–98.

Androff, D. & Tavassoli, K. (2012). Deaths in the desert: The human rights crisis on the U.S.-Mexico border. Social Work, 57(2), 165–173.

Bacon, D. (2008). Illegal people: How globalization creates migration and criminalizes immigrants. Boston: Beacon Press.

Becerra, D., Ayón, C., Gurrola, M., Androff, D. & Segal, E. (in press). Immigrants and poverty. In E. Giffords & K. Garber (eds.) The New Reality of Poverty. Boston: Pearson.

Bowen, K., & Marshall, W. (2008). Deaths of Mexican and Central American children along the US border: The Pima County Arizona experience. Journal of Immigrant Minority Health, 10, 17–21.

Briskman, L., Latham, S. & Goddard, C. (2008). Human Rights Overboard: Seeking asylum in Australia. Brunswick, Australia: Scribe.

Chacn, J. (2009). Managing migration through crime. Columbia Law Review, 109, 135–48.

Chaudry, A., Capps, R., Pedroza, J. M., Castañeda, R. M., Santos, R. & Scott, M. M. (2010). Facing our future. Children in the aftermath of immigration enforcement. The Urban Institute. Retrieved on May 1, 2010, http://www.urban.org/UploadedPDF/412020_FacingOurFuture_final.pdf.

Cholewinski, R. (2005). Protecting migrant workers in a globalized world. Migration Information Source, Migration Policy Institute. Retrieved February 2, 2012 from http://www.migrationinformation.org/Feature/display.cfm?id=293.

Cornelius, W. (2001). Death at the border: Efficacy and unintended consequences of US immigration control policy. Population and Development Review, 27, 661–685.

DeNavas-Walt, C. Proctor, B.D. & Smith, J.C. (2010). Income, poverty and health insurance coverage in the United States: 2009. P60–238. Washington, DC: US Census Bureau.

Graham, C.L. (2008). Relief for battered immigrants under the Violence Against Women Act. Delaware Law Review, 10 Del. L. Rev. 263, 1–13.

Grant, S. (2005). Migrants' human rights: From the marigns to the mainstream. Migration Information Source, Migration Policy Institute. Retrieved February 3, 2013 from http://www.migrationinformation.org/feature/display.cfm?id=291.

Haddal, C. (2010). Border Security: The role of the U.S. Border Patrol. Congressional Research Service.

Hagan, J., Eschbach, K. & Rodriguez, N. (2008). US deportation policy, family separation, and circular migration. International Migration Review, 42(1), 64–88.

Human Rights Watch (HRW). (2011). Hidden emergency: Migrant deaths in the Mediterranean. Retrieved February 2, 2013 from http://www.hrw.org/news/2012/08/16/hidden-emergency.

Jimenez, M. (2009). Humanitarian crisis: Migrant deaths at the U.S.–Mexico border. Retrieved from http://www.aclu.org/files/pdfs/immigrants/humanitariancrisisreport.pdf.

Lydgate, J. (2010). Assembly-line justice: A review of Operation Streamline, Policy Brief. University of California, Berkeley: Earl Warren Institute on Race, Ethnicity & Diversity.

National Immigration Forum. (2012). The "Border Bubble": A look at spending on U.S. Borders. Retrieved online February 2nd, 2012 at http://www.immigrationforum.org/images/uploads/2012/BorderBubble.pdf.

No Más Muertes (No More Deaths). (2008). Crossing the line: Human rights abuses of migrants in short-term custody on the Arizona/Sonora border. Tucson, AZ: Author.

Phillips, S., Hagan, J., & Rodriguez, N. (2006). Brutal borders? Examining the treatment of deportees during arrest and detention. Social Forces, 85(1), 93–109.

Rubio-Goldsmith, R., McCormick, M., Martinez, D., & Duarte, I. (2007). A humanitarian crisis at the border: New estimates of deaths among unauthorized immigrants. Washington, DC: Immigration Policy Center.

Sapkota, S., Kohl, H., Gilchrist, J., McAuliffe, J., Parks, B., England, B., Flood, T., Sewell, M., Perrotta, D., Escobedo, M., Stern, C., Zane, D. & Noite, K. (2006). Unauthorized border crossings and migrant deaths: Arizona, New Mexico, and El Paso, Texas, 2002–2003. American Journal of Public Health, 96(7), 1282–1287.

Southwest Institute for Research on Women. (2009). Unseen prisoners: A report on women in immigration detention facilities in Arizona. Retrieved from http://sirow.arizona.edu/files/UnseenPrisoners.pdf.

United Nations (UN). (1948). Universal Declaration of Human Rights. Retrieved January 23, 2011 from http://www.un.org/en/documents/udhr/index.shtml.

United Nations (UN). (1990). International convention on the protection of the rights of all migrants workers and members of their families. Retrieved January 23, 2011 from http://www2.ohchr.org/english/law/cmw.htm.

United Nations (UN). (2008). International Migrant Stock: The 2008 Revision. Retrieved January 23, 2011 from http://esa.un.org/migration/.

United Nations Development Program (UNDP). (2009). Human development report 2009: Overcoming barriers: Human mobility and development. New York: UNDP. Retrieved April 4, 2011 from http://hdr.undp.org/en/reports/global/hdr2009/.

United Nations (UN). (2012). Secretary-General's Message for 2012—International Migrants Day, 18 December. Retrieved March 18, 2013 from http://www.un.org/en/events/migrantsday/2012/sgmessage.shtml.

U.S. Department of Homeland Security. (2006). Treatment of immigration detainees housed at ICE facilities (OIG-07-01). Washington, DC: Author.

U.S. Department of Homeland Security. (2009). Annual report—Immigration enforcement actions: 2008. Retrieved from http://www.dhs.gov/xlibrary/assets/statistics/publications/enforcement_ar_08.pdf.

U.S. Government Accountability Office. (2006). Illegal immigration: Border-crossing deaths have doubled since 1995; Border Patrol's efforts to prevent deaths have not been fully evaluated (GAO-06-770). Washington, DC: Author.

U.S. Immigration and Customs Enforcement. (2008). Fiscal year 2008 annual report. Retrieved from http://www.ice.gov/doclib/pi/reports/ice_annual_report/pdf/ice08ar_final.pdf.

Wexler, L. (2007). The non-legal role of international human rights law in addressing immigration. University of Chicago Legal Forum, 360–403.

Williams, H. (2008). Statement to the US House of Representatives Subcommittee of Commercial and Administrative Law, June 25, 2008. Retrieved January 3, 2010 from http://judiciary.house.gov/hearings/pdf/Williams 080625.pdf.

Whitaker, J. (2009). Mexican deaths in the Arizona desert: The culpability of migrants, humanitarian workers, government, and business. Journal of Business Ethics, 88, 365–376.

Chapter Twelve

Transnational Dimensions of Mexican Migration at the Cusp of Comprehensive Immigration Reform

William Haller

Introduction

This chapter examines the development of transnationalism between the United States and Mexico in the context of U.S. policy, border control, and the unique historical relationship of the U.S. with Mexico. I argue that the criminalization of undocumented border crossing in the context of previously established transnational economic ties has led to the expansion of organized crime across a range of truly criminal sectors, including human trafficking, drug, and gun smuggling. The broader demographic, economic, and political forces that have shaped the transnational context of U.S./Mexican relations have also produced and expanded the patterns of both documented and undocumented migration from Mexico into the U.S. The vast majority of undocumented migrants and their children remain largely at the mercy of the transformations that have occurred in border control, immigration policy, and the outcomes associated with these.

Conceptually, transnationalism refers to "the continuing relations between immigrants and their places of origin and how this back- and-forth traffic builds complex social fields that straddle national borders" (Portes, Haller and Guarnizo 2002, p. 279). But given that most immigrants engage in at least some cross-border activity, such as sending remittances back to family or bringing back goods that are more expensive and difficult to obtain in their country of origin, an empirical question arises as to how much cross-border activity constitutes the development of a significant transnational social field. Research in the late 1990s and early 2000s from the Comparative Immigrant Entrepreneurship Project (CIEP) based at Princeton University and directed by Professor Alejandro Portes, used survey research in conjunction with local-level demographics from the U.S. Census, to establish that there is indeed significant grassroots-level transnational economic activity among immigrants of three nationalities (Salvadorans, Dominicans, and Colombians) in the communities where they were most highly concentrated.[1] Among the important findings of the CIEP was the discovery that most of the regular, sustained cross-border activity which defines transnationalism takes place within immigrant organizations (based mainly in the receiving country). Thus, the CIEP became the CIOP (Comparative Immigrant Organizations Project) and the subsequent research on transnationalism from this project focused on immigrant transnational organizations. Additionally, CIOP drew attention to the fact that more alert "sending country governments [such as the Mexican] began to interact proactively with their expatriates ... through representatives of the organizations created by the migrants themselves" due in no small measure to the dramatic increase of migrant remittances (which reached $336 billion globally in 2008; Portes and Zhou 2012, p. 192–193). In the case of Mexico, governmental attention to immigrant organizations has followed in line with its broader policy of acercamiento (approach or rapprochement) with the U.S. (Smith 2003, p. 306). In the case of Mexico, the proactive stance of the Mexican Federal Government is realized through the Institute of Mexicans Abroad. Besides the Mexican Federal Government, various state and municipal governments coordinate efforts with transnational Mexican migrant organizations. The services provided include mobile Mexican consulates providing access to consular services to Mexican communities dispersed across rural and other remote areas, legal and health services, language courses, etc. (Portes and Zhou, 2012, p. 199).

Given that Mexico is by far the top ranking country of origin for both legal and unauthorized immigration into the United States (approximately 11.4 million immigrants in 2010—with over one third in the United States without authorization—compared to second-ranking China's 2.2 million) Mexican migration represents the most significant country of origin for both documented and undocumented migration into the United States (Massey, 2007). Demographically, the total migrant flows from El Salvador, the Dominican

---

1. The Salvadoran communities were in Alexandria, VA, and the Pico Union area of Los Angeles; the Dominican communities were in Upper Manhattan and Providence, RI; and the Colombian community was in Queens, New York.

Republic, and Colombia amount to a small percentage of migration from Mexico (and because the scale and scope of Mexican/U.S. transnational activity is also larger than between immigrants from other countries and their home communities Mexico was added to CIOP). The unique complex of historical, geographical, political and economic relations between Mexico and the United States also require that this relationship be viewed separately from the relationship of the United States with other countries. The size and scale of the U.S.-Mexico border region also means that although the larger, national and global-level, forces that set the general parameters are essentially uniform there is great heterogeneity at the local level in the social, economic, and political dimensions of border region and its communities (Smith, 2000). The greater El Paso, Texas/Juarez, Chihuahua urbanized region is very different from the Nogales, Arizona/Nogales, Sonora region.

Background: The Border Region and its History

Today's American Southwest developed out of the frontiers contested by the descendants of both Anglo and Spanish colonists in the New World, demographically the largest and among the most recent cultural and historical layers of the region that comprise its deep history (Hall, 1989). Population movement and growth into the Southwest United States and Northern Mexico has transformed the once geographical frontiers of both nations into frontiers of social, cultural, political, economic dimensions of greater significance for both countries. The border between Mexico and the United is about 2,000 miles long and defines the largest disparity in levels of economic development between two adjacent nations with such long land borders. It is also the busiest international border with approximately 350 million authorized crossings annually through 46 U.S. points of entry and daily two-way trade is approximately one billion dollars (AFP Newswire, 2010).

U.S. immigration laws and policies have also run a different course with Mexican immigration than with immigration from other countries in ways that shaped the contours and scale of Mexican migration and transnationalism. The origins of the Mexican American population date back to the Treaty of Guadalupe Hidalgo which concluded the Mexican-American War in 1848 in which the present U.S. states of California, Arizona, New Mexico, Texas, and parts of Colorado, Nevada, and Utah were surrendered to the United States by Mexico. The establishment of these borders, along with Gadsden Purchase to create a rail line within U.S. boundaries from the Southern U.S. to San Diego, brought a small and remote group of Mexican citizens into the fold of the United States.

Estimates of the numbers of Mexicans who became Americans because of the new border are small, approximately 50,000 (Jaffe, Cullen, and Boswell 1980; Massey, Durand, and Malone 2002). The numbers of Anglo Americans moving into these newly acquired territories were also very small with California and Texas acquiring the major shares of permanent settlers during the 18th century. Prior to 1900 the Mexican-American borderlands were remote frontiers from the points of view of both the East Coast of the United States and Mexico City. Although Californians, alarmed by the increase of Chinese immigration, successfully lobbied to create the first major immigration legislation (the Chinese Exclusion Act of 1882) the bulk of concern among nativist groups of the 18th and early 19th centuries centered on the large numbers of Irish and continental Europeans, particularly those from predominately Catholic, Jewish, and Orthodox regions. Italians, Poles, Eastern European Jews, and Slavic peoples were the focus of immigration policy in the years leading up to and immediately following WWI. The greatest concern of the United States with respect to the frontier region of the Mexican border was with political insurgents' involvement in the Mexican Revolution and their raids into U.S. territory (such as Pancho Villa's razing of Columbus, New Mexico followed by a U.S. Army intervention led by General John J. Pershing into the mountains of Northern Mexico in a failed attempt to capture him). Aside from insurgents and persons fleeing the legal jurisdictions of U.S. or Mexican officials, the U.S.-Mexican border was porous and the small population movements crossing the border in either direction was largely considered trivial by the political elites of both countries.

As railroad infrastructure improved from central to northern Mexico and across the southern border states of the U.S. demand for labor increased on the northern side of the border. Labor recruitment attempted to meet growing demand for labor in southwestern agriculture, mining, construction, and railroads increasingly from Mexico—thus establishing a circular pattern of labor migration from Mexico into the U.S. characterized by sojourns north of the border with return migration back to Mexico (Massey, Durand and Malone 2002, p. 27).

In 1924 the United States passed the Immigration Act of 1924 which established highly restrictive immigration quotas by national origin based on the census of 1890, which sharply reduced additional immigration from Eastern and Southern Europe (because the greatest number of immigrants from these regions entered after 1890). "Even as Congress moved to close off European immigration by implementing strict quotas ... it remained silent on the issue of immigration from countries of the Western Hemisphere ... numerical limitations were never applied to Mexico, whose nationals were free to enter without quantitative restriction and did so in large numbers" (Massey, Durand and Malone 2002, p. 29).

Following the Great Depression, which included the Mexican Repatriation (forced expulsion of Mexican laborers back to Mexico motivated by high U.S. unemployment), WWII brought new labor shortages into the American Southwest. With so many American men conscripted into the war effort in both the Pacific and European theatres, and so many American women staffing the war industries to supply them, the need for increasing the number of agricultural workers in the U.S. became a matter of strategic concern. To answer this shortage of agricultural labor the Roosevelt Administration negotiated a treaty with Mexico in 1942 creating the Bracero Program, a formal temporary guestworker program. Initially it was to last only for the duration of the war but it persisted until 1964. Although highly exploitative and coercive (see Mize 2006), the Bracero program deepened and normalized the circular pattern of labor migration from Mexico into the U.S. Approximately 168,000 Braceros (manual laborers) worked in the United States under this program during WWII, the Korean War brought about additional labor shortages with an expansion of the program and later, from 1955 to 1960, Bracero migration increased to between 400,000 and 450,000 workers annually. Much of the authorization for these migrants occurred post facto and attempts at controlling the incidence of unauthorized migration increased. "At one point the INS [Immigration and Naturalization Service] was raiding agricultural fields in the southwestern United States, arresting undocumented workers, transporting them back to the border, and deporting them into the waiting arms of officials from the U.S. Department of Labor, who promptly processed them as Braceros and retransported them back to the very fields where they had been arrested in the first place" (Calavita, 1992, quoted in Massey, Durand, and Malone 2002, p. 37).

Driven Underground: Rupturing the Circulation and Continuity of Mexican Migrant Labor

Massey, Durand, and Malone (2002) described the subsequent changes to the Mexican-U.S. migration system in terms of two distinct periods: "The Undocumented Era" and "The Great Divide" defined by the implementation and consequences of immigration and economic policies vis-à-vis Mexico. The scale and practices of the Bracero Program normalized circular patterns of migration that also facilitated increases in unauthorized migration. By the end of the Bracero Program legal migration was curtailed and the stock of former migrants, their patterns of work sojourns in the U.S., and the knowledge of English and familiarity with basic work and consumption routines, represented a major resource for new migrants with social capital ties to them. As the ceiling for legal immigration visas from Mexico was lowered demand for these visas did not which led, not surprisingly, to increases in undocumented labor migration. Between the end of the Bracero Program in 1964 and passage of the Immigration Reform and Control Act (IRCA) in 1986 "roughly 28.0 million Mexicans entered the United States as undocumented migrants during this period." However, these "28.0 million entries were offset by 23.4 million departures, yielding a net increase of only 4.6 million." Massey, Durand, and Malone's (2002) estimate for this period was "probably on the order of 5.7 million, of whom 81 percent were undocumented" (p. 45). Border Patrol was able to provide some sense of security to the general public but was never given resources adequate to the task of denying willing employers of undocumented workers access to their labor. Increasing apprehensions of unauthorized entrants justified budget increases and expansions for the Border Patrol, resulting in larger numbers of arrests and quick turnaround time in processing and repatriation, typically according a "voluntary departure order" which allowed the migrant to forgo the inconvenience of a hearing. Upon repatriation the detainee was free to try again and would likely succeed on the second or third attempt.

The three major changes resulting from IRCA were increased funding for border security measures, legalization of "undocumented aliens who had been continuously unlawfully present since 1982" (U.S. Citizenship and Immigration Services web site), and provisions to fine employers who knowingly hired illegal immigrants. But, counter-intuitively, escalations in border security did more to deter the exits to back Mexico (associated with the previously established circular pattern of migration) than it did to deter new unauthorized entries into the United States. As border security measures increased and the experience of crossing the border to find work was made more difficult for individuals and small groups, the idea of returning home to Mexico with the possibility of repeating the experience in some future sojourn (an idea which was consistent with circularity of migration) was made increasingly unattractive. Furthermore, the disincentive created for returning to Mexico also removed advantages of convenient access to the border so that as the circularity of migration was ruptured so was the primary reason labor migrants had to stay near the border. This lead to the geographical spread of unauthorized labor migrants into new regions of settlement within the U.S. while, for others, the legalization of residency granted full freedom to relocate anywhere in the country which many exercised (Jiménez, 2010, p. 49). Once again, the goal of disentangling legal and unauthorized migrants (often members of the same towns and rural communities of origin) was stymied.

Tragically, the poignant irony of these unintended consequences of attempting to control Mexican immigration was not realized at the time and the efforts to establish a border control regime as if a prophylactic seal across 2000 miles of mainly rugged wilderness were possible continued. Furthermore, a vicious cycle was set in motion because the geographical spread of legal and unauthorized Mexicans living and working in the U.S. increased their visibility in the small towns and communities of the new regions of settlement, popularizing further calls for and attempts at heightened immigration restrictions from conservative politicians at the local level (e.g., Hazleton Pennsylvania's Illegal Immigration Relief Act of 2006, and the South Carolina Illegal Immigration Reform Act of 2011). The tragedy of the unforeseen consequences was realized in the increased rates of death and injury during unauthorized border crossing attempts. The dangers and difficulties of crossing the border as an unauthorized migrant in the years immediately following the closure of the Bracero Program were already significant during the "Undocumented Era" prior to the post-IRCA militarization of the border, as elaborated through participant-observation research (Samora, 1971). But because the security measures could not be escalated uniformly and concomitantly across the entire 2000 mile border, they were implemented first in the border cities and then expanded outward into increasingly remote and dangerous terrain.

A benign view of such policy and its implementation might excuse U.S. officials from responsibility for the increased death rate at the border. However, viewing unauthorized migrants as isolated individuals making rational cost/benefit calculations who would respond to the increased risk by foregoing the attempt was never realistic. Research on the motivations for migration has established that decisions at the family and household level (see Massey, et al. 1999, pp. 21–22) in order to diversify family income sources is the more typical reason for migration from rural Mexican households. Because the motivation is family wellbeing, this raises the stakes and migration to find work becomes a compelling need, far beyond what would be reasonably expected if individual cost/benefit were the only consideration. Rarely does unauthorized migration from Mexico take place as an individual's response to his or her circumstances in isolation from family circumstances. Thus, such escalation of border security as a deterrent against unauthorized crossing by individuals motivated by merely their own self-interest was fundamentally misconceived.

As the operating budget of the Border Patrol increased, so did apprehensions of unauthorized border crossers; but so, too, did death and injury of those seeking to evade the Border Patrol by attempting entry in increasingly remote and dangerous locales. Wayne Cornelius, Director of UCSD's Center for Comparative Immigration Studies, reported that deaths among unauthorized border crossers increased by 474% from 1996–2000, and by over 1180% in both the Texas and Arizona segments over the same period (Cornelius, 2001, p. 669). Cornelius continues,

> The most convincing evidence that concentrated border enforcement is largely responsible for the rise in migrant mortality is the change in causes of death among unauthorized border-crossers that can be observed since 1994. Most migrant deaths along the Mexico-California border between 1995 and 2000 (308 of them) were the result of "environmental causes": hypothermia (freezing to death in the mountains), dehydration, or heat stroke (after days of trudging through the desert). Another 177 migrants died by drowning.... ..Drowning is, in fact, the most frequent cause of death among migrants in the El Centro sector. This, too, is a direct consequence of the concentrated border enforcement strategy: migrants entering via the All American Canal and the New River are seeking to avoid the worst of a scorching, multi-day trek through the desert (pp. 670–671).

The crackdown on widespread "amateur" unauthorized entry following IRCA created demand and a marketplace for professional "coyotes" to create and maintain increasingly sophisticated smuggling routes and techniques. The "imbalance and the barriers that developed countries erect to keep people out create a lucrative niche for entrepreneurs dedicated to promoting international movement for profit, yielding a black market for migration services" (Massey, Durand, and Malone 2002, pp. 19–20). Expertise in smuggling among increasingly professional and organized criminals applied directly to other highly profitable ventures, such as smuggling drugs from Mexico into the U.S. with reverse flows of money and firearms (the latter being tightly regulated in Mexico). The mix of human, drug, and arms trafficking and the money it generated resulted in escalation of turf wars, widespread murder, assassinations, gang and cartel activity disproportionately centered on the border cities and town on the Mexican side, where the gangs and cartels could more effectively intimidate the local authorities and residents as they vied for dominance over invaluable crossing sites and each other. In 1990 Warren Reece, coordinator of Southwest Border Patrol High-Intensity Drug-Trafficking Area Program, reported to the House Select Committee on Narcotics Abuse and Control that "We are engaged in something akin to a guerilla war along the border against well-entrenched and well-organized trafficking groups" (Dunn, 1996, p. 2). Dunn continues indicating that "Complex international issues such as undocumented immigration and illegal drug trafficking were reduced to one-sided, domestic border control problems, and framed as potential or actual threats to national security, which in turn required strong law enforcement, or even military, responses. Less coercive approaches were de-emphasized or excluded from consideration" (Dunn, 1996, p. 2). With the flow of undocumented migrants (either helped by coyotes or, in some cases, kidnapped and trafficked by them) and drugs into the U.S., with a return flow of cash, assault rifles and other weaponry the unintended consequences of rupturing the circularity of Mexican/U.S. migration morphed into perverse consequences. Criminalizing undocumented migration, which had been essentially a civil offence, expanded opportunities for organized crime to flourish across a wider and far more serious range of criminal sectors. As nativist groups grew increasingly vocal and incalcitrant in their opposition to undocumented migration, the charged political atmosphere made it easy for law enforcement to adopt a zero-tolerance, one-size-fits-all approach to dealing with undocumented migrants. As easy as it is to adopt a hard line, and apply the law blindly, the cost of such convenience is outcomes that are inhumane and arguably unjust. For example, deportations of unauthorized immigrant parents of children who are U.S. citizens by virtue of the 14th Amendment has led to separating children from parents (when family reunification is one of the long-standing, core principals of U.S. immigration policy). Unauthorized migrants who were here to work and send earnings back to their family in Mexico would be deported, just as violent offenders who were involved in drug and gang activity.

More recently, however, there has been a positive trend among the law enforcement community of some locales in that the draconian, one-size-fits-all approach has been recalibrated by law enforcement in some jurisdictions in that they are setting enforcement priorities. For example, unauthorized migrant drug traffickers are being given high priority while those have committed driver's license violations are made low priority. Unauthorized migrants driving without a valid U.S. driver's license sometimes are shown more leniency if they are able to produce valid auto insurance papers or an international driver's license because they are demonstrating an attempt to comply with the law even if their efforts fall short. Among the major policy shifts is deferred Action for Childhood Arrivals (DACA), which does not grant legal status but does provide for "lawful presence."

Two Sides of Mexican/U.S. Transnationalism

In this chapter I have argued that the transnationalism of organized crime has been an outgrowth of misconceived U.S. policy targeting unauthorized crossings over the border with Mexico. But apart from the transnationalism of organized crime which often captures shocking headlines and feeds negative stereotypes, there is the far more widespread transnationalism of hometown associations and the policies and practices of various levels of the Mexican government (Federal, State, and Municipal) aiming to promote development in the communities of origin, to encourage continued engagement with Mexico on the part of its expatriate population, and to promote the recognition and respect of basic human rights towards Mexicans and Mexican Americans living in the U.S..

So what is this other face of Mexican/U.S. transnationalism that is far more widespread than the organized criminal activity which feeds public fears? To be sure, both legal and unauthorized immigration into the U.S. from Mexico in response to labor demand in the U.S. and the needs of family and community back in Mexico fed the growth of the Mexican and Mexican-American population in the U.S. over the course of the 20th and into the 21st century. The view of the expatriate population living and working in the U.S. among Mexican elites through much of the 20th century was that they were lower class, relatively few in number, and largely insignificant, and essentially devalued (pochos). But towards the end of the 20th century "The legalization of more than 3.5 million people — more than half of whom were Mexican — through the 'amnesty' provisions of [IRCA] shocked the Mexican elite out of their assumption that few migrants settled in the United States ... and by the early 1990s remittances to Mexico were ... conservatively 2 billion USD ... roughly equal to Mexico's earnings from agricultural export" (Smith, 2003, p. 307). The most up-to-date research on transnational Mexican immigrant organizations (CIOP) counted 1,290 such organizations in the United States (restricting the count to those that are large and well-established). Of these 64% were hometown associations, 10% were sports groups, and 9% were state-of-origin associations. The small 7% of transnational Mexican civic and cultural organizations stands in stark contrast to 47% of Colombian and 30% of Dominican groups in this category (Portes and Zhou, 2012, p. 197). "Mexican immigrant organizations in the U.S. are different from those created by other Latin American groups in several key respects. They are 1) predominantly rural, 2) highly concentrated on hometown civic associations, and 3) rely not on "raffles, dances, and similar events for fundraising" but view "such contributions as a continuation of their traditional duties (cargos) to their places of origin" (Portes and Zhou, 2012, p. 196; see also Sanchez, 2007).

Currently, the U.S. is once again at the cusp of comprehensive immigration reform, and possibly the most thoroughgoing immigration reform since the 1965 Hart-Cellar Act which overturned the Nationality Quotas Act of 1924.

At this time of writing the "Gang of Eight" U.S. Senators leading the bipartisan effort is holding together although strident opposition from the House of Representatives is expected. Whether we will retreat once more from significant immigration reform remains to be seen. Regularizing and legitimating the transnational flow of labor, just as NAFTA is doing for the flows of goods and services between Mexico and the U.S., is hardly even a remote possibility, but transnational migrant organizations are an important dimension of increasing cooperation between the United States and Mexico. Such cooperation is important for both countries not only in terms of promoting economic prosperity but also in terms of mutual security and peace.

Discussion Questions

1. What are the implications of the concept of transnationalism for immigration?
2. How can immigration reform be informed by globalization?
3. How does what you learned about the history of Mexicans in the United States impact your understanding of undocumented immigration?

References

Agence France Presse Newswire (2010). "U.S., Mexico open first new border crossing in 10 years." Washington: AFP Bureau.

Calavita, Kitty (1992). *Inside the State: The Bracero Program, Immigration, and the INS.* New York: Routledge.

Cornelius, Wayne (2001). "Death at the Border: Efficacy and Unintended Consequences of U.S. Immigration Control Policy." *Population and Development Review.* Vol. 27, No. 4, pp. 661–685.

Dunn, Timothy J. (1996). *The Militarization of the U.S.-Mexico Border, 1978–1992: Low-Intensity Conflict Doctrine Comes Home.* Austin: University of Texas Press.

Guarnizo, Luis, Alejandro Portes, and William J. Haller (2003) "Assimilation and Transnationalism: Determinants of Transnational Political Action among Contemporary Migrants." *American Journal of Sociology. Vol.* 108, No. 6, pp. 1211–1248.

Hall, Thomas D. (1989). *Social Change in the Southwest, 1350–1880.* Lawrence: University Press of Kansas.

Jaffe, A. J., Ruth M. Cullen, and Thomas D. Boswell (1980). *The Changing Demography of Spanish Americans.* New York: Academic Press.

Jiménenz, Tomás R. (2010). *Replenished Ethnicity: Mexican Americans, Immigration, and Identity*. Berkeley: University of California Press.

Massey, Douglas S. (2007). "Borderline Madness: America's Counterproductive Immigration Policy." Pp. 129–138 in C. M. Swain (ed.) *Debating Immigration*. New York: Cambridge University Press.

Massey, Douglas S., Joaquin Arango, Graeme Hugo, Ali Kouaouci, and Adela Pellegrino (1999). *Worlds in Motion: Understanding International Migration at the End of the Millennium*. Oxford: Oxford University Press.

Massey, Douglas S., Jorge Durand, and Nolan J. Malone (2002). *Beyond Smoke and Mirrors: Mexican Immigration in an Era of Economic Integration.* New York: Russell Sage Foundation.

Massey, Douglas S., Luin Goldring, and Jorge Durand (1994) "Continuities in Transnational Migration: An Analysis of Nineteen Mexican Communities." American Journal of Sociology. Vol. 99, No. 6, Pp. 1492–1533.

Mize, Ronald L. (2006). "Mexican Contract Workers and the U.S. Capitalist Agricultural Labor Process: The Formative Era, 1942–1964." Rural Sociology. 71(1): 85–107.

Portes, Alejandro, William J. Haller, and Luis Guarnizo (2002) "Transnational Entrepreneurs: An Alternative Form of Immigrant Adaptation." American Sociological Review. Vol. 67, No. 2, pp. 278–298.

Portes, Alejandro and Min Zhou. (2012). "Transnationalism and Development: Mexican and Chinese Immigrant Organizations in the United States." *Population and Development Review.* Vol. 38, No 2, pp. 191–220.

Samora, Julian (1971). *Los Mojados: The Wetback Story*. Notre Dame: University of Notre Dame Press.

Sanchez, Martha J. (2007) "La importancia del sistema de cargos en el entendimiento de los flujos migratorios indigenas." Pp. 349–390 in M. Ariza and A. Portes (eds.) *El Pais Transnacional*. Mexico D.F.: IIS/National University of Mexico Press.

Smith, Robert C. (2000) "How Durable and New Is Transnational Life? Historical Retrieval Through Local Comparison." Diaspora. Vol. 9, No. 2, pp. 203–233.

Smith, Robert C. (2003) "Migrant Membership as an Instituted Process: Transnationalization, the State and The Extra-Territorial Conduct of Mexican Politics." International Migration Review. Vol. 37, No. 2, pp. 297–343).

U.S. Citizenship and Immigration Services (retrieved 5/12/13): http://www.uscis.gov/portal/site/uscis/.

Chapter Thirteen

The "*Maras*": The Making of a Transnational Issue

Sonja Wolf

Street gangs, "durable, street-oriented youth group[s] whose involvement in illegal activity is part of [their] group identity" (Klein & Maxson, 2006, p. 4), have long existed in Central America and especially in the United States. The Dieciocho (18th Street Gang) and Mara Salvatrucha (MS-13), Los Angeles-born Latino gangs, have over the years grown in both size and complexity and today feature among the largest street gangs in North and Central America. Locally known as "maras," they are distinctive not only for the role that migration and deportation patterns played in their development, but also for the ways they have evolved —largely in response to repressive gang policies—from traditional street gangs into criminally more sophisticated entities. Whereas in the United States their members are involved in a wide range of offenses, in the Northern Triangle of Central America (Guatemala, El Salvador, and Honduras) they are chiefly known for their participation in homicides and extortions. In October 2012 the U.S. Treasury Department designated MS-13 a significant transnational criminal organization, yet the gangs' ties to, or possible transformation into, organized crime networks remain disputed.

Increasingly, the maras have also captured the imagination of filmmakers and journalists. Scores of documentaries seek, with greater or lesser success, to alert audiences to the gangs' origins, their threat levels, and available policy options (Wolf, 2011a). Media coverage, much of it sensationalist, inflates gang crimes, dehumanizes gang members, and has helped fan the notoriety of the maras (Wolf, 2012a). Due to some widely publicized killings in the Washington, D.C. area, MS-13 in particular has acquired a reputation for extreme brutality (Logan, 2009). The transnational gang menace has been fueled, because much of the public information about street gangs derives from police, who tend to equate all gang activity with delinquency and to attribute to the groups any offenses for which individual members stand suspected, charged, or convicted. Thus, all gang youth are stereotyped as hardened criminals who are capable of the most heinous crimes. At the same time, the law enforcement focus on MS-13 and other Latino gangs—at least in the United States—arises because minority youth are disproportionately identified as gang members (Wolf, 2012b, p. 90).

By and large, the maras have been met with ineffective measures or a policy of no policy. The United States pursues a suppressive approach and, on the unproven assumption that gangs are mostly composed of undocumented migrants, arrests and deports non-citizen gang members in an attempt to reduce what is perceived to be an imported problem. Central America, on the other hand, long ignored the gang phenomenon despite its growing security implications. It was not until the early 2000s that the governments of the Northern Triangle cracked down on gangs and gang crime through zero tolerance or mano dura policies, which prioritized the arrest and incarceration of gang members over prevention and rehabilitation programs. These strategies greatly exacerbated prison overcrowding, stimulated an increase in gang crime, failed to deter youth from joining gangs, and made the maras more structured and organized.

This chapter analyzes to what extent these groups have developed into transnational criminal entities and to what effect anti-gang strategies—both nationally and regionally—have been tackling them. It is argued that although the maras maintain a multi-country presence, they do not constitute a cross-border network with a single chain of command, but rather share a mostly normative, symbolic, and identity-based affiliation. Conversely, the emphasis on suppression has meant that the adopted policies reproduced the very problem they purported to contain. The chapter begins by situating the origins of the maras in southern California before explaining how they developed in northern Central America, where they have displayed greater levels of violence than elsewhere and pose a considerable challenge to still fragile and underresourced democracies. The chapter then examines the chief characteristics and consequences of the anti-gang strategies employed in Central America as well as the United States and ends by considering the nature of transnational anti-gang initiatives.

The Origins of the *Maras*

The development of the *maras* cannot be grasped without considering the role of migration and discrimination in gang formation. The United States, where both groups originated, has a long history of street gangs that dates back to the early 1800s. Over time, those entities have emerged mainly in low-income ethnic minority neighborhoods, where residents face substandard living conditions and tend to be barred from educational opportunities and gainful employment. Born among Irish, Italian, and Jewish immigrants in New York and Chicago, the earliest gangs dissipated as these communities assimilated into mainstream society. However, street gangs persisted with the continuous immigration of primarily Hispanic and Asian groups and their difficulties in adjusting to the host nation (Franzese, Covey, & Menard, 2006, pp. 111–24).

Writing about Los Angeles' ethnic minority communities, Vigil (2002, p. 7) concludes that street gangs are spawned by "multiple marginality," or exclusion leading to socioeconomic disadvantage, dysfunctional families, and psychological and emotional barriers that leave people with few resources to better their lives. The realization that others enjoy comparatively greater affluence but one's own aspirations are unattainable can cause alienation and resentment, especially among young people. Youth who are precluded from reaching a respectable status struggle to establish a social identity for themselves and often turn to street gangs in search of a place where they are not marginalized and ignored. Gangs not only offer familial bonding, friendship, and excitement, but also steer their members toward criminal activities through which they can acquire the respect and status that are otherwise unobtainable.

The processes that immigrants go through in adapting to life in the United States have remained unaltered, such that street gangs continue to be largely a byproduct of migration (Vigil, 2002, p. 3). Gang emergence, however, is primarily linked to marginality, which affects immigrants frequently, but not exclusively. Indeed, in many places around the world, people are abandoned by economic globalization and, considering their limited licit opportunities, may resort to gangs and the underground economy for survival (Hagedorn, 2008). Gang proliferation, though, has perhaps been most conspicuous in the United States.

Pico-Union, the heart of Los Angeles' Latino community, has long been an impoverished and densely populated area rife with gang activity. In the 1980s the district also absorbed many Central Americans who fled U.S.-backed military campaigns designed to defeat revolutionary forces. Most refugees moved north as undocumented migrants, and given the nature of the Reagan-era asylum policy, were often denied refugee status and forced to live clandestine lives (Johnson, 2006). Trapped in a neighborhood devoid of recreational facilities but sprawling with crime and gangs, these families not only struggled to overcome the trauma of war but also faced culture shock, language barriers, discrimination, crowded living conditions, and underpaid jobs. Combined with the specter of deportation, these strains often led to tensions, child neglect, and domestic abuse (Vigil, 2002, pp. 135-136).

In response to difficult personal circumstances and gang harassment, some youth joined existing street gangs, notably the Dieciocho, created by Mexican immigrants in the late 1950s. Others established Mara Salvatrucha, which in the early 1980s grew out of a crew of heavy metal aficionados that after some of its members' prison stints developed into the California-style gang it is today. Initially tied by a loose alliance, by 1992 MS-13 and the Dieciocho had formed the deadly enmity that has since characterized them (Zilberg, 2011, p. 28).

Once the Central American wars had drawn to a close, the U.S. authorities began targeting offending noncitizens more aggressively for repatriation. The federal Illegal Immigration Reform and Immigrant Responsibility Act (IIRAIRA) of 1996 facilitated this process in that it turned offenses that were neither aggravated nor felonies under criminal law into aggravated felonies within immigration law, thus expediting removal proceedings. Designed to reduce what the United States perceived as an imported problem, the deportations actually spread U.S. gang culture to Central America and made existing gang phenomena more virulent.

The *Maras'* Development in Northern Central America

MS-13 and the Dieciocho started to reach Central America in the early 1990s, but the isthmus saw street gangs first emerge in the 1960s. Based mainly in urban marginal communities, these barrio groups were mostly composed of male adolescents that hailed from lower-class or lower middle-class backgrounds, had grown up in dysfunctional families, lived in poor housing conditions, and possessed only modest educational levels. The majority of members were engaged in some kind of remunerated work, and those with a criminal record were struggling to secure decent employment. By and large these were youths who felt rejected or ignored by family and society and had turned to a gang in search of support, understanding, and fun (Wolf, 2011b). Gang members spent much of their time hanging out, partying and taking drugs, fighting their rivals, and committing robberies, the latter as a survival strategy to overcome discrimination and their inability to succeed in the job market.

Some of these territorial groups dissolved over time, but many were absorbed by the gangs U.S. deportees brought with them. Returning youth often felt disoriented in countries they had few memories of and alienated by the humble surroundings they encountered (Zilberg, 2011). Although many of them hoped to make a fresh start, weak family ties and continued marginalization prompted some to carry on with what they knew best. Their comparatively smarter dress, money, and romanticized versions of gang life held a fascination that local adolescents found hard to resist. Gradually, the latter adopted the identity of MS-13 or the Dieciocho and with it the hostility between the two. Two distinct phenomena merged, not through active recruitment or violent takeovers, but because Central America constituted fertile terrain for gang development.

MS-13 and Dieciocho were exhibiting notable dissimilarities with these traditional groups. Their gang garb had identification value, organizational levels were greater, internal norms were stricter and more violent, and adult responsibilities did not affect gang membership. More importantly, these youths used more sophisticated weapons, consumed costlier drugs, sold more illicit substances, and carried out large-scale robberies. Subsequent to the establishment of California-style gangs in Central America, local gang patterns began to change rapidly.

Today MS-13 and the Dieciocho are the largest street gangs in the isthmus. Other groups exist, but they have neither the public profile nor the security impact that characterize their U.S.-inspired counterparts. Given the difficulty of defining and counting gang members, reliable gang membership numbers are hard to obtain. Over the years the figures have oscillated around 70,000 gang members in Central America (Brenneman, 2012, p. 34). In the United States MS-13 alone is estimated (FBI, 2005, p. 3) to have some 10,000 active affiliates. Since both gangs also have an unknown number of sympathizers (youth who spend some time with these groups but may eventually choose not to join them) and an extensive social base (cooperating relatives), the true dimension of the phenomenon remains difficult to gauge.

Despite a generally greater geographical dispersion, the gangs continue to be concentrated in marginal urban communities. Gang youth are predominantly male and come from low-income, dysfunctional families. The average entry age is between eleven and fifteen years, but given the difficulty of leaving the gang and finding reinsertion opportunities, members are now largely young adults rather than adolescents. Most have reached only intermediate levels of education, although some have finished high school and a few have enrolled in university (Valencia, 2011).

Reasons for gang affiliation vary among individuals and have not substantially changed over the years. Key motivations remain el vacil (the range of licit and illicit pursuits that promise fun and excitement in a gang), family problems, a desire for support and respect, and peer pressure. Gang members are disenfranchised youth whose experience of social marginalization, family disintegration, and educational exclusion generates feelings of shame that the gang permits them to bypass by providing — through violence, sex, drugs, and group solidarity –alternative pathways to pride and respect (Brenneman, 2012, p. 74). Evidently, gang policies will need to consider these social contextual factors as well as individual-level experiences and psychological traits if they are to reduce the magnitude of the phenomenon.

Although solidarity, friendship, and identity remained important reasons for gang membership, what had once been secondary incentives, such as power, social visibility, and access to money and drugs, eventually assumed greater significance and denoted an apparent shift toward motivations that favored the exercise of criminal violence (Wolf, 2011b, p. 50). Due to their members' readiness to resort to violent behavior, the maras have always constituted a source of insecurity in Central American societies. With time, however, their involvement in violence and delinquency sharply augmented. The qualitative deterioration of the maras, made possible by incoherent if not absent gang policies, has — at least in Central America — posed an enormous challenge to law enforcement and gang interventionists alike.

Anti-Gang Strategies in Central America

For many years the Central American countries lacked a clearly-articulated gang strategy, a void that had partly been filled by non-governmental organizations that offered limited prevention and rehabilitation services to gang-prone and gang-involved youth. Between 2002 and 2003, however, the governments of the Northern Triangle introduced zero tolerance or mano dura policies that were to be a key factor in the gangs' organizational development and criminal professionalization. These plans favored joint police/military patrols, area sweeps, and mass detentions, while Honduras and El Salvador also adopted anti-gang legislation that sanctioned the arrest and prosecution of suspected gang members for their physical appearance alone.

The timing and content of these initiatives suggested that they had been adopted primarily for electoral purposes. Gang suppression certainly appealed to populations that had tired of constant insecurity, yet it was strikingly unsuccessful. Arrest figures spiraled, but most cases were dismissed for lack of evidence, overcrowded prisons were filled beyond capacity, and homicide figures escalated in all three countries (PNUD, 2009, p. 199). In response to civil society calls for alternative measures, some governments adjusted their gang policies, but state-led prevention and rehabilitation programs remained dispersed and underfunded (Jütersonke, Muggah, & Rodgers, 2009). Despite its ineffectiveness, mano dura policing has since remained the dominant approach to gang control. In tandem with this strategy, El Salvador has since March 2012 been experimenting with a government-supported gang truce, which has coincided with a drop in homicides from a daily average of 14 to 6 (El Faro, 2012). However, it is unclear to what extent other developments in what is a country with historically high levels of violence may have contributed to the decreasing murder rate.

As a result of mano dura, MS-13 and the Dieciocho experienced a number of important transformations, the unintended—but inevitable—consequences of deeply ideological plans. Both groups toughened their entry requirements and selection processes to reduce enemy infiltration and ensure greater internal control. Recruits are now more carefully screened and are assigned riskier initiation rites, including the physical elimination of a rival gang member (Aguilar, 2007, p. 881). Drug consumption became restricted, and the use of harder drugs was prohibited altogether, as it impaired the alertness of many youth and their deaths ultimately weakened the groups (Aguilar and Carranza, 2008, p. 11).

Gang youth turned from using knives and handmade weapons to employing industrial firearms, thus intensifying the lethality of gang violence (Aguilar and Carranza, 2008, p. 11). Gang members also adopted strategies that would make their detection more difficult and afford their operations greater secrecy. Tattoos ceased to be compulsory and are applied to less visible body parts; dress code and hairstyle became more conventional; and the public flashing of hand signs has largely stopped (PNUD, 2009, p. 111). Additionally, gang youth shifted their preferred hangouts from public to private locations to remain beyond the reach of the police (Cruz, 2007, p. 367).

Most crucially, the maras made the prisons their command centers. Gang members, especially leaders, were incarcerated in great numbers and separated by group to avoid clashes. But Central American jails are notorious not only for overcrowding and poor infrastructure, but also for lack of control, deficient rehabilitation programs, and poorly remunerated guards. Shared confinement, together with the prison conditions, allowed gang members to strengthen group cohesion and structure. Moreover, through intimidation and bribery, they managed to have cell phones smuggled into the precincts and to communicate with street-based gang members, ordering hits and managing extortions (Savenije, 2009, p. 148). Indeed, although gang members commit a wide variety of offenses, extortions become the chief source of illicit income for them and their families.

Anti-Gang Strategies in the United States

The United States has sought to tackle the maras through both national and transnational initiatives (considered below) which—as in Central America—have focused heavily on suppression. Domestically, anti-gang efforts have centered on three areas: databases, police gang units, and anti-gang legislation. In the 1990s law enforcement agencies began creating state-wide, facial recognition-enabled databases that tracked gang members and charted characteristics such as their tattoos and friends. These tools are problematic due to the lack of a universal definition of what constitutes a gang member. Gang experts have also criticized the databases, because individuals were rarely expunged once they had been included, and their gang population estimates were notoriously inaccurate (Garland, 2009, p. 166). The specialized police gang unit, for its part, was conceived in the 1980s by the Los Angeles Police Department and now serves as a model for local gang enforcement throughout the United States (Díaz, 2009, p. 80).

During the 1990s, most states enacted anti-gang legislation that defined—often differently—a gang, a gang member, and a gang crime (Garland, 2009, p. 195). The labeling efforts implied by both databases and laws, rather than facilitating policing and prosecution, may inadvertently foster gang cohesion and further distance youth from mainstream society. A widely used law enforcement tool is the gang injunction, a form of anti-loitering law that bans all forms of association and communication between two or more gang members in a particular geographical area and entails increased sentences for gang members found to be in violation of these restrictions. An injunction's chief objective is to ensure gang youth do not congregate in public space and thus to undercut one of the core activities of gang life. However, the measure does not prevent gang members from gathering in adjacent neighborhoods or from committing violence in rival gang territories (Zilberg, 2011, p. 94).

Anti-gang efforts that specifically target transnational Latino gangs, including MS-13 and the Dieciocho, revolve additionally around a federal task force, anti-immigrant sweeps, and prosecutions under organized crime statutes. Following some widely publicized incidents in the Washington, DC area, including the murder of former MS member and federal witness Brenda Paz, the Federal Bureau of Investigations (FBI) created the MS-13 National Gang Task Force. Launched in 2004, this body was designed exclusively to dismantle what was thought to be a particularly vicious and transnationally operating street gang. In 2007 the agency added the Dieciocho to its mandate (Díaz, 2009, p. 80). Aimed at improving information-sharing and intelligence-gathering among U.S. and Central American law enforcement officials, the task force has been marred by interagency disagreements on whether MS-13 is really more organized or dangerous than other street gangs (Díaz, 2009, p. 211).

In 2005 the Department of Homeland Security's Bureau of Immigrations and Customs Enforcement (ICE) initiated Operation Community Shield, a nationwide initiative that formed part of the Bush administration's anti-immigrant crackdown after the 9/11 terrorist attacks. The program, initially focused on MS-13 but later expanded to other gangs, consists of periodically conducted, highly publicized raids to arrest and subsequently deport gang members without legal status. However, it appears that the sweeps have also picked up undocumented migrants without gang affiliation and have exacerbated already strained policy-community relations in Latino neighborhoods (Díaz, 2009, pp. 212-213).

The prosecution of MS-13 and the Dieciocho under anti-racketeering statutes presupposes that these groups can be targeted as enterprises. The Racketeer Influenced and Corrupt Organizations (RICO) Act of 1970 and the Violent Crimes in Aid of Racketeering (VICAR) Act of 2006 consider an "enterprise" to be a "group of individuals associated in fact" or a structure for making decisions and a core of persons who function as a continuing unit (Díaz, 2009, 100). Using a series of investigative tools, the federal government hopes to put away as many members as the evidence allows.

The RICO Act, devised for and applied successfully in cases against the Italian mafia, was originally concerned with preventing the use of illicit funds for legal ventures and with prohibiting individuals from conspiring to do so. Their vague wording and stiff sentences made these statutes open to wider usage and converted them into instruments of unprecedented legal power. Any two or more crimes, one of which could be membership in the "enterprise," committed by a group of people could in principle be tried under RICO and result in a conviction for the death penalty (Garland, 2009, pp. 92-93). Applying organized crime statutes to the maras is, however, problematic since these entities have a shifting and shared leadership and the targeted arrests of leaders will likely result in the emergence of new shot callers.

Overall, the United States' domestic gang control efforts depart from the unproven assumption that MS-13 and the Dieciocho are composed primarily of undocumented immigrants and that arresting and deporting their members can prevent these groups from spreading and creating further mischief (Díaz, 2009, p. 106). This view ignores that gangs proliferate due to the socioeconomic dislocations prevailing in U.S. society (Garland, 2009). Thus far, this stance has done much to demonize the Latino population and stoke anti-immigrant sentiment, but little to reduce gang crime and violence. The missing element, in both national and U.S.-sponsored transnational anti-gang initiatives, is a commitment to prevention and rehabilitation.

The *Maras'* Transnational Dimension

The *maras'* perceived transnational nature is often inferred from their multi-country presence and a law enforcement belief that these groups use modern communications technology to recruit new members, exchange information, and coordinate criminal activities across frontiers. However, the research evidence on gang movements (including deportations) and cross-border links does not point to the existence of two transnational gang networks.

Regarding the influence of returning gang members in the Central American groups, the Guatemalan chapter of a regional gang study (Ranum, 2006) discovered that the deportees assumed positions such as palabrero (shot caller) (26.9 percent), soldado (territorial defender) (28.4 percent), or misionero (assignment executer) (3 percent). Yet while their status varies between cliques—depending on entry requirements, attainment of trust, and rapport with local gang leaders—generally the returnees' influence seems to have waned (pp. 21–22). In El Salvador, where deported gang members had once automatically become shot callers, the survey (Aguilar, 2006) suggested this is no longer the case: if they take up any positions, these are limited to palabrero (26.2 percent), soldado (16.3 percent), other (5.3 percent) or misionero (2.3 percent) (p. 28).

The existence of cross-border ties is unsurprising, especially since some gang members are deportees. However, the fact that youth in different countries claim affiliation with the same gang does not necessarily mirror the proliferation of a transnational gang network answering to a single chain of command. According to the El Salvador survey, 28.2 percent of interviewees admitted sustaining sporadic connections with their counterparts in other nations, notably the United States (37.2 percent), Mexico (19.9 percent), Guatemala (15.3 percent), and Honduras (15.3 percent) (Aguilar, 2006, p. 29). This coordination was pursued for a variety of purposes, especially to exchange intelligence (42.9 percent); to give or receive orders, codes of conduct, and action plans (23.1 percent); to send money and weapons (17.6 percent); and to help gang members leave the country (3.3 percent). However, the study found no evidence of systematic and institutionalized links between gang structures in North and Central America, let alone the existence of cross-border gang networks (Aguilar, 2006, p. 30).

In the Guatemala survey, 58.5 percent of respondents denied the existence of transnational links, while 41.5 percent of interviewees admitted sustaining such connections, most frequently with their peers in the United States, El Salvador, Honduras, and Mexico. Within this category, 66.7 percent indicated that these were mostly informal relations aimed at exchanging information and communicating with friends. By contrast, 18.5 percent acknowledged the existence of formal and structured ties aimed at receiving or giving orders, rules, and action plans, and for 7.4 percent, sending or receiving money, drugs, and weapons (Ranum, 2006, p. 23). The study concluded that the maras retained distinctive characteristics in each country and operated in ways that varied by cliques and gang leaders but did not reflect a deliberate gang strategy (Ranum, 2006, pp. 23–24).

In operational and structural terms, MS-13 and the Dieciocho remain networks of autonomous groups that share a symbolic, identifying, and normative affiliation (Cruz, 2007, pp. 363–64). They do not appear to recognize a transnational membership status, as evidenced by the fact that members jumped into the gangs in Central America must be reinitiated in the United States (Zilberg, 2011, p. 13). There is, however, a transnational facet to the gangs in that deported youth retain affective ties to family and friends in their former host country (Zilberg, 2011, pp. 148-149).

Transnational Anti-Gang Initiatives

Given the proximity of Central America, the United States has long been concerned about potential security threats from the region and has provided the southern nations with assistance to counter those threats. Official perceptions of the maras as transnational gangs, and a U.S. interest in preventing deported gang members from returning north, have stimulated a rise in regional anti-gang cooperation focused on information-sharing, an officer exchange program, a regional fingerprint database, and investigations of gangs as criminal enterprises (Ribando Seelke, 2013, pp. 17-18). The flagship programs are the International Law Enforcement Academy (ILEA) and the Transnational Anti-Gang Center (TAG).

Established in 2005 in San Salvador, the ILEA offers both general and specialized law enforcement training to police, prosecutors, and judges. Class priorities are defined by the United States, prioritize transnational crimes, and cover subjects such as street gangs, human trafficking, small arms trafficking, and crime scene investigations. The TAG began its operations in El Salvador in 2007 and later expanded to Guatemala and Honduras. The centers include vetted Central American police officers who—jointly with locally stationed FBI agents—investigate gang crimes that have a nexus with the United States.

While information-sharing remains an important element in gang control, it is unlikely to have a lasting effect on the maras. Few gang crimes are truly transnational in nature, and as long as the individual-level and community factors of the phenomenon are neglected, more youth may see in the gangs a source of social and economic support they are unable to obtain elsewhere. Indeed, the maras' extensive social base may well be a more significant hurdle to overcome than their sporadic cross-border connections. Alternative projects have been in short supply and produced little demonstrated success, partly due to the difficulty of gang exit, partly because of scarce resources and gang programming expertise.

The United States Agency for International Development (USAID) was, as of mid-2012, working in 175 communities to support municipal crime prevention initiatives such as crime observatories and community policing programs, and the establishment of outreach centers to provide recreational and educational opportunities for youth in high-crime areas (Ribando Seelke, 2013, pp. 19-20). Independent evaluations of these projects are not publicly available.

In Guatemala USAID produced Desafío 10-Paz para los Ex, a televised reality show that sought to help ex-gang members become self-reliant entrepreneurs, involve the country's private sector in gang reinsertion, and sensitize the public (Díaz, 2009, p. 261). Wearing colored eye masks to disguise their identity, the ten contestants shared a house, received small business mentoring, and were given two weeks to set up a small enterprise: a carwash for one team and a shoeshine stand for the other. Although USAID presented the show as a success, it was criticized for a number of reasons. The youth, initially enthusiastic about the project, gradually abandoned their ventures as these provided little opportunity for social and economic advancement. In fact, the menial jobs USAID had proposed did not meet the expectations of the more ambitious participants and only served to perpetuate the stigma surrounding gang youth. More important, as former gang members they remained vulnerable to social ostracism and attacks. By its very nature, the project provided no long-term support to ease their reintegration into society. Over time, several of the original ten participants were killed (Davenport, 2008).

El Salvador's now extinct National Council of Public Security had pursued a variety of gang prevention and rehabilitation activities as part of a five-year European Union-sponsored program. Between 2010 and 2011, 14 of its volunteers were killed (Chávez, 2011), suggesting that the Council had been insufficiently prepared for the complexities of the local environment. Conversely, the institution required the gangs' permission to conduct its prevention work in gang-affected neighborhoods and was unable to ensure that the youth involved in its rehabilitation projects were actually desisting from gang life. Ultimately, significant amounts of funding were channeled into sports infrastructure, but it remains unclear to what extent gang-prone and gang-involved youth and their communities were otherwise positively impacted (Zilberg, 2011, pp. 187-188).

Conclusion

The *maras*, born in southern California and transplanted to Central America through deportations of undocumented gang youth, found fertile ground for growth in marginalized communities where adolescents may consider them a pathway to identity and respect that are otherwise unattainable. Gang suppression, combined with chronic policy neglect, has permitted the gangs –particularly in the Northern Triangle—to evolve into more organized and criminally sophisticated entities whose affiliates display progressively greater levels of brutality. Gang members engage in a variety of criminal offenses and in Central America have made extortions the chief source of illicit income for themselves and their families. However, crime and violence are only byproducts of gang life, committed to demonstrate loyalty to, and gain respect within, the group. Youth turn to gangs for a combination of individual-level socio-psychological as well as community-level factors, and these need to be taken into account in the search for effective gang policies.

The *maras'* presence in multiple countries throughout North and Central America has led law enforcement, policy and journalistic circles to believe that these gangs constitute transnational criminal networks. Yet, the available research evidence indicates that while gang members and cliques maintain affective and sometimes instrumental cross-border ties, these relationships remain limited and largely informal. Instead, MS-13 and the Dieciocho operate autonomously in each country and are bound by a symbolic, normative and identity-based affiliation. Official perceptions have, however, given rise to a gamut of transnational anti-gang initiatives that, like domestic measures, privilege information-sharing and investigations that seek convictions of entire cliques under organized crime statutes. Law enforcement is required, but it will achieve more lasting results if it departs from a more nuanced understanding of gang dynamics and entails targeted apprehensions, not mass arrests and deportations. Prevention and rehabilitation, on the other hand, have been pursued with much less enthusiasm. The projects that have been executed fell short of the resources, expertise, and long-term support that gang-prone and gang-involved youth and their communities require to forge a different future for themselves.

Media coverage and documentaries of the maras, in principle designed to educate the audiences, have disseminated distorted interpretations of the gangs' origins, their members' motivations, and the policies that are required to reduce the magnitude of the phenomenon. Worse yet, they have helped produce public tolerance, if not support, of misguided gang policies. By implication, if truthful representations of the maras managed to sensitize societies to members' individual-level experiences and the social contexts that shape them, pressure for alternative strategies might build. The force of this pressure, in turn, might make possible the sustained implementation of comprehensive gang policies that combined community policing, prevention, and rehabilitation. Suppression has enjoyed widespread approval, because it promises quick solutions to an apparently intractable problem. Yet, the record indicates that this approach is ultimately counterproductive and does nothing to keep youth out of gangs or to make communities safer and more inclusive. Prevention and rehabilitation efforts that are limited in time and scale, offered as a concession to critics of suppression, are but a palliative and inadequate given the extent and impact of gangs. The maras will not go away if left to fester. Rather, they constitute a test of whether governments that tend to be focused on short-term priorities can muster the political will to reverse the socio-economic dislocations that ultimately engender gangs.

Discussion Questions

1. What factors have contributed to the development and proliferation of the maras?
2. Are the maras a Central American or a U.S.-made problem?
3. In what sense are the maras a transnational issue?
4. To what extent might the maras be described as organized crime networks?
5. What policies might reduce the magnitude and impact of the maras?

References

Aguilar, J. (2006). Pandillas juveniles transnacionales en Centroamérica, México y Estados Unidos: diagnóstico de El Salvador. San Salvador: IUDOP.

Aguilar, J. & Carranza, M. (2008). Las maras y pandillas como actores ilegales de la región. Report prepared for the Informe Estado de la región en desarrollo humano sostenible 2008. San Salvador: IUDOP.

Brenneman, R. (2012). Homies and Hermanos: God and Gangs in Central America. New York: Oxford University Press.

Chávez, S. (2011). 14 voluntarios de prevención de la violencia asesinados. La Prensa Gráfica. 15 February. http://www.laprensagrafica.com/el-salvador/judicial/171915-14-voluntarios-de-prevencion-de-la-violencia-asesinados.html.

Cruz, J.M. (2007). El barrio transnacional. In F. Pisani, N. Saltalamacchia, A. Tickner, & N. Barnes (Eds.), Redes transnacionales en la cuenca de los huracanes (pp. 357–382). Mexico City: ITAM/Porrúa.

Davenport, R. (2008). Reality Show. http://www.youtube.com/watch?hl=en-GB&gl=IN&feature=user&v=eSQfni7Xyuk.

Diaz, T. (2009). No Boundaries: Transnational Latino Gangs and American Law Enforcement. Ann Arbor, MI: University of Michigan Press.

El Faro. (2012). Funes destaca ante ONU reducción de homicidios gracias a tregua entre pandillas. 25 September. http://www.elfaro.net/es/201209/noticias/9760/.

Federal Bureau of Investigation (FBI). (2005). Mara Salvatrucha (MS-13): An International Perspective. Washington, DC: FBI.

Franzese, R, Covey, H., & Menard, S. (Eds.). (2006). Youth Gangs. 3rd ed. Springfield, IL: C. Thomas.

Garland, S. (2009). Gangs in Garden City: How Immigration, Segregation, and Youth Violence are Changing America's Suburbs. New York: Nation Books.

Hagedorn, J. (2008). Making Sense of Central America Maras. Air & Space Power Journal (Summer), Spanish ed. www.airpower.au.af.mil/apjinternational/apj-s/2008/2tri08/hagedorneng.htm.

Johnson, M. (2006). National Policies and the Rise of Transnational Gangs. Washington, DC: MPI. www.migrationinformation.org.

Jütersonke, O., Muggah, R., & Rodgers, D. (2009). Gangs, Urban Violence, and Security Interventions in Central America. Security Dialogue 40, 373–97.

Klein, M. & Maxson, C. (2006). Street Gang Patterns and Policies. New York: Oxford University Press.

Logan, S. (2009). This is for the Mara Salvatrucha: Inside the MS-13, America's Most Violent Gang. New York: Hyperion.

Programa de las Naciones Unidas para el Desarrollo (PNUD). (2009). Informe sobre desarrollo humano para América Central 2009–2010. San José: PNUD.

Ranum, E. (2006). Pandillas juveniles transnacionales en Centroamérica, México y Estados Unidos: diagnóstico nacional Guatemala. San Salvador: IUDOP.

Ribando Seelke, C. (2013). Gangs in Central America. CRS Report for Congress RL34112, 28 January. Washington, DC: Congressional Research Service (CRS).

Savenije, W. (2009). Maras y barras. Pandillas y violencia juvenil en los barrios marginales de Centroamérica. San Salvador: FLACSO.

Valencia, R. (2011). El pandillero universitario. El Faro. 14 October. http://salanegra.elfaro.net/es/201110/bitacora/6128/.

Vigil, J. (2002). A Rainbow of Gangs: Street Cultures in the Mega-City. Austin: University of Texas Press.

Wolf, S. (2012a). Creating Folk Devils: Street Gang Representations in El Salvador's Print Media. Journal of Human Security 8(2), 36–63.

Wolf, S. (2012b). Mara Salvatrucha: The Most Dangerous Street Gang in the Americas? Latin American Politics & Society 54(1), 65–99.

Wolf, S. (2011a). Living and Dying for the Crazy Life: Exploring Documentary Representations of the Central American Maras. Revista Centroamericana de Ciencias Sociales 8(2), 23–52.

Wolf, S. (2011b). Street Gangs of El Salvador. In T. Bruneau, L. Dammert, & E. Skinner (Eds.), Maras: Gang Violence and Security in Central America (pp. 43–69). Austin, TX: University of Texas Press.

Zilberg, E. (2011). Space of Detention: The Making of a Transnational Gang Crisis Between Los Angeles and San Salvador. Durham, NC: Duke University Press.

Chapter Fourteen

The Criminalization of Immigration in the United Kingdom

Ana Aliverti

In recent years, migration and refugee studies have attracted a great deal of attention from criminology and criminal law scholars to the extent that some lay claim to the emergence of a subfield within criminology on migration controls: the 'criminology of mobility' (Aas & Bosworth, 2013). For some time, scholars have pointed to the increasing 'criminalization of immigration' as states in Western, rich countries endeavor to control immigration flows by deploying the criminal justice system and its agencies for immigration purposes, or by appealing to other forms of punitive measures—such as deportation and detention (e.g. Medina, 1997; Calavita, 2003; Stumpf, 2007; De Giorgi, 2010). Other authors point to a further symbolic dimension of this phenomenon. As migrants are increasingly dealt with by the penal system, or by measures and institutions which resemble imprisonment and prisons and by police-like enforcement agencies, a new construct has been created which portrays them as dangerous and criminal (Wacquant, 1999; Melossi, 2000; Pratt & Valverde, 2002).

In this chapter, I will focus on a specific aspect of the criminalization phenomenon, namely the formal criminalization of immigration breaches. As in the US (Stumpf, 2009), the UK has relied on the criminal law for immigration purposes for some time (Aliverti, 2013). While immigration-related offences have been part of almost every piece of legislation passed by the British Parliament since the eighteenth century, most of these offences were seldom enforced in practice until the mid-1990s. In the last two decades the catalogue of immigration offences has not only grown exponentially, but also some of these offences—particularly crimes penalizing immigration fraud—have started to be more systematically enforced. Unlike the US where immigration prosecutions represent the largest category of federal criminal prosecutions (Legomsky, 2007, 479; Eagly, 2010, 1282; Chacón, 2012, 614), in the UK immigration prosecution rates are still considerably low in comparison with other crimes, such as drug-related or property offences.

In the first part of the chapter, I trace the history of immigration policy and the role that criminal law played in the enforcement of entry controls. I argue that, in the absence of institutional arrangements to police foreigners, criminal law played a crucial role in the enforcement of border controls from the late 1700s until the early 1900s. In the second part, I explain that as the category of exclusionable subjects expanded in the 1960s to encompass Commonwealth citizens, immigration-based crimes proved instrumental to draw a new boundary of belonging. As priorities shifted from controlling immigration from the Commonwealth to managing the growing number of people claiming asylum, I show that criminal law started to be used more systematically against undocumented migrants. In the final part, I move to more recent policy developments which led to the creation of an immigration force, modelled on a crime enforcement agency. I conclude by sketching continuities in the use of criminal law powers to police non-nationals and the functions that it plays in contemporary conditions.

The Foundations of Britain's System of Immigration Controls

Britain has a long history as a country of immigration. Since the late eighteenth century, French radicals, Jews, Polish, Irish and Commonwealth citizens arrived in the UK in large numbers escaping persecution, or seeking economic and social betterment. The influx of people from different cultures, languages and races did not go unnoticed. Foreigners were met with hostility and anxiety by natives. This prompted Parliament to pass legislation to control the entry of foreigners and regulate their residence. The first law to control immigration was passed in 1793 and targeted in particular suspected French insurgents involved in the French Revolution. The Aliens Act 1793 tightly regulated the conditions for landing, registration with the authorities and residence, and obliged all foreigners to obtain and carry a passport issued by the British authorities. People in breach of these rules were subject to detention without bail and, if convicted, to a term in prison. They were also liable to be 'sent out' from the Realm after a court recommendation. Likewise, sea captains and housekeepers at dwelling houses were liable to a fine for breaching these rules. Similar laws were passed during the nineteenth century, but were seldom enforced particularly during the second half of the 1800s.

It was not, however, until the enactment of the Aliens Act 1905 that a comprehensive system of immigration controls was established. This act set the legislative basis for Britain's modern system of immigration controls (Evans, 1983, 4; Cohen, 1994, 41). It was enacted in response to the arrival of Jews expelled from Russia and Eastern Europe since the late 1890s. Like the previous laws, the 1905 act imposed criminal sanctions on foreigners who entered the country unlawfully or breached their conditions of stay. It also granted the Executive the power to expel noncitizens considered 'undesirable', such as people without financial means of support, those who were likely to be a public burden due to a disease or mental conditions, people with criminal convictions and those who had been previously deported from the country. Foreigners against whom an expulsion order was made were kept in custody until they were shipped away from the UK. As there were no special premises, they were held in ordinary prisons.[1] Ships bringing people considered 'undesirable' to the country were also liable to a fine of up to £100.

The act was deemed as ineffective due to the lack of capacity to enforce it. Immigrants could easily evade controls or have refusal decisions overturned by the appeal board (Troup, 1925, 143). Even though the 1905 act created the Aliens Inspectorate formed by immigration officers in charge of conducting immigration controls on all ships and vessels arriving to Britain, it was claimed that many passengers managed to avoid controls. In 1920, a special Immigration Branch within the Home Office was established to conduct immigration controls in all sea and air ports. It was formed by a Chief Inspector, based in London, and an army of immigration officers located at the ports of entry. They were empowered to refuse or grant leave to enter the country (Home Office, 2004, 3). Until 1970 when it was replaced by the Immigration Service, the Immigration Branch was in charge of the decision to grant or refuse leave to foreigners wishing to enter the UK. In turn, the police was responsible for inland immigration controls, which included the registration of foreigners in the country, and the identification and deportation of non-citizens in breach of immigration rules or considered 'undesirable' (Troup, 1925; Newsam, 1954).

The outbreak of the First World War prompted further legislation which imposed tighter controls on the conditions of entry and residence, and it was overwhelmingly applied against Germans (Holmes, 1988, 96). While the Aliens Restriction Act 1914 was first passed as a temporary emergency measure, it was extended after the war by the Aliens Restriction (Amendment) Act 1919

---

1. The first special immigration detention centre was opened in 1969, near Heathrow airport, when due to its size the detention of immigrants in prisons became unworkable.

which retained the powers introduced in the 1914 act. The 1919 act was also meant to be temporary but it was extended annually until 1971—when Parliament passed permanent legislation. It was supplemented by orders-in-council which incorporated criminal offences and conferred on the Executive a wide power to deport foreigners from the country when their presence was not 'conducive to the public good'. This ground for deportation could be invoked even though the deportee had never been convicted for a crime. It was frequently used against illegal entrants or people who overstayed their leave as it proved a more straightforward and simpler way to deal with them compared to a criminal prosecution (Troup, 1925, 148). The 1919 act also introduced two broad provisions which criminalized any contravention or failure to comply with the act 'or of any order or rules made or conditions imposed thereunder', as well as assisting, abetting or harbouring those in contravention. Foreigners were obliged to register with the police and to carry their certificate of registration, under threat of criminal punishment. Post-war legislation granted the Executive broad powers over foreigners without subjecting it to any form of legislative or judicial oversight.

Although every act passed since the eighteenth century contained various immigration crimes, the criminal law powers introduced were seldom questioned or discussed in Parliament. Back then, attaching a criminal sanction to an immigration norm was considered a necessary enforcement mechanism. This rationale was not unique to immigration law. Rather it underpinned early factory legislation and it is one of the reasons for the expansion of English substantive criminal law since the mid-nineteenth century. Many regulatory offences were introduced in legislation passed during this period when arguably, without the threat of criminal sanctions, regulation would have been difficult to enforce (Lacey, 2008, 2012). Prior to 1905, there was no specialized body to enforce immigration controls. With the enactment of the 1905 act and subsequent legislation, the creation of a special branch in charge of immigration controls and the introduction of a power to deport non-citizens on 'conductive to public good' grounds, the criminal law powers contained in immigration legislation became redundant and at best reduced to mere deterrence on would-be unauthorized migrants.

Expanding the Category of Exclusionable Aliens: Commonwealth Citizens

While immigration legislation applied only to non-citizens until the 1960s, the right to entry and residence of certain British subjects started to be restricted. In the 1950s, large numbers of Commonwealth citizens immigrated to Britain, particularly from former British colonies in South Asia, the Caribbean and Africa. At that point, Commonwealth citizens were British subjects and hence free to enter and stay in the Motherland. Such unrestricted policy towards Commonwealth citizens upheld in the British Nationality Act 1948 started to be questioned by some members of Parliament while the arrival of non-white immigration generated public outcry (Hansen, 2000). In this context, the Commonwealth Immigrants Acts (CIA) 1962 and 1968 were passed which applied immigration controls to British subjects, except for those born in the UK or for British passport holders who had a least one parent or grandparent born, adopted or naturalized as a British citizen in the UK. This exclusionary rule disproportionately affected non-white Commonwealth citizens who were less likely to have relatives born or naturalized in the UK. 'Non-patrial' Commonwealth citizens (including those without British ancestors) were later on equated to non-citizens by the Immigration Act 1971 (IA 1971).

From then on, certain Commonwealth citizens were subject to deportation and criminally liable for entering the country illegally or breaching their conditions of leave. Both acts incorporated a number of criminal offences. The CIA 1962 created 14 different criminal offences. In addition, the CIA 1968 introduced the offence of landing without proper examination by an immigration officer. Commonwealth citizens were guilty of such offence if they could not demonstrate that they were properly inspected upon arrival. This offence not only reversed the burden of proof; it also lacked the subjective or mental element (mens rea). The act also made the master of the ship or aircraft who allowed the landing criminally liable.

Even though both acts criminalized a number of breaches by Commonwealth citizens, it was only the offence of harbouring immigrants in breach in the CIA 1962 which raised questions by parliamentarians. One of them considered it unnecessary for achieving 'What the authorities are legitimately after[:] the apprehension of, and penalty for, the illegal immigrant' (Hansard, HC Deb 7/02/1962, col. 436). Others criticized it for the potential to lead to discrimination. In response, the representatives of the government argued that prosecutions for this offence were unlikely to be used due to evidentiary difficulties. However, the provision was still necessary because 'if you have a control, you must be seen to have the machinery to enforce it' (Hansard, HL Deb 20/03/1962, col. 476). The debate around the harbouring offence reflects the rationale underlining most immigration-related offences. First, the criminalization of 'third parties' aims primarily to control illegal immigration rather than to punish third parties' wrongdoing; second, immigration offences are, first and foremost, 'necessary ancillary provisions' of the legislation—if there is a law there should be a mechanism to enforce it; and third, they serve as a deterrent to ensure compliance with immigration norms.

Indeed, although statistics prior to 1980 do not compile information on the prosecution and conviction of people for offences under immigration acts, the limited data available from this period suggests that immigration crimes were barely used. For instance, it was mentioned in parliamentary debates that between March 1968 and December 1972 only 74 cases of 'illegal immigration offences' were brought before the courts involving 307 illegal immigrants (Hansard, HC Deb 31/01/1973, col. 1532). Even though the IA 1971 incorporated 21 different offences (including illegal entry, assisting illegal entry and harbouring a person who illegally entered the UK or overstayed), the number of people prosecuted from 1979 until 1983—and even more so convicted—for these offences was very low. Except for the offences of overstaying and the failure to observe the conditions attached to a leave, the number of prosecutions for other offences was far below one hundred (Home Office, 1985, Table 21).

Until 1988, over-stayers were the exception to this rule. Well into the 1980s, the large number of people staying in the country beyond the time limit stated in their leave constituted the greatest challenge in terms of internal enforcement. Overstaying was the most frequently prosecuted immigration offence. In 1988 this started to change. Section 5 of the Immigration Act 1988 introduced restrictions on appeal rights to deportation decisions against overstayers, which made those decisions more strictly enforceable. As deportation became an easier and smoother way to deal with over-stayers than criminal prosecutions, the latter fell considerably after 1988: from 509 prosecutions in 1986 to 45 in 1990. This example shows how interconnected immigration and criminal law regimes are. It also shows that criminal law plays a merely instrumental role in immigration enforcement: it is resorted to as long as it is effective for achieving particular immigration goals.

The Asylum Crisis and the (Re)discovery of the Criminal Law for Immigration Purposes

Since the mid-1980s the increase in asylum applications and the concern within the government that the asylum system was being abused by 'bogus' asylum seekers prompted further legislation. From 1985, visas were introduced for nationals of several countries—including many former colonies such as India, Sri Lanka, Bangladesh, Pakistan and Nigeria—which were considered 'producers' of asylum seekers. In addition, carrier liability legislation made transportation companies which did not properly check passengers' documents on embarkation liable to fines. Further criminal offences were introduced to tackle the use of deception in the quest for asylum and assisting asylum seekers into the country. In 2002, the latter offence was modified to penalise those who help asylum seekers 'knowingly and for gain', that is 'commercial smugglers'. Yet, this offence is seldom enforced, presumably because of the difficulty in proving 'gain'. People assisting asylum seekers, either for gain or for humanitarian purposes, can instead be prosecuted for assisting unlawful immigration when there is no proof of gain and the claimant is considered an 'illegal entrant' (R v. Alps [2001] All ER (D) 29 (Feb)). Both offences (helping asylum seekers and assisting unlawful immigration) carry a maximum penalty of 14 years imprisonment.

Paradoxically, even though by the time the catalogue of immigration-related offences was expanding, immigrants and asylum seekers trying to enter or leave the country with false documents were charged with offences in non-immigration statutes. From 1994, a growing number of people were caught in British airports—mainly Heathrow—using false documents and were charged, imprisoned and convicted for the use of false instruments under the Forgery and Counterfeiting Act 1981 or for attempting to obtain services by deception under the Criminal Attempts Act 1981 (Hales, 1996). In 1993, there were 53 arrests under these offences. In the subsequent two years, arrests increased to 126 in 1994 and 376 in 1995 (Dunstan, 1998, 208). The rise in the enforcement of fraud-based offences was a reaction to the growing number of asylum claimants resorting to smugglers and false documents to enter the country. It also signals a change in the response by the government which became more determined to appeal to criminal law against migrants and asylum seekers using false documents.

The number of asylum applications received grew substantially between 1997 and 2002: from 32,500 to 84,130 (Home Office, 2006, Table 3.1). Following the war in the ex-Yugoslavia, new applications peaked in 2002. This period coincided with the first term in office of centre-left New Labour government which came into power in 1997 after almost two decades of Conservative rule. While immigration was initially not high on the political agenda, soon after New Labour took office it became one of the priorities of Prime Minister Tory Blair. The government's policy toward illegal immigration was largely driven by concern about asylum abuse. Faced with criticism by the opposition and the popular press, in 1998 the government launched a programme of reforms of the immigration and asylum system. It was by far the most ambitious in the history of the immigration service and included the resort to criminal law for 'stamping out abuse of immigration control' (Home Office, 1998, ch. 11). Similarly, when then Home Secretary Jack Straw presented the bill laying down the proposed reforms, he announced that 'Enforcement must be backed by the criminal law'. This announcement was followed by the largest expansion in the catalogue of immigration crimes ever and a steady increase in the number of prosecutions and convictions for these offences.

The first piece of legislation passed under New Labour, the Immigration and Asylum Act 1999, introduced 35 different criminal offences, most of them targeting abuse in the quest for asylum, such as deception, false representation, dishonest representation, and causing delays or obstructions. In addition, in section 31 the 1999 act incorporated a defence based on article 31 of the 1951 Convention Relating to the Status of Refugees which prevents Member States from imposing penalties on refugees on account of their illegal entry or presence.

Unlike the US, where immigration policy has been predominantly concerned with illegal border crossing, the main motivation of British policies and debates in this field have been dominated by the abuse of the asylum system by economic migrants, especially from the mid-1980s up until the mid-2000s. This feature has placed a number of legal challenges for the government in terms of the use of criminal law against people who had applied for asylum. Yet, as Catherine Dauvergne (2008, 60) bluntly put it, Britain—as other western states—has successfully managed to progressively resile from the central commitments of refugee law without actually 'walking away from' the Refugee Convention.

By making refugee status a defence rather than a ban to prosecution and by restricting this defence to certain fraud-based offences, the UK has significantly limited the protection against prosecution afforded by the Refugee Convention to good faith claimants. Further, one of the most often prosecuted immigration offences—being unable to produce a passport at an asylum interview—explicitly excludes the defence based on the Refugee Convention. People who arrive in the country without a genuine document cannot invoke their asylum case in order to be exempted from punishment. There is a further, more subtle implication of the way immigration and criminal law regimes interact. Asylum seekers cannot be removed until their applications are decided and their appeal rights exhausted. Neither can they be detained if their removal cannot take place within a reasonable period. Many of them have no valid documents and so they need to be re-documented before removal action can be carried out. Faced with the impossibility to detain, people in this condition are often prosecuted (Aliverti, 2012). A criminal conviction, which almost always entails imprisonment in cases involving undocumented migrants, serves the purpose of preventing claimants from going underground while awaiting the decision in the asylum case. Perversely, then, the protection of refugees against non-refoulment turns in practice against them.

Shifting the Sight: Inland Controls and Immigration-Criminal Enforcement

In the mid-2000s when the numbers of asylum applications started to go down, attention turned to those who were illegally in the country after their claims were refused. This period marks a beginning of a shift in British traditional strategy hinged on external border controls to a more integrated policy encompassing the policing of immigrants within the country. Until the 1980s, immigration enforcement was very much limited to admission controls on ports of entry, while the police was in charge of internal enforcement, particularly the detection of immigration wrongdoers. Since then and particularly from the 2000s onwards, the Immigration and Nationality Directorate steadily expanded its remit to inland immigration enforcement, targeting in particular illegal working, 'sham' marriages and 'bogus' colleges (Jordan & Düvell, 2002). So, too, organized crime—such as people smuggling and trafficking—became another top priority not only at home but also at the European Union level (Kostakopoulou, 2006). Criminal gangs, it was argued, were behind three quarters of unlawful immigration, so disrupting their networks was important not only as an end in itself but also as a means to curve down illegal flows (Home Office, 2010a, 8).

The institutional move towards internal enforcement was further accelerated by the foreign national prisoners' crisis. In April 2006 it was revealed that over 1,000 foreign national prisoners (FNPs) were released from prison before the Immigration and Nationality Department had considered them for deportation. This revelation prompted the resignation of then Home Secretary Charles Clarke and raised serious questions about the competence and fitness of the immigration department. This crisis brought about important institutional changes. The resulting focus on FNPs in immigration policy led to changes in the enforcement approach and priorities of the department which was replaced in April 2007 by the Border Immigration Agency and in 2008 by the UK Border Agency.

The Enforcement Division was particularly boosted. In 2004, this division was only in charge of the detention and removal of immigration offenders (particularly failed asylum seekers). Its operations were mainly centred in London (Home Office, 2004, 5). Nowadays, the equivalent section of the UKBA is better resourced and larger in scope. Its new tasks include criminal enforcement and criminal casework. Further, it has substantially increased its geographical reach by regionalizing its operations into different Local Immigration Teams in charge of low-level immigration offences—mainly dealt with by administrative action. It has also progressively strengthened inter-agency cooperation with the police by establishing 'join ventures' formed by immigration and police officers to tackle serious immigration crimes—so-called Immigration Crime Teams—throughout the country (Home Office, 2008, 2010a). Overall the agency grew from around 11,000 staff in 2003 to 18,246 in 2007 and 24,511 in 2009—of whom 1,198 were in the Criminality & Detention Group (House of Commons, 2001, Appendix 2; Home Office, 2009, 34; 2010b, 56).

Along with its expansion, the immigration agency was reshuffled to be more like a police force. It established prosecution targets to measure the agency's performance and hired new prosecution staff to increase the rate of prosecutions against immigration offenders (Home Office, 2007, 25; 2008, Appex. C; also Home Office, 2009, 21). Consistent with this approach, immigration officials have progressively gained police-like powers with respect to many immigration offences, such as powers to arrest, detain, enter and search premises, and seize evidence. Bestowing immigration officers with these powers has decreased the dependency on the police in the arrest and removal of immigration offenders which is now carried out almost entirely without police intervention and has virtually transformed the agency into an 'immigration police force' (Macdonald, 2010, Ch. 14.11; also Vogel et al., 2009, 218).

The new approach to immigration enforcement has not resulted in a significant addition of immigration crimes to the statute book. Neither has it involved a substantial increase in prosecution and conviction rates for immigration offences. While there was a steady increase in these rates from the mid-1990s until the mid-2000s, since then they started to fall. Rather, the new enforcement style has contributed to a more targeted approach towards immigration wrongdoing, with those causing the most harm prioritized for prosecution, detention and removal (Home Office, 2007, 5; 2010a, 10). This drop in prosecution rates is in part due to the realization that criminal proceedings are expensive and time-consuming, and prosecutions are not necessarily more effective than removals in deterring asylum seekers and unwelcome migrants from coming to the country.

Conclusion

As the brief historical account in the first section of this paper shows, immigration-related offences are not new. They constituted an important enforcement tool to deal with unwanted immigration flows when there was no organized police force or specialized law enforcement body. Because immigration wrongdoing was penalized since early days with criminal sanctions, it is no coincidence that immigration offences have been inserted to almost every single law on this field passed after 1905. As David Cesarani (1993, 31) observes '[t]he existence of a statute and the administrative machinery to enforce it provided the basis for continuity'. The perpetuation of a system in which a criminal sanction is attached to an immigration rule, though, is not completely explained by the existence of a legal tradition or an administrative apparatus in place.

Immigration-related offences play important pragmatic and symbolic functions. They have been conceived as merely threats or as secondary, backup sanctions to the primary administrative sanction of removal or deportation. This instrumental dimension of the criminal law is clear from the decline in prosecutions against over-stayers following the restriction of appeal rights against deportation orders which made the administrative channel preferable. Similarly, people who cannot be deported or removed are usually prosecuted instead, such as undocumented foreigners or asylum seekers who have an application under consideration. From this perspective, criminal law powers are interchangeable enforcement tools resorted to whenever they prove useful or effective to achieve a particular immigration goal (Sklansky, 2012).

On the other hand, criminal law plays a further symbolic function. Making immigrants criminal conveys a powerful message about the gravity of immigration-related transgression and the stake of the state in stamping it out. Indeed, the criminalization of immigration breaches is not only about the mere transgression of immigration rules. As Katja Franko Aas (2013, 12) writes, it 'denotes a more pervasive and insidious connection between migration, crime, and insecurity'.

Discussion Questions

1. What should be the role of the criminal law in the regulation of immigration?
2. Is it desirable or necessary to punish certain immigration breaches with punishment? If so, in which cases?
3. How does the use of criminal law powers to control immigration in Britain differ from that in the US?

References

Aas, K. F. (2013). The ordered and the bordered society: migration control, citizenship and the Northern penal state. In K. F. Aas & M. Bosworth (Eds.), The Borders of Punishment: Criminal justice, citizenship and social exclusion. Oxford: Oxford University Press.

Aas, K. F., & Bosworth, M. (Eds.). (2013). The Borders of Punishment: criminal justice, citizenship and social exclusion. Oxford: Oxford University Press.

Aliverti, A. (2012). Exploring the function of criminal law in the policing of foreigners: the decision to prosecute immigration-related offences. Social & Legal Studies, forthcoming.

Aliverti, A. (2013). Crimes of Mobility: Criminal Law and the Regulation of Immigration. Abingdon: Routledge (forthcoming).

Calavita, K. (2003). A 'Reserve Army of Delinquents:' The Criminalization and Economic Punishment of Immigrants in Spain. Punishment & Society, 5(4), 399–413. doi: 10.1177/14624745030054002.

Cesarani, D. (1993). An Alien Concept? The Continuity of Anti-Alienism in British Society before 1940. In D. Cesarani & T. Kushner (Eds.), The Internment of Aliens in Twentieth Century Britain: Frank Cass.

Chacón, J. (2012). Overcriminalizing Immigration. Journal of Criminal Law & Criminology, 102(3), 613–652.

Cohen, R. (1994). Frontiers of Identity. The British and the Others. Harlow, Essex: Longman.

Dauvergne, C. (2008). Making People Illegal. What Globalization Means for Migration and Law. New York: Cambridge University Press.

De Giorgi, A. (2010). Immigration control, post-Fordism, and less eligibility: A materialist critique of the criminalization of immigration across Europe. Punishment & Society, 12(2), 147–167. doi: 10.1177/1462474509357378.

Dunstan, R. (1998). United Kingdom: Breaches of Article 31 of the 1951 Refugee Convention. International Journal of Refugee Law, 10(1–2), 205–213. doi: 10.1093/ijrl/10.1–2.205.

Eagly, I. (2010). Prosecuting Immigration. Northwestern University Law Review, 104(4), 1281–1360.

Evans, J. (1983). Immigration law (2nd. ed.). London: Sweet & Maxwell.

Hales, L. (1996). Refugees and criminal justice? Cropwood occasional paper No 21. Institute of Criminology, University of Cambridge.

Hansen, R. (2000). Citizenship and immigration in post-war Britain: the institutional origins of a multicultural nation. Oxford: Oxford University Press.

Holmes, C. (1988). John Bull's island: immigration and British society, 1871–1971. Basingstoke: Macmillan.

Home Office. (1985). Control of Immigration: Statistics United Kingdom 1984. London: Home Office.

Home Office. (1998). Fairer, Faster and Firmer. A Modern Approach to Immigration and Asylum. London: Home Office. Cmnd 4018.

Home Office. (2004). United Kingdom Immigration Service. London: IND.

Home Office. (2006). Control of Immigration: Statistics United Kingdom 2005. London: Home Office. Cmnd 6904.

Home Office. (2007). Enforcing the rules. A strategy to ensure and enforce compliance with our immigration laws. London: Home Office.

Home Office. (2008). Enforcing the Deal. Our Plans for Enforcing the Immigration Laws in the United Kingdom's Communities. London: Home Office.

Home Office. (2009). UK Border Agency Business Plan April 2008—March 2011. London: Home Office.

Home Office. (2010a). Protecting Our Border, Protecting the Public. The UK Border Agency's five year strategy for enforcing our immigration rules and addressing immigration and cross border crime. London: Home Office.

Home Office. (2010b). UK Border Agency Business Plan April 2009—March 2012. London: Home Office.

Home Office. (2011). Tackling immigration crime. A guide for police. London: Home Office.

House of Commons. (2001). First Report. Border Controls: Report and Proceedings of the Committee. London: Home Affairs Committee, House of Commons, UK Parliament. HC 163-II.

Jordan, B., & Düvell, F. (2002). Irregular migration: the dilemmas of transnational mobility. Cheltenham: Edward Elgar.

Kostakopoulou, D. (2006). Trafficking and smuggling human beings: the British perspective. In E. Guild & P. Minderhoud (Eds.), Immigration and Criminal Law in the European Union. The Legal Measures and Social Consequences of Criminal Law in Member States on Trafficking and Smuggling in Human Beings (pp. 345–370). Leiden: Martinus Nijhoff.

Lacey, N. (2008). The Prisoners' Dilemma. Political Economy and Punishment in Contemporary Democracies. New York: Cambridge University Press.

Lacey, N. (2012). Principles, Policies, and Politics of Criminal Law. In L. Zedner & J. Roberts (Eds.), Principles and Values in Criminal Law and Criminal Justice. Essays in Honour of Andrew Ashworth. Oxford: Oxford University Press.

Legomsky, S. (2007). The New Path of Immigration Law: Asymmetric Incorporation of Criminal Justice Norms. Washington & Lee Law Review, 64, 469–528.

Macdonald, I. (2010). MacDonald's Immigration Law and Practice (8th ed.). London: LexisNexis.

Medina, I. (1997). The Criminalization of Immigration Law: Employment Sanctions and Marriage Fraud. George Mason Law Review, 5(4), 669–731.

Melossi, D. (2000). The Other in the New Europe: Migrations, Deviance, Social Order. In P. Green & A. Rutherford (Eds.), Criminal Policy in Transition (pp. 151–166). Oxford: Hart.

Newsam, F. (1954). The Home Office. London: Allen & Unwin.

Pratt, A., & Valverde, M. (2002). From Deserving Victims to 'Masters of Confusion': Redefining Refugees in the 1990s. The Canadian Journal of Sociology, 27(2), 135–161.

Sklansky, D. (2012). Crime, Immigration, and Ad Hoc Instrumentalism. New Criminal Law Review, 15(2), 157–223.

Stumpf, J. (2007). The Crimmigration Crisis: Immigrants, Crime, and Sovereign State. Lewis & Clark Law School Legal Research Paper Series, 2007–2, 1–44.

Stumpf, J. (2009). Fitting Punishment. Washington & Lee Law Review, 66, 1683–1741.

Troup, C. (1925). The Home Office. London & New York: G.P.Putnam's sons ltd.

Vogel, D., McDonald, W., Düvell, F., Jordan, B., Kovacheva, V., & Vollmer, B. (2009). Police Cooperation in Internal Enforcement of Immigration Control: Learning from International Comparison. Sociology of Crime, Law and Deviance, 13, 207–244.

Wacquant, L. (1999). 'Suitable Enemies': Foreigners and Immigrants in the Prisons of Europe. Punishment & Society, 1(2), 215–222. doi: 10.1177/14624749922227784.

Case Examples: The Human Cost of the Criminalization of Immigration

Chapter Fifteen

Systemic Parallels: The Impact of Criminalizing Immigration on Work with Asian Victims of Intimate Partner Violence

Tien Ung

Approximately 18.2 million Asian Americans live in the United States reflecting 5.8% of the population (Census, 2011). This has been attributed to a rise in Asian immigration in the last decade. Asians make up 36% of new immigrants, both documented and undocumented, roughly 430,000 (Pew, 2012). Over the next 40 years, Asian American population rates are projected to grow 134 percent. Despite recent reports about success and achievement among the Asian American community in the United States (ibid), serious social problems confronting this community become more apparent when data about Asian Americans are isolated and analyzed by ethnic groups (Office for Minority Health, 2012).

One such problem facing the Asian American community is intimate partner violence (IPV). For the Asian immigrant community this problem has historically been exacerbated by a woman's legal status. Consequently when Congress passed the Violence Against Women Act in 1994 (VAWA), specific provisions pertaining exclusively to immigrant women were included offering protection from violence without prejudice by legal status (Conyers, 2007). In 2000, and 2005, when the bill was up for renewal, expanded protections specifically for abused immigrant women were proposed and passed both times, without incident (ibid).

In 2011, VAWA was up for renewal again, and expired. Congress was unable to reach consensus in part because of requests for ongoing and increased protection to immigrant victims. An alternative version of the bill was consequently put forward. In the alternative version, provisions to increase the number of visas law enforcement officials can offer to protect immigrant victims from threats to their life for reporting crimes such as sexual and physical assault were removed. Although it took one and a half years, the bill did finally pass. However, the controversy and fierce debate surrounding its process of review and renewal, the first ever in its history since 1994, is a strong indicator of the inextricable ways in which the socio-cultural climate intertwines with the political landscape. Specifically, what happened with VAWA is illustrative of the relationship between anti-immigration sentiment and policy and lawmaking. The present shift in thinking relative to immigration reform, particularly of criminalizing the immigrant under the rationalization of protection, nearly scuppered over two decades of VAWA sanctioned protection for immigrant women in the United States.

There has been much discussion, both in the news as well as the professional literature, about the impact of criminalization of immigration on victims of IPV. Very little has been explored in relation to its impact on the actual workers and work of protecting abused immigrant women. This chapter draws on the ideas of chaos, complexity, and trauma theory embodied in the work of Sandra Bloom (2000) to suggest the current criminalization movement serves as a trauma catalyst that has negative impact on the capacity of professionals doing frontline work. Drawing on interviews with professionals who work with Asian women abused in their intimate relationships as well as two decades of the author's field experience, I illustrate how criminalization complicates rather than clarifies events that surround the experiences of documented and undocumented Asian women battered by their partners. In addition, I propose that current immigration reform compromises decision making for professionals and organizations by narrowing rather than broadening opportunities for innovation and collaboration.

Working with Asian Survivors: The Professional Landscape

While abuse by an intimate partner is something that immigrant women and men face, the focus of this chapter is specific to work with Asian American women. To this end, the use of the term immigrant throughout this chapter includes women refugees and asylees from Asia who also experience intimate partner violence. However, it is important to note that in so doing, I am not suggesting that the experiences of Asian refugees and asylees are similar to the experiences of documented and undocumented Asian women migrants and immigrants as they are not. Their inclusion reflects the position that violence against Asian women may be complicated by one's migration status, and the type or reason for migration, but should not be distinguished by it.

The prevalence of violence against Asian women by their partners is difficult to accurately estimate because of the absence of linguistic and culturally responsive methods of data collection and sampling. Current literature regarding intimate partner violence (IPV) in the Asian community estimates rates for IPV range from 12% to 71% (Raj & Silverman, 2002; Tjaden & Thoennes, 2000; Yoshihama, 1999). The case of battered Asian women is unique in that ethnic diversity makes the provision of adequate and culturally relevant services to these women a significant challenge. Within the Asian community in the United States for example, there are over 30 countries represented with nationals speaking over 100 different languages (White House, (nd)). In addition, like other immigrants, Asian women are vulnerable to multiple conditions that heighten their vulnerability such as social isolation, legal status complications, cultural conflicts, limited mobility, and compromised work opportunities (Lee & Hadeed, 2009).

Safety and recovery for immigrant victims of partner violence involves acculturation strategies that include, in part, learning about new cultural standards, different ways of socializing, and about new perspectives regarding their rights under the law. Professionals involved on behalf of battered Asian women therefore need to understand the social, cultural, and political contexts that surround their work (Kim, 2006). This includes assessing how the women's experiences are confounded or helped by cultural variation and norms, complex social interactions and systems, social welfare policy, and immigration legislation and reform. Cultivating networks across professional domains, raising awareness about the dynamics of abuse and its impact on women, and finding allies become non-negotiable practice behaviors or work-related skills that enable effective intervention. As one practitioner noted:

> Without insurance it is impossible to help (immigrant Asian) women get necessary care. I mean in hospitals and clinics you can find ways to find women free care. I had a client who really needed dental work, you know, her husband had really done a number on her teeth—broke one of them when he assaulted her. And it was impossible to find her anyone who could help her. Anyone who knew anyone who was doing any type of probono work was already full. So one day I was at my own dentist and started to talk to him about what I do and then one

thing led to another and I just asked him—you know, would he treat this client and he said yes.

Yet, when this type of work takes place against a backdrop of heightened anti-immigration sentiment, authorized by changes in federal and state legislation where protecting and empowering the victim can be interpreted as harboring the undocumented (Arcidiacono, 2010; Rieser-Murphy & DeMarco, 2012), the practitioner, like the victim herself, can find themselves entangled in a practice environment where allies are harder to find, resources even more scarce, and collaboration and networking not possible (Erez & Globokar, 2009). In the above situation for example, it is reasonable to imagine a reluctance among dentists in private practice to come forward.

Consequently, the professional ecology or work-related conditions and systems surrounding documented and undocumented Asians reflect an elaborate and complex labyrinth involving politics, economics, and values (Wong, 2012). Ensuring the safety and needs of battered Asian women therefore requires specialized skills and knowledge that include but are not limited to cultural brokering, language matching, legal and policy acuity, systemic sagacity, and interdisciplinary competence. Recent changes in immigration legislation has shifted the professional climate within this ecology from one of support driven by underlying commitments to human rights and justice to one of criminalization driven by underlying anti-immigration sentiments. Against this context, a new conceptualization of abused Asian women emerges. Rather than victims of violence, immigrant women are instead perceived as economic burdens, illegal and fraudulent, pernicious competitors for scarce resources, or invisible casualties of war. Such a backlash makes the complex work of human service professionals in this field even more onerous. Offering help and resources under current immigration enforcement laws could easily lead to controversy, complications, and hassles that would be best if avoided altogether. One community agency member shares how avoidance of such hassles prevents them from growth and service.

> Our funding comes totally from private funders and community . fundraisers. All of our services are provided in house and through a volunteer network. We serve close to 150 women each year and there are more we are unable to serve. The effect (of criminalization of immigration) is that we can not grow ... we were thinking about using state and federal funds but now in this climate ... it is not so easy.

Under current workforce conditions practitioners working on behalf of immigrant Asian survivors find themselves in a professional climate where they are isolated, and sometimes unaware of loopholes and contradictions in current immigration legislation. Combined, this makes it difficult to mobilize resources in support of client safety and difficult to determine what clients' rights legitimately are (Erez & Globokar, 2009). The parallel to intimate partner violence is understandable and hard to miss. Intimate partner violence is about the intentional use of psychological coercion, degradation, and physical and sexual assault to injure, threaten, instill fear in, and control another. Criminalizing immigrants and extending the authoritative domain of the Immigration and Customs Enforcement agency (ICE) to other public institutions creates a social-cultural professional environment for the advocate or human service professional that mirrors the unpredictable, chaotic, and oppressive home climate of Asian women who are abused by their partners.

An Alternative Landscape: Exploring Systemic Parallels to Manage Work with Asian Victims

The experience of intimate partner violence is compounded by social forces such as the criminalization of immigration, thereby making approaches that contend with traumatization essential to work with Asian immigrants who experience IPV. Sandra Bloom (1997) developed The Sanctuary Model, an evidence informed approach for working with survivors of trauma. This model provides a powerful framework that explains why consideration of trauma is necessary not only for victims of violence but also for the organizations and systems that are created to deal with violence in the lives of people.

Bloom's framework builds on principles of chaos and complexity theory and the idea that social phenomena are multidimensional and intricately interconnected. Consequently, she contends, linear models that lay out direct cause and effect trajectories cannot be used to effectively explain the nature of relationships involved in our social worlds. While it may be clear that community, and politics are social, Bloom effectively argues that organizations and institutions are also social, dynamic, essentially alive.

Central to the model is the idea that decision making is organized around parallel forces defined by characteristics of trauma. Subsequently, social and service delivery systems will organize around traumatic themes essentially mirroring and manifesting the dynamics of trauma that clients suffer. Much like processes and functioning in a violent family organizing around the perpetration of violence and the experience of trauma (e.g., the abusive partner whose unpredictable outbursts effectively creates a climate of control over their spouse, who uses love for and commitment to the children to manipulate an agenda, or who manages the flow of information that both enters and leaves the home), a culture or an agency will organize its operations and functioning around trauma-induced dynamics. For example, organizations can enforce a climate of don't ask don't tell, of punishing rather than learning from mistakes, and generate secrecy around departmental processes that cultivates an atmosphere of control and isolation. Such organizational processes create a climate that endorses anxiety and demoralization among employees.

At the core of Bloom's work is self-organization, or "the notion that new levels of form, organization, and complexity, often arise out of the interchanges between organisms and their contexts" (Bloom, 2000, p. 3). The degree to which we oversimplify this process or embrace the inherent complexities will directly affect the sophistication with which we make decisions, solve problems, and resolve conflict. In her work we discover a pathway by which to bridge what she calls "the simultaneously existing worlds of psychological knowledge and political action (2004, pg. 80)" in service of more effective social and cultural scaffolding at the organizational and community level. The primary purpose of human service delivery systems Bloom suggests is creating sanctuary for healing and innovation. Sanctuary is critical. According to Bloom and Farragher (2010) the status quo exemplifies complex ethical dilemmas ignored by good intentions, at best. At worst they suggest current social institutions reflect tyrannical efforts to pursue safety at the cost of liberty, resulting paradoxically in less safety for everyone.

> Trauma theory makes it clear that political and social policy decisions are intimately connected to people's experience of—and exposure to— traumatic experience. The impact of combat on Vietnam veterans cannot be separated from the political furvor associated with that conflict. Violence against women and children can only be addressed through a discourse centering on patriarchal power and the abuse of that power (Bloom, 2004, p. 80).

Immigration reform examined through this lens makes it clear that legislation and policies surrounding border control, residency, and citizenship are inextricably linked to women's well-being, their health and mental health, and more importantly, their safety and protection from trauma, especially in the context of intimate personal violence. Bloom's framework extends this point to the professional landscape that surrounds battered Asian women. It calls on us to consider how immigration reform, and specifically the criminalization of immigration will not only affect immigrant women and their safety, but also the workforce and the processes embedded in the systems that are erected to serve them.

Fear Begets Fear, Isolation, and Stagnancy: The Consequences of Criminalization

Criminalization backfires against the process of helping battered Asian women in three ways: 1) it heightens fear and promotes weariness in the professional community, 2) increases isolation, and 3) fosters reluctance that can contribute to systemic or service stagnancy. Expanding patrol authority beyond border control by requiring proof of documentation, and broadening mechanisms for immigration status enforcement to public institutions heightens fear both within the immigrant community (Erez & Globokar, 2009; Owen, 2006; Ray, 2011), as well as within the service community. Threat of deportation is one of the most frequently used tactics of control that batterers use against Asian immigrant women (Lee & Hadeed, 2009). Consequently, fear of deportation is the most common reason provided by women for not disclosing abuse, not calling police, not participating in the legal proceedings once abuse has been disclosed, and not seeking or accepting help to address abuse related issues (ibid).

The authors of VAWA (1994) recognized that effective implementation of safeguards to protect immigrant women against violence would require among other things collaboration among advocates and professionals in the criminal justice system. Therefore specific monies are earmarked to be used for the training of criminal justice professionals and for research pertaining to collaboration between professionals working with abuse victims. In the two decades since VAWA's passage, encouraging immigrant women to work within both the criminal justice and legal systems and to call the police are actions that many advocates strive to empower Asian clients to take. In so doing, advocates draw on their own knowledge of immigrant women's rights, and on their understanding of the law. To this end, they rely on policy and legislation to protect women and to work in their favor. However, with the passage of current immigration legislation, such as Secure Communities where law enforcement personnel are required to collaborate with ICE officials, professionals working with Asian victims of IPV are left worried and afraid.

It is so hard, so hard. You know Asian woman does not come forward. She does not talk about abuse. She doesn't want to bring shame to

> her family. She will sacrifice herself like that. And sometimes she does not understand you know what her rights are in this country. She does not speak the language. And before (Secure Communities legislation) you know I would always say to them, you have to call the police. They will help you, they will protect you. But now you know, I can not be sure. I just don't know you know. Will they protect them or will they turn them in (to ICE). I'm afraid for my clients because of this you know. I really just don't know.

Criminalization undermines the relationship with law enforcement by placing the criminal justice professional in the dual bind of having to choose between one's duty to protect and one's duty to enforce.

In addition to fear, isolation is another consequence of criminalization that negatively impacts work with Asian victims of IPV. Between 2011 and 2012, 2,403 bills and resolutions involving immigrants and refugees were under consideration across more than 45 state legislatures (National Conference of State Legislatures, 2012). As a whole the proposed bills covered immigration reform in the areas of health care, education, public benefits, and enforcement. A review of the proposals illustrates the pervasiveness of the intent to criminalize immigrants. Some of the bills under consideration for example would enable state residents to sue local and public agencies for failure to comply with enforcement regulations (ibid). Other proposals would make it illegal to transport or harbor immigrants unless documentation could be established (ibid). Moreover, current immigration laws prohibit anyone receiving federal funding from working with immigrants unless proof of documentation can be established (Arcidiacono, 2010; Rieser-Murphy & DeMarco, 2012).

Such proposals and legislation interferes with the generation of social capital and the building of social networks. Social capital and social networks in the field of IPV serve as critical formal and informal infrastructure that tends to the needs of Asian victims when more formal public and welfare institutions cannot. Current immigration reform and policies compromise and obstruct collaboration between community partners in service of safety and protection for Asian victims of IPV. This makes it difficult for professionals working with Asian women in need of IPV services to locate and leverage resources to protect women and children from abuse in their homes.

> I work like don't ask, don't tell, you know. I just don't ask them and I don't tell other people I have to work with and I just pray they don't ask me. You know. It is hard of course. Sometimes I feel like why do we have to be having such secrets you know. These women are abused

you know—that is their only crime. Why can't we help them you know. I heard you know that some states say you can't shelter and drive these women. You know and I think oh my God, what are we going to do? Our entire service is made of volunteers you know. People who drive the women for job interview, for court, for medical appointments. The volunteer sometimes let woman live with them. You know, who is going to volunteer with us now?

When combined or taken as a whole, current immigration legislation to include many pending proposals erect barriers to effective strategies and intervention on behalf of Asian victims and obstruct the flow of service delivery. Many Asian victims of IPV are not English speaking, making it very difficult for them to navigate the system. Therefore, they rely on legal and social institutions for safety and protection. When current reform places a heavier emphasis on immigrant removal rather than immigrant safety, and when helping an immigrant becomes a crime unless proof of documentation is established, humanitarian aid is essentially thwarted. Consequently, Asian victims of IPV could face more vulnerability, risk, and fear.

Such a state of affairs decreases help seeking and cooperation rather than facilitate it. It is commonly accepted that protecting battered immigrant women involves complex decision making and is most effective when collaboration is not only possible, but the driving motivation underlying intervention efforts. However, current immigration reform discourages and creates barriers to complex, cross disciplinary decision making and collaboration. Rather, for the case of battered Asian women, under current legally sanctioned anti-immigration sentiment, professionals are forced to organize complex decision-making and service planning around documentation status rather than around protection and safety. As a result, the complexities involved in a case multiplies, lag times for services increases, and in some cases no services are even possible (Arcidiacono, 2010; Rieser-Murphy & DeMarco, 2012). These work conditions can wear down the hope of professionals who are trying to support women out of abusive relationships or push a more simple, bifurcated approach to problem assessment and decision making in general. Direct implications of this can be seen in screening and case management decisions mentioned earlier. Whereas organizations may have accepted a referral for a woman and worked on figuring out the complexities of the situation later, now under current anti-immigration sentiment endorsed by local, state, and federal laws, organizations find themselves questioning whether they can actually help the woman, or how many women they must turn away in order to be of use to one.

It is hard. I know of a law firm that makes a conscious choice not to accept any federal funding so they don't have to ask women about their legal status. This limits the number of cases they can take, but this is what they do so they can take the cases without worry.

Conclusion

Criminalizing immigration has negative repercussions for documented and undocumented Asian women in spite of federal safeguards intended to protect women from abuse and violence. In this chapter I have discussed how criminalization of immigration also has negative repercussions for the workforce. Using federal and state legislation to enforce border control, immigrant detention, and immigrant removal at the local and state level, amidst public and social institutions, and among citizens, significantly heightens the sense of patrol and control over immigrant communities (Arcidiacono, 2010; Owen, 2006; Rieser-Murphy & DeMarco, 2012). This places the professional working with battered Asian women in the unexpected irony of perpetuating the very conditions of threat and controls that victims experience at the hands of their batterers when they are being called upon to help the women address these issues.

Under the Violence against Women Act, prior to current immigration reform, women who came forward in the U.S. to report abuse found a system of diverse professionals positioned and ready to protect them from further harm. Between 1994 and 2012, since VAWA has been in effect, the Department of Justice has reported a 64% decrease in violence against women in the United States. Enacting legislation that requires immigrants living in the United States to be forced to carry documentation and that makes immigrant women vulnerable to pretext arrests undermines the significant progress that has evolved over 20 years as a result of meaningful legislation in service of protection of women—citizens, documented, and undocumented, against violence. Current shifts in immigration reform which prioritizes women's status over their rights to freedom from violence essentially dismantles a legally sanctioned social fabric which communicated unequivocally that in the United States, we will not tolerate violence against women and we will work together to ensure their safety.

Criminal justice professionals such as police, probation and parole officers, attorneys, and advocates are among some of the first responders to Asian immigrant victims of intimate partner violence. In order for these professionals to effectively protect women from further violence, they must also be empowered to understand the complexities of these women's needs, and to collaborate in order to create a climate where the women feel safe to come forward and cooperate in service of their own protection. Services for these women are at their most effective when criminal justice professionals have the authority under the law to act in socially just ways, focusing on the safety and protection of documented and undocumented women. Current reform unfortunately puts the criminal justice professional in the middle of a larger controversy about the legitimacy and make up of the larger U.S. population. Under such conditions, government and institutions do not allow criminal justice professionals to leverage their expertise and skills into best practices at the ground level. Instead, criminal justice professionals will find themselves caught in an unresolvable ethical dilemma, stuck between safeguarding women from violence in their own homes, or violating women's rights to protection in service of alleged national security.

Discussion Questions

1. With recent passage and implementation of Secure Communities legislation, criminal justice and law enforcement officials find themselves caught between the duty to protect and a duty to enforce, yet these professionals are among the first responders to Asian women who are battered by their intimate partners. What factors must professionals consider and weigh to manage this dilemma?
2. Policy analysts emphasize the importance of establishing practice protocols to guide decision making as a means to ensure immigration focused legislation does not compromise the physical safety of immigrants who are victims of a crime, like domestic assault. What might an effective practice protocol include and look like? Why?
3. Is social justice critical to criminal justice practice? Why or why not?

Author's note: The author would like to thank and acknowledge Rita Shah, Family Services Coordinator at Saheli and Uyen Tran, Shelter Manager & Legal Advocacy Services Coordinator Asian Task Force Against Domestic Violence for their invaluable contributions to my conceptualization of this chapter.

References

Adams, M.E., and Campbell, J. (2012). Being undocumented and intimate partner violence (IPV): Multiple vulnerabilities through the lens of Feminist Intersectionality. Women's Health and Urban Life, 11(1), pp. 15–34.

Arcidiacono, A. (2010). Silencing the voices of battered women: How Arizona's new anti-immigration law "SB1070" prevents undocumented women from seeking relief under the Violence Against Women Act. California Western Law Review, 47(1), p. 173.

Bloom, S. L. (1997) Creating Sanctuary: Toward the Evolution of Sane Societies. New York: Routledge.

Bloom, S. (2004). Neither liberty nor safety: The impact of fear on individuals, institutions, and societies, Part 1. Psychotherapy and politics international, 2(2), pp. 78–98.

Bloom, S. and Farragher, B. (2010). Destroying Sanctuary: The Crisis in Human Service Delivery Systems. New York. Oxford University Press.

Conyers, J. (2007). The re-authorization of the Violence Against Women Act— Why Congress acted to expand protection to immigrant victims. Violence Against Women, 13(5), pp. 457–468.

Dahlberg, L.L. and Mercy, J.A. (2009). History of violence as a public health issue. AMA Virtual Mentor, 11(2), pp. 167–172. Retrieved from: http://virtualmentor.ama-assn.org/2009/02/mhst1-0902.html.

Erez, E. and Globokar, J. (2009). Compounding vulnerabilities: The impact of immigration status and circumstances on battered immigrant women. Sociology of crime, law, and deviance, 13, pp. 129–145.

Ingram, M., McClelland, D.J., Martin, J., Cabellero, M., Mayorga, M., and Gillespie, K. (2010). Experiences of women who self-petition under the Violence Against Women Act. Violence against women, 16(8), pp. 858–880.

Heilbroner, R. and Thurow, L. (1998). Economics explained: Everything you need to know about how the economy works and where it is going. Touchstone Rockfeller Center: New York, NY.

Kim, M. (2006). Alternative interventions to violence: Creative interventions. The International Journal of Narrative Therapy and Community Work, 4, pp. 45–52.

Lee, Y. S., & Hadeed, L. (2009). Intimate Partner Violence Among Asian Immigrant Communities Health/Mental Health Consequences, Help-Seeking Behaviors, and Service Utilization. Trauma, Violence, & Abuse, 10(2), pp. 143–170.

National Conference of State Legislatures. (May, 2012). 2012 Immigration-related laws, bills, and resolutions in the States: Jan.1–March 31, 2012. Retrieved from: http://www.ncsl.org/issues-research/immig/2012-immigration-laws-bills-and-resolutions.aspx.

Owen, L.J. (2006). Forced through the cracks: Deprivation of the Violence Against Women's Act's immigration relief in San Francisco Bay Area immigrant domestic violence survivor's cases. Berkeley Journal of Gender, Law, and Justice, 21, pp. 13–37.

Ray, R. (2011). Insecure Communities: Examining local government participation in US Immigration and Customs Enforcement's "Secure Communities" Program. Seattle Journal for Social Justice, 10(1), p. 23.

Rieser-Murphy, E. M., & DeMarco, K. D. (2012). The Unintended Consequences of Alabama's Immigration Law on Domestic Violence Victims. University of Miami Law Review, 66, pp. 1059–1183.

The White House, Initiative on Asian Americans and Pacific Islanders. (nd). Critical issues facing Asian Americans and Pacific Islanders. Retrieved from: http://www.whitehouse.gov/administration/eop/aapi/data/critical-issues.

Wong, T. (2012). 287(g) and the Politics of Interior Immigration Control in the United States: Explaining Local Cooperation with Federal Immigration Authorities. Journal of ethnic and migration studies, 38(5), pp. 737–756.

Chapter Sixteen

The Crime of Presence: Latino Meatpacking Workers in Iowa

Mark A. Grey & Michele Devlin

Iowa is an important part of that region of the United States often referred to as "flyover" country. Many who refer to the region this way may concede that Iowa and its neighboring states also form the "heartland" but that may not be sufficient to spark their interest in visiting the state, much less living here. The geography is not attractive for many: vast expanses of corn fields, small towns populated by boring provincials, and no large cities. The place is easy to stereotype for these reasons and for a perceived lack of ethnic diversity.

It is the case that Iowa has been, and will continue to be, overwhelmingly white. Although small populations of native peoples—like the Meskwaki—have and do live in Iowa, the vast majority of the population consists of the descendants of European immigrants who arrived en masse in the mid- to late-1800s. Indeed, in 1836 Iowa's total population was a mere 10,531. But by 1855, the population grew to 500,000 and by 1890, it had mushroomed to 2,231,853.

This dramatic population growth was due to aggressive recruitment of immigrants to the state and high fertility rates after they settled. Recruitment of immigrants was often orchestrated by railroads that sought labor and people to settle and develop communities along their routes. Recruiting materials often took the form of handbooks with long, descriptive titles like "Iowa as it is in 1856; a gazetteer for citizens, and a hand-book for immigrants, embracing a full description of the state of Iowa ... Information for the immigrant respecting the selection, entry, and cultivation of prairie soil; a list of unentered lands in the state...." Immigrants started pouring into the state. One principal place of entry was the Mississippi River town of Dubuque where one local newspaper described the mass arrival of immigrants as an "endless procession ... a mighty army of invasion, which, were its objects other than peace, and holy, fraternal, cordial league with its predecessors, their joint aim to conquer this fair and alluring domain from the wild dominion of nature, would strike terror into the boldest hearts."

Although efforts to lure immigrants to Iowa prior to the Civil War led to "a mighty army of invasion," Iowa leaders after the Civil War recognized the need for even more people. In 1969, The Iowa state legislature formed a Board of Immigration. The following year, this Board published a thin book with the title Iowa: The Home for Immigrants. Using the comma-heavy, flowery language of the time, "this little book, with the information it imparts, and the counsel it gives, is respectfully offered." It appealed "To all Landless Men and Women, of both the Old World and the New, who desire beautiful homes in the fairest portion of the green earth; [and] To all Good Men and Women, who aspire to independence, either for themselves or their children after them, and who will contribute, either of mind or muscle, to carry Iowa forward to her grand and glorious destiny."

The vast majority of newcomers settled with those who hailed from the same nations or regions, spoke the same language, and practiced the same religions. Small towns across the state were in fact ethnic enclaves of made of Swedes, Norwegians, Germans, Slavs, Danes, Dutch and many others. There were also a handful of African American settlements—like Buxton in Southern Iowa—created by migrants from Virginia and elsewhere. Most settlers to the state were European and racially white but they were ethnically very diverse. The state's history is replete with stories about how parents from one town refused to allow their daughters to date or marry boys from nearby towns because of their different ethnicity and language.

Of course, several decades later, the importance of these ethnic differences among white people have diminished as have the use of Europeans languages other than English. Iowa hosts an impressive number of immigrant heritage museums, like the Danish Immigrant Museum, the Czech and Slovak Museum in Cedar Rapids, and the Vesterheim Norwegian-American museum. As interest in these ethnic immigrant heritages has faded, attendance at these museums has fallen dramatically in recent years. These days, about the only way to discover the immigrant heritage of many Iowa towns is to see their "Welcome" signs displayed in German, Dutch, Swedish, or some other European language.

In contrast to this historic backdrop characterized by a state that encouraged and supported immigration, the state's more recent experience with immigration has not always been so welcoming. In the 1990s, Iowa began to experience rapid growth in its Latino population. In the 1990 Census only 32,822

Hispanics lived in Iowa, less than one percent of the state's total population. But by 2000 the Census counted 81,188 Latinos and by 2010 more than 151,000. The most dramatic growth took place in several meatpacking towns, some of which saw their Latino populations grow in excess of 1,000 percent in a few short years (Grey & Woodrick, 2005). Marshalltown provides one example. In 1990 there were a few dozen Latinos in the community, but by about 1995 or 1996, there were about 5,000.

The Latino Boom in Iowa was part of the same growth pattern experienced throughout the Midwest. This migration in Iowa was made up mostly—but not exclusively—by Mexicans who left the western states of Michoacán, Jalisco and Guanajuato. They left behind high unemployment, low wages for those who had work, poor schools, and poor economic prospects for themselves and their children. They came to take jobs in large meatpacking and other food processing plants that offered wages of $10 or more per hour and did not require education, previous experience, or English skills. Employers needed to tap a labor force willing to take difficult, distasteful jobs at wages that made the jobs unattractive to those few Iowans willing to apply. They found a deep reserve of these eager workers in rural Mexico and—despite their denials to the contrary—they were willing to hire them despite the lack of clearly legitimate immigration papers. In other words, they employed a workforce that was largely in the country illegally.

Estimates about the percentage of Iowa's Latino newcomers who were in the country illegally ranged widely but they said a lot about the degree to which individuals and policy makers were willing to criminalize the presence of Latinos and their agendas for doing so. Many immigrant advocates refused to estimate entirely, insisting that "no human being is illegal" or that if they did admit an illegal presence in the United States, these newcomers were not illegal but "undocumented." Social scientists and demographers usually acknowledged that some proportion of Latinos was in the country illegally but admitting the lack of sound data, we usually gave a range between 30 and 70 percent of Latino adults.

At the far end of this spectrum were those who insisted every Mexican newcomer was an "illegal." For years, as an immigration expert, it was quite common to visit some service club or speak to a professional association in Iowa and be confronted—often in heated, angry terms—about how "illegal means illegal," that these newcomers were only in Iowa because "they think they can get away with it," and that they were "making fun of us [Iowans] because they know we can't understand what they're saying!" Thus, Latinos committed the dual crimes of being in the country illegally and not speaking English.

Part of this rancor against Latino newcomers gained legitimacy with comparisons to previous generations of American immigrants. Older Iowans are often more keenly aware of their European heritages than more recent generations. They remember some of the family lore about how one's great-grandfather came here from Norway with three dollars in his pocket but he learned English and became an American. Of course, these immigrant stories tend to be romanticized, overly simplified, and naïve. What is often left out of the story is that most immigrant Iowans clung stubbornly to their languages. Indeed, there were many newspapers printed in Danish, German and other European languages well into the 1940s and 1950s. Some churches still provided services in Norwegian and other languages until about 15 or 20 years ago. Clubs like the Cedar Valley Danes and the Sons of Norway are still regular venders at community festivals and county fairs.

Latinos were also regularly compared to other, more recent but smaller waves of "legitimate" immigrants, namely refugees. Iowa became a major resettling site for Tai Dam, Vietnamese "boat people" and other refugees from Indochina with the end of the Vietnam War. Iowa state government even created an agency to promote refugee resettlement in the state. This agency was eventually named the Iowa Bureau of Refugee Services and became part of the state's Department of Human Services.

In the 1970s, 1980s and early part of the 1990s, support for refugee resettlement at the federal, state and local level was high. Adequate federal funding assured the provision of services lasting two years or more to help refugees learn English, get jobs, and integrate. Most importantly, refugees who arrived in those days also greatly benefited from sponsorships in their resettlement communities. These sponsorships typically came from churches and individual families who often committed monetary support but most importantly assistance with the day-to-day process of settling into a new society. These refugees were, in this sense, not only welcomed but invited and underwritten.

Although adjustment to their new lives in Iowa was often difficult and challenging for host sponsors and communities, these invited refugees provided local residents with opportunities to exercise their cultural largesse and patronage. In return, the refugees were expected to become model immigrants, learning English, acting like Americans, and expressing gratitude for their new lives. Of course, many of these refugees did fulfill these expectations. But whether individual refugees did or did not live up to all of these expectations, as a group, they became the model by which Latinos and other subsequent waves of immigrants were often judged.

For the Southeast Asian refugees, there was an expectation that they learn English, but this was often accompanied by the provision of volunteers and sponsors to help them learn the language. No doubt this encouraged many refugees to learn English and most of their young children—educated in Iowa schools—became fluent English speakers. In the greater scheme of things, many adult refugees did not learn English but this fact did not prompt citizens and policy makers to criticize them in the media and public. The reluctance or inability of Asian refugees to speak English did also not contribute to efforts to make English the state's official language. But this is exactly what happened with the arrival of Latinos.

How speaking Spanish (and other languages) became a crime in Iowa must be explained within the context of efforts in the early 2000s to once again make Iowa a state that welcomes immigrants. When he was elected Governor in 1998, Tom Vilsack sought advice about how to best position the state for the future. He formed a Strategic Planning Council. This council was made of an important and high-level mix of university presidents, business leaders, community leaders, and policy makers. Their charge was to travel around the state and hear from Iowans about their vision for the state, collect and analyze relevant data, and make recommendations for how Iowa can position itself as a thriving, progressive state in 2010. For this reason, the council became known as the 2010 Commission.

The council issued their report in the summer of 2000 with the title Iowa 2010: The New Face of Iowa. Typical of this kind of report, it addressed such issues as economic development, schools, the environment and so forth. However, all issues in the report become overshadowed by the most important issue facing Iowa, namely its looming population and workforce shortages. The council projected that by 2010, the state would need an additional 310,000 new workers to assure the state's long-term social and economic well being. This projection alone did not raise many hackles, nor did their suggestions to achieve their population goals by encouraging Iowans who left the state to come home or encouraging young Iowans to stay. But their third recommendation, namely to attract more immigrants to the state, unleashed a storm of controversy.

In the heady days that followed the 2000 council's recommendation about immigration, there was talk of making Iowa the "Ellis Island of the Midwest." The council specifically recommended approaching the Immigration and Naturalization Service (INS) to request a special designation for Iowa as an "immigration enterprise zone" free of federal quotas on visa and fueled by INS prompt processing of visa requests by immigrants moving to Iowa.

At first, Governor Vilsack enthusiastically embraced these recommendations and he announced a bold plan to recruit immigrants. He even raised the projected number of needed workers to 563,000 to bolster his case. He, his lieutenant governor, and their staffs even waved facsimile copies of the 1870 Iowa Board of Immigration book to demonstrate that recruiting immigrants to Iowa has deep historic roots. National and international media began tracking the story. Even the New York Times—resorting to its own stereotypes about Iowa— claimed "no one would call Iowa a melting pot," but the immigration initiative was "something no other state has done." The international media made Iowa look like welcoming state and prematurely and inaccurately announced special opportunities for immigrants to gain a foothold in the United States in Iowa. For months, the governor's office and members of the 2010 Council received emails, letters, and resumes from people from several nations asking how they could take advantage of Iowa's special opportunities.

Of course, the widespread media attention attracted the interest anti-immigration forces as well. The Federation for American Immigration Reform (FAIR) and Project USA poured money into the state for print and electronic advertisements fighting the immigration initiative and they trained activists to work against the plan at the local level. As one of their trained operatives stated in a town hall meeting in Mason City put it, Governor Vilsack wanted to "turn Iowa into another California" (Grey, 2006).

The political backlash against Iowa's immigration plan grew weekly and by the spring and summer of 2001, the plan was doomed. Union opposition to the plan grew and the AFL-CIO threatened to pull its support for the Democratic governor if he did not drop the plan. After he was accused of working for the "low-wage labor lobby," Vilsack changed his rhetoric from recruiting immigrants in general to recruiting "skilled immigrants." This change reflected growing opposition to the immigration plan couched in heated rhetoric about how the majority of immigrants in the state were poorly educated Latinos who did not speak English and took low-wage jobs requiring no specific skills in meatpacking and similar industries. It also reflected deep concerns about the Latinos' immigration status. The title of a Washington Post article in August 2001 articulated the controversy this way: "Immigration Foes Find Platform in Iowa, National Groups Fight Governor on Recruiting Workers from Abroad." In this article, Vilsack himself admitted that Iowa's meatpacking industry "has become the poster child for immigration problems, with some justification." He also started insisting that communities designated as "models" in the plan were not, after all "required to actively recruit foreign workers but are merely intended to be 'welcoming' to immigrants." Weeks later, he backed off even further, insisting the goal of the "model" communities was not to recruit immigrants but to "establish a dialog."

About the time Governor Vilsack's rhetoric backed off the immigration plan, the terror attacks of September 11, 2001 took place, driving one final nail in the plan's coffin. In the wake of 9/11, Iowa's once grand and innovative immigration initiative could have been allowed to die a relatively quiet death. But Vilsack was up for re-election in 2002 and he knew returning to office was jeopardized by the immigration initiative. He also knew his ambitions to run for president would be jeopardized as well. Even though the plan was dying and the governor stopped talking about the initiative in public and his staff stopped attending meetings, pubic and political pressure did not go away and even grew louder (Grey, 2006)

Not only did vocal Iowans not want new immigration, they were unhappy about many of the immigrants already living in the state. Calls for tougher state enforcement of immigration laws were met with reminders that immigration laws were the domain of federal authorities. Some local law enforcement agencies did begin their own immigration enforcement efforts but others refused because, as one police chief said, "It's not illegal to be 'illegal' in my town" as long as they did not commit other crimes. Work place enforcement was also deferred to federal authorities.

Latinos were criminals because they were in the country illegally, but since the state refused to enforce immigration law, immigration opponents had to find another angle and another hook for their hostility towards Latinos. So, in order to criminalize Latinos they urged the creation of laws that would make what Latinos do become—at least in some cases—illegal, namely speaking Spanish. Thus, the Iowa legislature passed the Iowa English Language Reaffirmation Act of 2002. Clearly aimed at Latino Spanish-speakers, the bill enjoyed the support of 86 percent of polled Iowans. Immigrants, their advocates, and even members of his own 2010 Council urged the governor to veto the bill, but he signed it anyway, quietly, on a Friday afternoon with no fanfare and no media. The following November he was re-elected governor of Iowa. He did run for president but dropped out of the race early in the primary process. In 2009, Vilsack was appointed Secretary of Agriculture under the Obama administration.

Iowa had its chance to shine by actually leading the nation on the critical issue of immigration. Instead, this unfortunate chapter in Iowa's history showed how forward-looking, progressive thinking about immigration often gave way to popular anger in the heartland. It also reinforced stereotypes by urban, liberal metropolitan areas on the East and West Coast about Iowa being a "backwards" state. The irony is not lost, then, when Iowa became a lightning rod for immigration in the nation once again in 2008 through the now infamous Postville immigration raid, which came to represent for many why American immigration policy is in such dire need of reform.

Postville is a small town in the extreme northeast corner of Iowa, about 20 minutes drive to the Mississippi River. The town garnered national and international attention prior to 2008 because this otherwise stereotypical Midwestern town hosted a large number of Hasidic or Orthodox Jews among its population. With a few exceptions, these Jews lived in Postville because they worked at the local Agriprocessors meatpacking plant in town, which for many years was the largest kosher plant in the world. Documentary films, books and countless electronic and print media stories covered the town's unusual mix of people, including an article in National Geographic.

The town's largest non-white population was Latino, which was primarily Mexican up until 2000, and then by 2008 was heavily Guatemalan. It was an open secret in town that most were using fake documents and that many immigrants working in the kosher plant were employed illegally with social security numbers that they bought through black market venues. In a sense, everyone involved got what they wanted. Cattle ranchers from counties away had a local market for their livestock; Latinos and other immigrants had jobs that helped support their families back home; plant managers had a sufficient supply of cheap labor; local business owners had a healthy population of customers; property owners had plenty of people to pay rent; and consumers the world over were able to buy affordable Kosher meat products. The town's school system, tiny and shrinking even further in years past, even grew and bucked a rural Iowa trend by actually hiring more teachers.

Despite the odd controversy, which almost always seemed to garner outsized media attention because of the fascinating cultural juxtaposition between the local Iowan townspeople and the orthodox Jews, Postville provided a model for how multicultural populations could co-exist and even thrive in small, rural communities. Over the years, Postville had developed truly innovative diversity programs, including a local radio station in four languages, a community center downtown that celebrated everyone's ethnic heritage, a major multicultural food festival every year, model school curriculum to address the needs of non-English speaking children, a multicultural community diversity garden, and other unique initiatives.

But this bucolic charm was shattered on May 12, 2008 when federal agents raided the kosher meatpacking plant with nearly 700 warrants for immigrants that were working illegally. In the end, nearly 400 workers were arrested, almost all Guatemalan from several different Central American indigenous tribes. To date, it is the largest single-site immigration raid in United States history. The raid fit the classic military-style scenario for such an action: a helicopter flew over head, hundreds of law enforcement agents from state and federal agencies descended on the town, buses with Department of Homeland Security logo drove arrestees to holding centers, and dozens of well armed federal immigration agents led hundreds of immigrants out of the factory chained at their ankles and wrists (Grey, Devlin & Goldsmith, 2009).

Iowa had experienced large worksite immigration raids in the past, such as those in Marshalltown in 2006 and Storm Lake in 1996. In these previous cases, however, the end result for most immigrants arrested was deportation, mostly to Mexico. Unless they were wanted for other crimes, they were generally placed into deportation proceedings and sent home. The Postville raid was very different. Instead of placing the arrested immigrants in deportation proceedings, they were charged with felony crimes, talked into pleading guilty to these charges, and marched through a makeshift, temporary federal court on the county fair grounds of the National Cattle Congress in nearby Waterloo, Iowa. Unlike their predecessors who were sent home, the majority of immigrants arrested in Postville spent five months in prison and then were sent back to Guatemala.

When the raid took place, it was assumed by advocates that arrestees would be charged with violation of federal immigration law, as was the case with previous raids: i.e. entering the country "without inspection" by a border patrol agent, for which the penalty in first-time cases was deportation. Entering the country without inspection is a minor violation of administrative law and is not a felony. But immigration activists were surprised and deeply outraged when it became obvious that federal authorities never intended to file immigration charges. Instead, those arrested were offered a choice to plead guilty to one set of felony charges, go to jail for five months and then be deported, or go to trial on more serious charges and face potentially longer felony jail terms. The more serious charge was of "aggravated identity theft" which carried a mandatory minimum sentence of two years in prison. To avoid this charge, the defendants were offered the opportunity to plead guilty to the lesser charge of using a false social security number. However, this lesser charge usually only carries a discretionary prison sentence of zero to six months. Yet, the plea agreement offered to arrestees included an obligatory five-month prison term and deportation. Faced with the potential of being in prison for two years or more or signing the plea agreement and getting back with their families in five months, almost every defendant signed the agreement. All that was left for the judges to do was to repeat the terms of the agreement for the record. They had no discretion whatsoever.

Public defenders were brought in to defend arrestees at the last moment, but to their surprise were handed a playbook created ahead of time by the U.S. Attorney's office outlining the charges, the plea agreement offer, and how the court proceedings would take place. Among other unusual happenings, the public defenders and court interpreters found themselves working with ten defendants at a time, marched together like a chain-gang through a temporary court room set up on the Cattle Congress county fairgrounds in Waterloo.

Many of the public defenders and court appointed interpreters were outraged by the process. Dr. Erik Camayd-Freixas was one of the 26 federal court-certified Spanish interpreters flown to Waterloo to process detainees through the makeshift court. As a respected professor at Florida International University, he was dismayed at being part of these felony criminal proceedings against the immigrants and felt that the process was highly flawed in its violation of the civil and human rights of the detainees. Camayd wrote a June 13, 2008, essay entitled "Interpreting after the Largest ICE Raid in U.S. History: A Personal Account." His story was ultimately featured by the New York Times, and he was asked to testify before Congress.

Camayd described his three principal concerns about the Postville detainees' treatment. First, he argued that most of the immigrants were Guatemalan tribal people who were functionally illiterate in their own indigenous languages, let alone Spanish and English. Most were unaware that they needed Social Security numbers to work in the United States, and could certainly not even read the cards. Second, he felt that the legal proceedings were deeply flawed and provided no due process to the detainees. He was particularly concerned about the immigrants facing charges together in a group of ten, having almost no time to meet with their attorneys, and not having their individual cases investigated. Third, immigration lawyers were ultimately denied access to these nearly 400 clients because attorneys for ICE never intended to charge the detainees with immigration violations. In a rare twist, ICE and the federal court in the local area worked together before the event to set up the detainees. In the majority of immigration raids prior to Postville, detainees were generally charged with administrative immigration violations and deported. But in the Postville case, as noted, the majority of detainees were forced into a plea bargain agreement in which one way or another they were facing felony charges for identity theft of social security numbers. No matter which option they chose, they would be spending at least five months in a federal prison, if not longer.

In Camayd's essay, he noted, "By handing down the inflated charge of 'aggravated identity theft,' which carries a mandatory minimum sentence of two years in prison, the government forced the defendants into pleading guilty to the lesser charge and accepting five months in jail. Clearly, without the inflated charge, the government had no bargaining leverage, because the lesser charge by itself, using a false Social Security number, carries only a discretionary sentence of zero to six months. The judges would be free to impose sentence within those guidelines, depending on the circumstances of each case and any prior record. Virtually all the defendants would have received only probation and been immediately deported. In fact, the government's offer at the higher end of the guidelines (one month shy of the maximum sentence) was indeed no bargain. What is worse, the inflated charge, via the binding 11(C)(1)(c) Plea Agreement, reduced the judges to mere bureaucrats, pronouncing the same litany over and over for the record in order to legalize the proceedings, but having absolutely no discretion or decision-making power. As a citizen, I want our judges to administer justice, not a federal agency" (Camayd, 2008).

In a virtually unprecedented scenario, the court clearly knew in advance about the Postville raid, and worked with federal prosecutors to ensure that the immigrants would more than likely have to plea guilty to felonies. As such, critics felt that the court, rather than being an impartial deliberator, decided well in advance that the detainees were guilty and did not allow the immigrants to seek justice through a fair hearing. However, Attorney Peter Moyers, Clerk of the Court of the Northern District of Iowa during the raid, wrote in his own analysis of the situation, "The coercion involved flowed from the law itself.... The defendants understood their limited choices all too well: put the government to its proof and exercise one's rights, and risk at least two years imprisonment, or take the deal and spend no more than five months out of work." The attorneys Moyers interviewed "emphasized the importance of certainty for their clients, who were anxious about when they could return to their families ... the prospect of a minimum two-year prison term made the offer of five months exceedingly attractive" (Moyers, 2009).

In the annals of American immigration history, many that are familiar with the Postville raid have asked why the immigrant workers in the Kosher meatpacking plant were forced into the plea bargain in the first place and their actions were criminalized, when previous raids had just deported "illegals" as violators of misdemeanor administrative law. Fundamentally, according to a number of federal immigration officials and lawyers, Postville was a test case by the federal government to see if felony identity theft charges could be leveled on immigrants working illegally in the country. By charging these immigrants with felonies and forcing them to serve serious prison time rather than just face deportation, the government essentially hoped to make an example out of the Postville immigrants. Indeed, as one defense attorney Moyers interviewed told a client that the U.S. Attorney's Office "hoped that upon their return to their countries of origin, [they] would tell their stories and thereby discourage others from seeking unlawful entry and employment in the Northern District of Iowa" (Moyers, 2009).

Human rights advocates, social service workers, Hispanic politicians, public defenders, immigration attorneys, and many in church ministries ultimately objected loudly and strongly to the legal treatment of the Postville immigrants. They felt that the forced plea bargains and federal prison sentences raised concerns about civil rights, and gave the impression that the real issue was illegal immigration, not illegal employment. The legal protests against the Postville case even went as far as the United States Supreme Court, which ultimately ruled that charging such detainees with knowingly and willingly stealing identity cards to work was inappropriate for many immigrants, particularly those that were illiterate and could not understand the documents they bought illegally in the black market to work in the United States.

On top of the very serious legal objections to the Postville raid, the immigration offensive on the town had significant socioeconomic impacts that continue to be felt today. In the end, 25% of the town's population was ultimately arrested for illegal activity in the meatpacking plant, including its infamous owner, Shalom Rubashkin, who is now serving 27 years of federal prison time. After the raid and the legal charges against many of the workers and management members for a variety of fraudulent schemes, Agriprocessors ultimately went bankrupt. As it was the anchor company for the small town of Postville, many local stores went bankrupt too, particularly those that were owned by immigrants. Many local Iowan farmers that sold poultry or beef to the plant never got paid for their goods for many miles away in the supply chain. A significant percentage of houses in the town experienced foreclosure, as most immigrant renters fled the community or were arrested, and no one seemed to be left to pay mortgages. Even the banks that held the mortgages suffered financially, as did the city government itself that went into debt due to all the unpaid utility bills and lower tax revenues. And personal tensions in the town became very high after the raid, with friends and family members taking different sides of the immigration debate. Opinions about who to blame for the raid ran the gamut, and included the plant owners, ICE, the illegal workers, the consumers that wanted cheap kosher meat, and even the townspeople themselves that looked the other way while the plant operated for years primarily with immigrant workers (Grey, et al, 2009).

Interestingly, the federal government has not tried to "criminalize the presence" of immigrants in the manner it did in Postville since this highly controversial effort of 2008. In light of harsh criticism regarding the militaristic tactics of the raid, the lack of due process given to the detainees, and the Supreme Court's rejection of the use of felony charges for identity theft by illiterate immigrants, the United States government has retrenched and returned to many of its less controversial immigration enforcement practices prior to the Postville raid. For instance, only two months after the Postville raid, ICE conducted an even larger immigration raid in Mississippi. But this time, the federal court judge was not informed about the raid until the day it happened, and cooperated in full with the local public defenders. Almost all the Mississippi detainees were charged with misdemeanor violations of administrative law and deported as usual, just as other immigrants working in the United States had been for years. Militaristic-style, "hard" immigration raids like Postville have also not happened in the country since 2008, although the Obama administration has replaced them with "soft" or "silent" raids that involve surprise checks on companies and time to terminate employees working illegally, without destroying the economic vitality of a company and the community in which it resides. (Ironically, however, the liberal Obama administration has deported more immigrants through frequent low-publicity soft raids than the conservative Bush administration ever did with hard raids like Postville.)

The United States clearly requires significant immigration reform that aligns the new economic realities of globalization with an expanded international pool of laborers to keep up with growing consumer demand and worker shortages in aging countries. When all was said and done, the Postville raid was a very costly test case in the criminalization of presence. The Des Moines Register filed a Freedom of Information suit in order to determine the economic cost of the enforcement act. ICE reluctantly issued a press release, noting that it had spent $5.2 million of taxpayer funds on the Postville raid. This estimate did not even begin to include other related costs, such as those associated with the Cattle Congress trial by the Federal Court of Iowa's Northern District, court interpreters, public defenders, detainee imprisonment, and deportation costs. Detainee prison costs alone were estimated to be nearly $600,000 a month by mid-summer, and the Register noted that taxpayers were spending an average of $13,396 for each of the 389 illegal immigrants taken into custody and imprisoned with felonies in an effort to send an anti-immigration message to foreign nations in this country and in their home nations.

Small towns in rural Iowa today are struggling to serve the immense cultural, social, and linguistic needs of the thousands of legal refugees now pouring into the state as secondary migrants from remote nations. These refugees come from dozens and dozens of countries ranging from Somalia to Bhutan, and Burma to Ethiopia, and are contributing to a new phenomenon of microplurality in the state. These new legal refugee populations are being recruited heavily to work in meatpacking plants in the state as replacements for the illegal immigrants who were chased out of Iowa by the Postville raid. In a classic case depicting the law of unintended consequences and summarized by the statement "be careful what you wish for," many local Iowans are now whispering, "Life was so much easier when we had just one new group in town. We miss our illegal Mexicans!"

Discussion Questions

1. Based upon this chapter, what might be some useful policies to help undocumented meatpackers?
2. How do the dynamics of undocumented workers differ in states like Iowa from more traditional immigrant receiving states?
3. Discuss the social justice implications of this chapter.

References

Caymayd-Freixa, E. (2008). Interpreting after the Largest ICE Raid in U.S. History: A Personal Account. Monthly Review, 7 December.

Grey, M.A. (2006). State and Local Immigration Policy in Iowa. In G. Anrig ad T.A. Wang (Eds), Immigration's New Frontiers: Experiences from the Emerging Gateway States (pp. 33–66) New York: The Century Foundation Press.

Grey, M.A. and Woodrick, A. (2005). Latinos Have Revitalized our Community. In V. Zuniga and R. Hernandez-Leon (Eds.), New Destinations: Mexican Immigration in the United States (pp. 133–154). New York: Russell Sage Foundation.

Grey, M.A., Devlin, M. and Goldsmith, A. (2009). Postville USA: Surviving Diversity in Small-Town America. Boston: Gemma Media.

Moyers, P.R. (2009). Butchering Statutes: The Postville Raid and the Misinterpretation of Federal Criminal Law. Seattle University Law Review 32, 3 April.

Chapter Seventeen

Children of the Unauthorized: Domains of Compromise in Development

Carola Suárez-Orozco
Marcelo Suárez-Orozco
Dalal Katsiaficas
University of California, Los Angeles

Global migrations transform the structure, processes, and ethos of the family as "familyhood" is experienced by hundreds of millions of families across national borders (Foner, 2009; Suárez-Orozco & Suárez-Orozco, 2013). While most think of immigration as driven by labor, demographic, and economic factors, its enduring root is in the family. Immigration is, indeed most often, an ethical act motivated for the wellbeing of family. The bittersweet paradox of immigration is that, despite the centrality of the family in the making of migrant chains, the process often wrenches the family apart. The experience of transnational migrants can be characterized as a cycle of "separation and reunification of different members of the family unit over time" (Tyyskä, 2009). Typically, migrations take place in a "stepwise" fashion with one or two family member going ahead, later followed by others (Hondagneu-Sotelo & Avila, 1997). As migrant households gain a firmer foot in the country of immigration, new children are born. Complex-blended families arise incorporating settled migrants, new arrivals, and citizen children, as they are born in the new land (Suárez-Orozco & Suárez-Orozco, 2013). With the growth of unauthorized immigration over the last generation, and a concurrent growth in deportations of the unauthorized, families headed by unauthorized parents have been involuntarily torn apart by workplace as well as in-home raids. This leaves citizen children behind, sometimes in the care of relatives, sometimes in the care of foster homes, while sometimes citizen children are forced to relocate to a country they have never known (Capps, et al., 2007).

In recent years, "illegal immigration" has become the subject of increasing concern with negative media coverage (Massey, 2010), growing rates of hate crimes (Leadership Conference on Civil Rights Education Fund, 2009), and exclusionary political legislation (Carter, Lawrence, & Morse, 2011). Preoccupation with the issue has largely been about adults with little consideration of two groups of children and youth who contend with the wake of unauthorized status (Chavez et al., 2012). Approximately 1.5 million are children and emerging adults brought over without papers sometime during their childhoods. Then there are citizen children of unauthorized parents numbering an additional estimated 4.5 million (Passel, & Cohn, 2010). Their numbers have grown substantially in the past decade (Donato & Armenta, 2012). Millions more live in some sort of mixed-status home (Passel, 2006) where at least one member of the family is unauthorized (Fix & Zimmerman, 2001). These mixed-status households involve a range of documentation patterns: some siblings are born in the US with birthright citizenship, some are in the process of attempting to obtain documentation, and some lack any legal documentation (Fix & Zimmerman, 2001).

For children of unauthorized parents, the legal status of their parents creates a web of compromised contexts of development. Families with unauthorized parents often contend with extreme poverty, often limiting their access to resources necessary for healthy development of children (Barrera et al., 2002; Yoshikawa, 2011). In addition, many families, children, and youth exist in a state of "liminal legality" (Menjivar, 2006) with ambiguous documentation, waiting in the stagnant queues of a broken immigration system (Suárez-Orozco, Yoshikawa, Teranishi, & Suárez-Orozco, 2011). Living in the shadow of illegality, these families grapple with the ever-present threat of deportation of unauthorized family members (APA, 2012). The duress that such liminal status produces can significantly impact the family and, as children develop into young adults, create a sense of "perpetual outsiderhood" for many (Gonzales, Suárez-Orozco, & Dedios-Sangotti, under review).

Such conditions produce far from optimal developmental contexts for children of unauthorized parents, evidenced through an emerging body of literature demonstrating the links between unauthorized status and a series of negative developmental outcomes including educational access, psychological wellbeing, and transitions to the labor market (Gonzales et al., 2009; Suárez-Orozco et al., 2011; Yoshikawa, 2011). In this chapter we examine the various domains comprising the contexts of development for the children of the unauthorized. Furthermore we outline how each domain of compromise mediates various psychosocial outcomes, often creating a perfect storm of compromised contexts of development that can negatively affect the lives of the children of the unauthorized.

Compromised Access to Resources

Immigrants are disproportionately likely to live in poverty (US Census, 2007) and when compared to permanent residents or naturalized immigrants, the unauthorized tend to have the lowest socio-economic status of all groups (Padilla et al., 2006; Tienda & Mitchell, 2006). In fact, families with at least one parent who is unauthorized have an average income that is 40 percent lower than that of their legal immigrant and native-born counterparts (Passel, 2006). Furthermore unauthorized families are more likely to settle in segregated areas of dense poverty (Chavez, 1998, Zoliniski, 2006) and concentrated disadvantage.

Unauthorized status further compounds poverty, as parents' legal status creates a lack of access to and array of resources from public assistance and health benefits to such necessities of everyday life like valid social security numbers, driver's licenses, and bank accounts. Furthermore the poverty of the unauthorized creates its own strain of chronic job insecurity and low-wage work (Barrera et al., 2002) resulting in excessive anxiety and malaise. Many families face serious declines in their economic wellbeing as they endure economic hardships due to the apprehension of a parent in an ICE raid, including costly efforts to contest deportation, and job loss (with concurrent steep declines in income) as a result of workplace raids (Chaudry et al., 2010).

These economic hardships often give way to food and housing instabilities (Chaudry et al., 2010). Furthermore, unauthorized families may live in crowded conditions, as they often have to "double up" with relatives to afford the rent. In addition they are prone to frequent moving either by being asked to leave by landlords who fear ICE raids, continually moving to avoid such encounters with ICE officials, or by unauthorized family members voluntarily moving to protect their loved ones (Chaudry et al., 2010). The economic constraints of unauthorized status, particularly in the wake of a parent's detainment, create difficulties affording food, with rates of hunger for unauthorized families far above the national norms (Chaudry et al., 2010).

Citizen children of unauthorized parents are less likely to be enrolled in programs that help to foster their early learning, such as pre-school, or to have access to healthcare (Yoshikawa, 2011). Through an extensive study of a New York-based birth cohort, Yoshikawa (2011) identified important mechanisms related to these outcomes. At twenty-four months of age, parental legal status affected children's cognitive skills through parental economic constraints, compounded by the psychological distress of negative work conditions. Extended family and community networks are often disrupted during immigration posing a lack of social support to help with childcare, as well as a lack of access to information regarding public resources (Yoshikawa, 2011). At thirty-six months of age, difficult working conditions were associated with low enrollment in center-based child care (Yoshikawa, 2011).

Such compromised access in early life is further compounded when children begin to enter school. The unauthorized are at a disadvantage as far as school readiness when compared to children of the authorized (Crosnoe, 2007). Schools where many unauthorized families enroll their children are often characterized by higher dropout rates, inadequate postsecondary educational preparation, and lower rates of matriculation into college (Teranishi, Allen, & Solorzano, 2004). Thus, unauthorized status can have educational ramifications that can last a lifetime.

Lack of access to healthcare also poses formidable risks to optimal development. Currently, unauthorized parents and children are ineligible for government healthcare benefits (with the exception of perinatal and emergency room care). Research has revealed that unauthorized Latino immigrants in the US visit doctors less frequently than immigrants who have legal status (Berk, 2000; Ortega et al., 2007). Citizen children of unauthorized parents are eligible for such benefits, however their parents are often fearful of revealing their own legal status and thus avoid receiving such benefits for their children (Chavez et al., 2012). Caring for a sick child is already anxiety producing for parents, but unauthorized parents must also weigh the risks of forgoing healthcare benefits and protecting themselves from deportation (Chavez et al., 2012).

Given their parents' limited options in the labor market and inability to access public assistance, many youth take on additional financial responsibilities for their family. They may have access to job opportunities that their unauthorized family members do not (Fuligni & Pedersen, 2002; Gonzalez, 2011; Rumbaut & Komaie, 2010). For many, the limited access to such resources is further compounded by the burden of living in the shadow of illegality.

Living in the Shadow of Illegality

Unauthorized status often gives way to transnationally separated families. Many families find themselves not only living apart from their extended families, but also with parents and siblings, split between the U.S. and the country of origin (Suárez-Orozco, Bang, & Kim, 2011). Long backlogs, a byzantine bureaucracy, and high rates of denials are fomenting growing numbers of transnationally separated mixed-status families (Anderson, 2012; Suárez-Orozco, Bang, & Kim, 2011). Family separations come about for an array of reasons. A father may go ahead, with the plan to find a job and then send for his wife and children. A widowed mother may be forced to leave behind her children with her mother while earning enough to support them and save to send for them. Both parents may be paying off their passage fees and may recognize their U.S. citizen infant will get more consistent care from a grandmother in the country of origin than in an overcrowded day-care in an American city. For others the asylum application may take more than half a childhood to be approved. Facing long delays and the realization that they are missing their children's childhood, some parents make the difficult decision to bring their children to the United States without papers.

Unauthorized status has a pervasive impact on the quality and size of social support networks, not only through transnational separations, but also through alienating families, children, and youth from supporting relationships by fostering a constant fear of "being discovered" (Abrego, 2006; Gonzales, 2011; Gonzales, Suárez-Orozco, & Dedios-Sangotti, under review). Many unauthorized families report minimizing time in public space as well as intense feelings of isolation and hopelessness derived from concealment, self-censure, and hyper-awareness about others discovering "who they really are" (Gonzales et al., under review). Many youth note a difficulty to trust and count on their friends, in addition to having to conceal important details about their own lives which often leads to the severing of important networks of support (Gonzales et al., under review). Such self-censorship and lack of spontaneous authenticity may lead to social isolation.

As unauthorized youth begin to come of age, they bump up against a series of barriers that prohibit them from participating in normative coming of age rituals and prevent them from reaching markers of adulthood. Unable to get a driver's license, apply for financial aid for college, or get a job drastically reduces their future prospects as they transition into adulthood (See Suárez-Orozco et al., 2011 for detail) and contributes to a greater sense of social isolation from their peers (Gonzalez, et al., under review). As youth grow older and begin to encounter the social stigma of unauthorized status, feelings of social isolation surface and grow, as they are unable to participate in culturally proscribed rites of passage. Chronic stress has implications for identity development and has been linked to both externalizing and internalizing psychological symptoms (Gonzales, Suárez-Orozco, & Dedios-Sangotti, under review). Instead of emerging into adulthood like many of their peers, they often begin a process of hiding their legal status with feelings of shame and fear, into a liminal period of "(sub)merging adulthood" (Suárez-Orozco et al., 2011). An unauthorized teen, Grace, described the impact on her interpersonal life, "I just stopped going out. I was tired of asking for a ride and coming up with excuses ... It's such a hassle to explain everything to people. And it has affected the way I am when I meet new people. I used to be very outgoing, but I try to keep my guard up, try not to get too close to people" (Gonzales et al., under review). Identities thus become cockled in protective but ultimately isolating armor.

Even if the legal status of these children and youth is resolved with the passing of the DREAM Act (or similar measure) the negative developmental sequelae of years in the shadows will be felt. Furthermore, without comprehensive immigration reform, their parent's status will keep millions of youth in a labyrinth of compromised contexts.

The Ever-Present Threat of Deportation

Unauthorized parents, with or without citizen children, are at high risk of deportation (APA, 2012; Homeland Security, 2012). Heidi, for example, described in a Congressional Hearing her experience repeated in hundreds of thousands of families every year: "At only 10 years of age ... I woke up and found out that my mother had been arrested" (U.S. Congress, 2011) and soon thereafter deported. As a result, it fell upon her shoulders to care of her younger siblings including an infant. A year and a half after her heart-wrenching testimony, Heidi and her siblings have not seen their mother again. Under the current policy framework, the prospects of reunification are slim.

The daily lives of children of unauthorized parents, citizens and unauthorized children alike, reflect the ever-present threat and often realities of the separation/deportation of a loved one. From January to June in 2011, US Immigration and Customs enforcement removed 46,486 unauthorized parents who claimed to have at least on child who is an American citizen (US Department of Homeland Security, 2012). Multiple negative psychological outcomes have been linked to such forced separations (see Urban Institute Report, 2010). There is, for example, a high incidence of negative psychological consequences for children who have had a parent detained by ICE. Research shows an array of negative behavioral changes including changes in eating and sleeping patterns, frequent crying, being afraid, anxious, withdrawn, as well as patterns of clingy and or aggressive behavior (Chaudry et al., 2010). In one research study children aged 6-11 experienced the highest levels of behavioral change two to three months after the apprehension of a parent. Furthermore, negative physical and psychological outcomes persisted for children at nine months after their parental separation, especially for older children aged 6-17 years (Chaudry et al., 2010).

For children and youth in households with unauthorized family members, the legal status of those family members weighs heavily on their daily routines. The children of unauthorized parents report living in constant fear that their parents or other family members will vanish and never be seen again (Capps, Castaneda, Chaudry, & Santos, 2007). As Mateo explained to members of Congress in his testimony: "I am always worried when my family leaves the house that something might happen to them. I think about it when my dad goes to work that he might not come back or when I go to school that there might not be someone to pick me up when I get out" (U.S. Congress, 2010). The effects of these raids not only affect the individuals who have been detained and their families but resonate across the community as well (Juby & Kaplan, 2011).

In the face of such events, families must make difficult decisions about the fate of their children should the dreaded apprehension and deportation unfold. Often parents discuss contingency plans with their children in case they are detained or deported. A recent study of Latino families found that among unauthorized parents, more than half (58 percent) had a plan in place for their children's care in case they were detained, and 40 percent had discussed such plan with their children (Brabeck & Xu, 2010). As Chavez and colleagues (2012) found in their interviews with unauthorized parents, while many parents were unsure of their own futures, their main concern was providing their children with stability in their futures. Still for others, the threat of separation becomes a reality all too soon, as children suddenly find that a parent has disappeared. Families must make the difficult choice of whether their children should stay with a remaining relative in the US or go to the country of origin with the deported parent. For children raised in the US, the ancestral country is a foreign land. Many youth may have spent the majority, if not all, of their life in the US and have few if any memories of their parents' native country (Chavez et al., 2012).

For a mixed-status family, routine activities in the public sphere present a constant danger of confrontation with law enforcement and evokes fear of the possible separation of family members. Living in a culture of compromised contexts of development, where family members and other kin and kith have been detained or deported heightens insecurity, undermine a sense of belonging, and can erode basic trust in the institutions of society. If the child is a citizen, her sense of belonging to the nation is thus undermined as authorities actively seek to expel his or her parents, siblings, and other loved ones (Gonzales, et al., under review). Basic distrust suffuses from Immigration and Customs Enforcement, onto policy officers, school guards, and other authority figures and representatives of the State. Thus, even if these youth can come out of the shadows, the concerns over continued threats to the integrity of the family will feed a pervasive fear and mistrust of the authorities.

Liminal Status & Perpetual Outsider-Hood

Unauthorized status creates a sense of what scholars have termed "liminality" (Suárez-Orozco et al., 2011)—belonging neither to the society they left behind or the society they entered into. The duress of liminal status (Menjívar, 2006; Suárez-Orozco, et al. 2011) takes a heavy toll on the socio-emotional development of children of unauthorized parents. Previous research has demonstrated that stressed and depressed parents have compromised parenting abilities (Ashman et al., 2002). Concreted disadvantage places unauthorized parents at risk of stress and depression. Parental detention has well-documented negative consequences on children across a range of ages, including a high incidence of reported depressive, anxiety, and post-traumatic stress disorder (PTSD) symptoms (Chaudry, et al., 2010). Furthermore living in a community where family members or friends' parents have been detained or deported heightens insecurity while corroding the sense of social safety and belonging. If the child is herself unauthorized, belonging is elusive as she is unable to participate in the social rituals that define personhood. Although she may deeply long for belonging, it will remain a frustrated ambition. Identity formation, already a complicated task for immigrant youth (Fuligini, 2010; Suárez-Orozco, 2004), will be particularly frustrated in the face of hostile and disparaging social, political, and media representations (Suárez-Orozco, 2004), creating a continual state of "perpetual outsider-hood" (Suárez-Orozco, et al., 2011).

The myriad of stresses that the children of unauthorized immigrants are exposed to as a result of such liminal status is linked to complex symptomologies. Significant increases in stress levels during childhood and adolescence have far-reaching neurobiological and psychological implications including structural changes in stress and emotion reactive systems (Stortelder & Ploegmaker-Burg, 2010). For some it leads to externalizing and acting out behaviors such as substance abuse or engaging in sexual behaviors that are especially relevant and threatening during adolescence and emerging adulthood (Gonzales, et al., under review). For many others, however, the pattern is one of internalizing, or turning distress inward. Typical complaints include shame, anxiety, and chronic sadness, over or under eating, difficulties sleeping or a desire to never get out of bed (Gonzales, et al., under review). Particularly for this population, somatic complaints are common, including but not limited to high blood pressure, chronic headaches, toothaches, stomach aches, back aches, and the like (Bui, 2011; Gonzales et al., under review). Of deepest concern is the giving up of hope and the inability to project oneself into the future which has led to thoughts, gestures, or acts of suicide among some unauthorized youth (Gonzales et al., under review).

Resiliency & DREAMing for the Future

While these domains of compromise produce far from optimal developmental contexts not all children exhibit negative outcomes. Some youth are remarkably resilient in spite of the odds (Masten, 2001). The capacity to maintain hope is essential to mental health (Seligman, 1990). For children of unauthorized parents, without a sense of where and how they belong in society, maintaining a sense of hopefulness can be severely compromised. Those who are able to maintain strong friendships or have caring adults (teachers, counselors, mentors, therapists) with whom they can talk openly about their struggles, share their distress, and receive guidance, are more likely to remain engaged in school (Gonzales et al., under review). Youth that are able to share their identity with others in similar circumstances become less isolated. For example, self-identified "DREAMers"—unauthorized youth who would benefit from the passing of the Development, Relief, & Education for Alien Minors (DREAM Act) find purpose and solidarity among others who share their plight. Together they have come to form a civil rights movement and to engage with like-minded partners for a better future. Bella, a twenty-year-old DREAMer, explains:

> Like when I say I am a DREAMer, I mean I am undocumented, so I understand the struggles. I understand what it means to be frustrated.

> I understand why others like me are depressed, why it's so frustrating to feel like you want to do so much but you can't. You are so close but yet so far ... So I want to work with others like me to help us have an optimistic view ... I got involved and it has been helpful because it has helped me mature and grow as a person.

Participation in civic activities to affect change can serve as a catalyst out of "learned helplessness" (Peterson, Maier, & Seligman, 1993) into "learned hopefulness" (Zimmerman, 1990).

This kind of civic work can turn into a virtuous circle whereby by helping themselves and others, unauthorized youth find purpose and a role that serves to augment their own wellbeing. For these youth "coming out" unauthorized is a journey from the shadows to the light of the public sphere. This is a journey structured by what the Brazilian scholar Paulo Freire termed conscientização—roughly translated as "critical consciousness." The socially dispossessed, living in "a culture of silence," come to experience their condition as self-failing. Coming to see in the plight of others the plight of the self is a first step in developing critical consciousness. In his Pedagogy of the Oppressed (1970) Freire argued that when those who are socially dispossessed come to the insight that their own oppression is shared and take collective action they are able to move into a generative space not only for themselves but also for others. By coming together and sharing their predicament and seeing their frustrations and social anomie through the eyes of others, DREAMers gain a public voice and begin an unstoppable march towards dignity, self-authoring, and liberation. Their struggles embody, indeed perform, the very promise of citizenship.

Conclusion

For the growing number of children growing up in a household headed by an unauthorized parent, contending with a variety of compromised contexts of development is a way of life. While extant literature suggests that for some, these compromised contexts may take a heavy toll on socio-emotional development (Suárez-Orozco & Yoshikawa, in press), others demonstrate incredible resiliency despite these barriers. To date, little empirical research has been conducted on the psychosocial implications of unauthorized status, especially longitudinally as these young people develop over time. Future research is needed in this area to help inform clinical practice when working with this vulnerable population.

Discussion Questions

1. What compromised contexts of development, over and above poverty, affect the lives of children of unauthorized immigrant parents?
2. What are the similarities and differences in developmental challenges faced by unauthorized children, citizen children of unauthorized parents, and children growing up in mixed-status homes?
3. What considerations should be taken into account in clinical practice when working with these populations?

References

Abrego, L. J. (2006). I can't go to college because I don't have papers: Incorporation patterns of Latino unauthorized youth. Latino Studies, 4, 212–231.

Anderson, S. (2012). America's incoherent immigration system. Cato Journal, 32, 71–84.

APA Crossroads: The psychology of immigration in the new century—The Report of the Presidential Task Force on Immigration. (2012). Washington, DC: American Psychological Association.

Ashman, S. B., Dawson, G., Panagiotides, H., Yamada, E., & Wilkins, C. W. (2002). Stress hormone levels of children of depressed mothers. Development and Psychopathology, 14,(2), 333–349.

Brabeck, K., & Xu, Q. (2010). The impact of detention and deportation on Latino immigrant children and families: A quantitative exploration. Hispanic Journal of Behavioral Sciences, 32(3), 341–361.

Bui, H. N. (2011). Immigrant generational status and delinquency in adolescence: Segmented assimilation and racial-ethnic differences. In C. Garcia Coll & A. K. Marks, The Immigrant Paradox in Children and Adolescents: Is Becoming American a Developmental Risk? Washington, D.C.: APA.

Carter, A., Lawrence, M., & Morse, A. (2011).2011 Immigration-related laws, bills, and resolutions in the states: Jan. 1–March 31, 2011. Washington, DC: National Conference of State Legislatures. Retrieved from: http://www.ncsl.org/default.aspx?tabid=13114.

Capps, R., Castañeda, R. M., Chaudry, A., & Santos, R. (2007). Paying the price: The impact of immigration raids on America's children. Retrieved from http://www.urban.org/publications/411566.html.

Chaudry, A., Capps, R., Pedroza, J., Castañeda, R. M., Santos, R., & Scott, M. M. (2010). Facing our future: Children in the aftermath of immigration enforcement. Washington, DC: Urban Institute. Retrieved from http://www.urban.org/publications/412020.html.

Chavez, J.M., Lopez, A., Engelcrecht, C.M. & Viramontez Anguiano, R. P. (2012). Sufren los ninos: Exploring the impact of unauthorized immigration status on children's well-being. Family Court Review, 50 (4), 638–649.

Chavez, J. M., & Provine, D. M. (2009). Race and the response of state legislatures to unauthorized immigrants. The ANNALS of the American Academy of Political and Social Science, 623, 78–92.

Crosnoe, R. (2007). Early child care and the school readiness of children from Mexican immigrant families. International Migration Review, 41(1), 152–181.

Donato, K. M., & Armenta, A. (2011). What we know about unauthorized immigration. The Annual Review of Sociology, 37, 529–43. Doi: 10.1146/annurev-soc-081309-150216.

Fix, M., & Zimmerman, W. (2001). All under one roof: Mixed-status families in an era of reform. International Migration Review, 35(2), 397–419.

Foner, N. (2009). "Introduction: Intergenerational relations in immigrant families," in Across generations: Immigrant families in America. (Ed.) Foner, N. New York: New York University Press, 1–20.

Freire, P. (1970). Pedagogy of the oppressed. New York: Continuum.

Fuligni, A. J. (2010). Social identity, motivation, and well-being among adolescents from Asian and Latin American backgrounds. In G. Carlo, N. J. Crockett, & M. A. Carranza (Eds), Health disparities in youth and families: Research and applications. Nebraska Symposium on Motivation, Vol. 57 (pp. 97–120. New York: Springer Science.

Gonzales, R. G. (2009). Young lives on hold: The college dream of unauthorized students. Washington, DC: College Board. Retrieved from http://professionals.collegeboard.com/profdownload/young-lives-on-hold-college-board.pdf.

Gonzales, R. G. (2011). Learning to be illegal: Unauthorized youth and shifting legal context in the transition to adulthood. American Sociological Review, 76 , 602–619.

Gonzales, R., Suárez-Orozco, C., & Dedios-Sangotti, M.C., (under review). No place to belong: Contextualizing concepts of mental health among unauthorized immigrant youth in the United States. To appear in American Behavioral Scientist.

Homeland Security (2012). Deportation of parents of U.S. born citizen children: Fiscal year 2011 report to the U.S. Congress Semi annual report. Retrieved from: http://www.lirs.org/wp-content/uploads/2012/07/ICE-DEPORT-OF-PARENTS-OF-US-CIT-FY-2011.pdf.

Hondagneu-Sotelo,P. & Avila, E. (1997). "'I'm here, but I'm there: The meanings of Latina transnational motherhood," Gender and Society 11 (5), 548–571.

Juby, C., & Kaplan, L. E. (2011). Potsville: The effects of an immigration raid. Families in Society: The Journal of Contemporary Social Services, 92(2), 147–153.

Leadership Conference on Civil Rights Education Fund (2009). Confronting the new faces of hate: Hate crimes in America—2009. Washington, DC: Author. Retrieved from http://www.civilrights.org/publications/hate-crimes/lccref_hate_crimes_report.pdf.

Massey, D. S. (2010). New faces in new places: The changing geography of American immigration. New York, NY: Russell Sage Foundation.

Masten, M. S. (2001). Ordinary magic: resilience processes in development. American Psychologist, 56(3) 227–238.

Menjívar, C. (2006). Liminal legality: Salvadoran and Guatemalan immigrants' lives in the United States. American Journal of Sociology, 111, 999–1037.

Ortega, A.N., Horwitz, S. M., Fang, H., Perez, V. H., Kuo, A. A., Wallace, S. P., & Inkelas, M. (2009). Documentation status and parental converns about development in young US children of Mexican origin. Academic Pediatrics, 9 (4), 278–282.

Padilla, Y.C., Radey, M. D., Hummer, R. A., Kim, E. (2006). The living conditions of US born children of Mexican immigrants in unmarried families. Journal of Hispanic Behavioral Sciences, 28(3), 331–349.

Passel, J. S. (2006).The size and characteristics of the unauthorized migrant population in the U.S: Estimates based on the March 2005 current population survey. Washington, DC: Pew Hispanic Center. Retrieved from http://pewhispanic.org/files/reports/61.pdf.

Passel, J. S., & Cohn, D. (2010). Unauthorized immigrant population: National and state trends. Washington, DC: Pew Hispanic Center. Retrieved from http://pewhispanic.org/reports/report.php?ReportID=133.

Peterson, C., Maier, S. F., & Seligman, M. E. P. (1993). Learned helplessness: a theory for the age of personal control Oxford University Press. New York, 60–97.

Rumbaut, R., & Komaie, G. (2010). Immigration and adult transitions. The Future of Children, 20(1), 43–66.

Stortelder, F., Ploegmakers-Burg, M. (2010). Adolescence and the reorganization of infant development: A neuro-psychoanalytic model. Journal of American Academy of Psychoanalysis, 38:503–531.

Suárez-Orozco, C. (2004). Formulating identity in a globalized world. In M. Suárez-Orozco & D. B. Qin-Hilliard (Eds.), Globalization: Culture and education in the new millennium (pp. 173–202). Berkley: University of California Press.

Suárez-Orozco, C., Bang, H. J., & Kim, H.Y. (2011). "I felt like my heart was staying behind": Psychological implications of immigrant family separations and reunifications. Journal of Adolescent Research, 26(1), 22–257.

Suárez-Orozco, C. Yoshikawa, H. Teranishi, T. & Suárez-Orozco. M. (2011). Living in the Shadows: The developmental implications of unauthorized status. Harvard Education Review, special issue on immigrant students in education, 81(3) 438–472.

Suárez-Orozco, C. Yoshikawa, H. (in press). Children growing up in unauthorized families: developmental challenges. New Directions for Child Development.

Suárez-Orozco, C. & Suárez-Orozco. M. (2013). Transnationalism of the heart: Familyhood across borders. In What is parenthood?: Competing models for understanding today's revolution in parenthood. Cere, D. & McClain, L. (Eds.). New York: New York University Press.

Teranishi, R. T., Allen, W. R., & Solorzano, D. G. (2004). Opportunities at the crossroads: Racial inequality, school segregation, and higher education in California. Teachers College Record, 106(11), 2224–2245.

Tienda, M. & Mitchell, F. (2006). Hispanics and the future of America. Washington D.C.: National Academy Press.

Tyyskä, V. (2007)."Immigrant families in sociology." In Immigrant families in contemporary society, (Eds). Lansford, J.E., Deater-Deckard, K. & Bornstein, M.H. New York: Guilford Press, 91.

U.S. Congress. (2010, July 15). In the best interest of our children: Examining our immigration enforcement policy (Ad-hoc hearing). U.S. House of Representatives, Washington, DC. Retrieved from http://www.apa.org/about/gr/issues/cyf/immigration- enforcement.aspx.

U.S. Census. (2007). Selected characteristics of the native and foreign-born populations. American Community Survey. Retrieved from http://factfinder.census.gov/servlet/STTable?_bm=y&-geo_id=01000US&-qr_name=ACS_2007_1YR_G00_S0501&-ds_name=ACS_2007_1YR_G00_&-_lang=en&-redoLog=false.

Wagmiller, R. L., Lennon, M. C., Kuang, L., Alberti, P. M., &Aber, L. (2006). The dynamics of economic disadvantage and children's life chances. American Sociological Review, 71(5), 847–866.

Yoshikawa, H. (2011). Immigrants raising citizens: Unauthorized parents and their young children. New York: Russell Sage.

Zimmerman, M. A. (1990). Toward a theory of learned hopefulness: A structural model analysis of participation and empowerment. Journal of Research in Personality, 24(1), 71–86.

Chapter Eighteen

No Somos Vagabundos ("We Are Not Loiterers"): The Impact of Anti-Immigrant Policies on the Lives of Latino Day Laborers in the United States

Nalini Negi & Neely Mahapatra

Day labor work is growing nationally and predominantly consists of Latino men who solicit work on busy street corners and storefronts. Latino day laborers (LDLs) work in the informal economy in jobs that are often too dirty, too dangerous, and too poorly paid for local workers (Walter, Bourgois, Loinaz, & Schillinger, 2002). Day labor work is difficult and includes significant abuse of worker rights, routine denial of payment for work, dangerous work conditions, employer abuse, as well as poorly paid and inconsistent employment opportunities (Quesada, 1999). The dangerous conditions of day labor work often expose LDLs to work injury at higher rates than those working in more regulated conditions yet LDLs have limited access to medical care (Walter et al., 2002).

Undocumented immigration status heighten the challenging circumstances of LDLs' daily lives as they often experience being "treated as a reserve of flexible labor, outside the protection of labor safety, health, and minimum wage and other standards, and are easily deportable" (Taran, 2000, p. 7). In the face of scarce information, community members and law enforcement often develop misperceptions about LDLs as troublemakers, criminals, and loiterers (Quesada, 1999; Turnovsky, 2006). LDLs also have to contend with policies that often criminalize their ability to procure work. In light of these negative misperceptions and policies, social workers and other service providers may find it difficult to advocate for LDLs and implement effective programs for them. This chapter focuses on presenting LDLs as a special population of interest for those working in social services. Next, it provides information on how policies have contributed to the criminalization of this population with severe and adverse consequences on this population's well-being as well as their marginalization. A vignette will be provided with discussion on how social service providers and advocates can better advocate for the improved work and life conditions of LDLs as well as discussion regarding the use of human rights to leverage the well-being of this population.

Literature Review

Day Laborers in the United States

A formal definition of day labor does not exist despite the significant growth of day labor (Valenzuela, 2003). In fact, neither the U.S. Census Bureau nor the Department of Labor includes day labor in its official classifications of work. However, the first and only national study of day laborers, conducted by Valenzuela, Theodore, Melendez, and Gonzalez (2006), has contributed significantly to understanding the characteristics of this population. These researchers randomly selected 2,660 day laborers from 264 hiring sties in 139 municipalities in 20 states and the District of Columbia to reveal the first comprehensive portrait of day laborers in the United States. Below we provide a summary of Valenzuela et al.'s (2006) study, as it is the only national study to date of day laborers, to offer a contextual understanding of day labor corners, this population's demographic characteristics, and the challenging work conditions of day labor work.

Valenzuela (2003) classifies day labor industries into two categories: informal and formal. Informal day labor is characterized by the congregation of men (and in some exceptional cases, women) who gather in open spaces or visible markets such as empty lots, street corners, parking lots, store fronts, or other public spaces to solicit temporary daily work. Formal day labor is generally organized by for-profit temp agencies or enclosed "hiring halls." Although both informal and formal day labor industries share similar characteristics such as unstable employment opportunities, worker abuse, and dangerous work, formal day labor sites tend to include a more ethnically/racially diverse work force that includes American born workers. Formal day labor sites also differ from informal day labor sites through the enforcement of structure and rules regarding employment seeking. In sharp contrast, informal day labor sites operate in a more unstructured fashion with no explicit rules regulating workers' participation.

Valenzuela et al. (2006) found that approximately 117, 600 workers nationally are looking for day labor work or working as a day laborer on any given day. Day laborers are predominately male and Latino immigrants, mainly from Mexico and Central America. Over half (59%) were born in Mexico, 14% in Guatemala, and 8% in Honduras, with a small percentage born in the U.S.A (7%). Most (three-quarters) of the day labor force is undocumented. Every morning, Monday through Sunday, workers gather at the hundreds of day labor markets found nationally and solicit work. These day labor markets are generally open air spaces where workers and employers meet to negotiate employment that often includes construction, landscaping, painting, cleaning, and moving, among other tasks. Employers are usually residential construction contractors, homeowners, or sub-contractors. These day labor sites form at strategic parts of the city such as near home improvement stores, parks, and other public spaces. The numbers of workers who gather at each site daily vary considerably from over 200 workers at some sites to a handful at others.

Employment contracts at informal day labor corners are usually made verbally and are often unsecured and open-ended. As a result, day laborers are highly dependent on the conditions the contractor creates. According to Valenzuela et al. (2006), 70% of day laborers search for work five or more days a week, while only nine percent seek work one or two days a week. The median hourly wage of day labor assignments is $10, with the low end range at $5.15–$9.99 an hour; and the upper end range being between $10–$12 an hour. While a majority of day labor work pays $10 an hour, the monthly and yearly earning of day laborers are comparable to the working poor as employment and wages are often inconsistent, work days are lost due to work-related injury, and employers often do not pay workers the wages they earn. In fact, Valenzuela et al. found that in good months (months where employment and worker demand is high), day laborers' median income is $1400, while in bad months (months where employment and worker demand is low), their median income is only $500 per month. They conclude that even if workers had more good months than bad, the annual earning of most workers is not likely to exceed $15,000 a year. Most day laborers are then living under the federal poverty threshold as work is seasonal and highly contingent on the weather and the local economy (Valenzuela, 2000).

Furthermore, day laborers are generally employed to do the most dangerous jobs in situations where health and safety codes are not often enforced and have high incidence of workplace injury. Day laborers are often exposed to chemicals and toxic emissions and faulty equipment as well as lack of safety training but may feel unable to complain out of fear of being fired or not being paid for their work (Buchanan, Nichols & Morello, 2005). Despite such high rates of work-related injury, Valenzuela et al. (2006) found that more than half of injured day laborers do not receive medical treatment for their injuries. The underutilization of medical services can be attributed to the fact that most workers' have no medical insurance, cannot afford the high cost of medical care and employers may generally refuse to pay for their workers' medical treatment. Walter et al.'s (2002) ethnographic study of San Francisco's LDLs reveals that many indigenous workers who had never received medical care from a physician before were the most apprehensive about receiving medical services in the United States. A majority of the workers also expressed anxiety about their immigration status, i.e., that seeking medical care may make them vulnerable to incarceration or deportation. Walter et al. further found that LDLs often did not want to seek medical treatment as they did not want to lose potential earnings that may be lost by a hospital stay. Additional barriers to healthcare included lack of information regarding medical services and language barriers.

The nature of day labor work and their undocumented status makes day laborers highly vulnerable to employer violations of worker rights. According to Valenzuela et al. (2006), wage theft or unpaid earned wages is the most common abuse day laborers experience. They found that nearly half (49%) of all day laborers surveyed nationally reported having been denied payment by an employer for work rendered and completed. Valenzuela et al. further revealed an almost complete lack of any labor standards applied to day laborers. Their study revealed that out of 2,660 day laborers, 44% of workers were denied food and water breaks; 32% worked overtime without overtime pay; 28% were threatened by their employer with physical or verbal abuse; and 27% of workers were abandoned at the work-site without the means to get back to their home. Most disturbingly, 18% of day laborers reported having been violently victimized by an employer.

Anti-Solicitation Policies and LDLs

LDLs vulnerability is exacerbated by the often hostile treatment they receive by local and state governments, and law enforcements including federal immigration officials, anti-immigrant activists, and citizens (Campbell, 2010). In fact, there has been a move by cities to attempt to criminalize LDLs' ability to procure work, the very reason that many LDLs migrate to the United States, through anti-solicitation policies. Such policies are aimed to cause "attrition through enforcement" (Immigration Policy Center: American Immigration Council-Special Report, 2012). That is, the systematic creation of conditions so unwelcoming for immigrants in the state that it not only discourages new immigrants from entering the state but it would also force those who are already there to leave voluntarily or "self deport" (Immigration Policy Center: American Immigration Council-Special Report). While it is unclear how many immigrants "self-deport," it is evident that restriction on LDL's right to work has a significant impact on their economic well-being as well as the families they support. Furthermore, such policies, perceived to be discriminatory by LDLs, have a significant impact on the mental health of this population as they report feelings of desesperación or despair (Negi, 2012). Studies further indicate that LDLs may self-isolate themselves from mainstream social institutions or recreational places as they experience a fear of "being caught as illegal" (Negi, 2011). The implications of the rise of such anti-immigrant policies then extend to the psychosocial well-being of this population.

Advocates have fought against anti-solicitation ordinances by disputing the constitutionality of such policies. Specifically, advocates have utilized the First Amendment, that is, all persons have the right to speech, to argue that "persons" includes undocumented immigrants therefore they are entitled to constitutional protections contained in the Bill of Rights once they are physically present within the borders of United States (Campbell, 2010). Furthermore, advocates contend that solicitation speech is protected by the First Amendment and should be subject to reasonable time, place, and manner restrictions by the government.

Thereby, the constitutionality of anti-solicitation ordinances has been mainly discussed on grounds that these governmental restrictions, "must be content-neutral, narrowly tailored to serve a significant governmental interest, and must leave ample alternative channels for communication" (Campbell, 2010, p. 1). Much of the debate about the legality of anti-solicitation ordinances has been around the free speech right to work, and whether or not anti-solicitation ordinances are content-based, content-neutral, or commercial speech (Feere,

2007). Content-based speech is subjected to strict scrutiny while content-neutral is subjected to lesser scrutiny. In most cases, the federal courts have held that anti-solicitation ordinances be thoroughly analyzed as content-neutral restrictions on speech. The courts then have the responsibility to determine whether the restriction of solicitation speech is not in fact undue restriction by the government and therefore an attempt to suppress a particular message or restrictions on a particular group of people from speaking which would be content-based restriction on speech and therefore unconstitutional.

Most recently, a provision of Arizona's controversial immigration law, "Support Our Law Enforcement and Safe Neighborhoods Act," or, as it is commonly known, Senate Bill 1070 that addresses the hiring of illegal day laborers was ruled as unconstitutional as it was found to infringe on First Amendment rights. The State attorneys argued that it was important to have the law in place in order to guarantee that traffic at day labor corners (often in public streets or storefronts) was not blocked but the Defense successfully argued that the unconstitutionality of this law as it targeted only day laborers instead of making it illegal for anyone to block traffic (American Civil Liberties Union, 2013).

Earlier, the U.S. Supreme Court had upheld a key section of the bill, but struck down three other sections. The justices decided by a 5-3 margin that the Section 2(B) of SB 1070, which requires state and local law enforcement agencies (LEAs) to check the immigration status of anyone they encounter during a lawful stop or arrest on the basis of "reasonable suspicion" if they are lacking valid immigration status or are in the country illegally, was upheld as it does not conflict with federal law. Nevertheless, Section 3, which would make it a state crime for undocumented immigrants not to carry an alien registration document, was struck down as it is preempted by federal laws. Section 5(C), which would have made it a state crime for undocumented immigrants to apply for work, solicit work in a public place, or work within Arizona was also not upheld. Lastly, Section 6, which would have authorized state and local police to arrest immigrants without a warrant where there is "probable cause" that the person committed an offense that would make them deportable was also struck down as it is preempted by federal laws (Mershon, 2012). However, the law allows for disparate sentencing for example, day laborers and other undocumented immigrants can receive up to six months in jail while others, for the same violation, can receive a comparatively reduced sentence of up to 30 days maximum for a traffic violation (Fischer, 2012).

This is only one of many efforts to pass anti-solicitation ordinances to regulate day laborers lives. For the most part, such efforts by local and state governments have been struck down by federal courts and therefore have upheld day laborers' right to seek employment in public day labor corners. These types of ordinances have varied in their strictness and severity. Some other important court cases include the case of the American Civil Liberties Union (ACLU) of Nevada v. City of Las Vegas (9th Cir. 2006). In this case, the Ninth Circuit Court of Appeals struck down the city's anti-solicitation ordinance as unconstitutional and content-based restriction of protected speech under the First Amendment of United States Constitution. The court believed that the ordinance was content-based, i.e. targeted towards one group, because it prohibited distribution of handbills that contained financial requests while permitted other types of bills (citation). Other cities that tried to pass anti-solicitation ordinances such as Cave Creek in the case of Lopez v. Town of Cave Creek (D. Ariz. 2008) and Seattle in the case of Berger v. City of Seattle (9th Cir. 2009) also met with similar fates and were declared unconstitutional. These cities singled out a particular group of people (day laborers) and were attempting to prohibit the solicitation speech of day laborers while allowing for other kinds of solicitation speech. In other cases such as the Coalition for Human Immigrant Rights of Los Angeles (CHIRLA) v. Burke (C.D. Cal. Sept. 12, 2000) the court struck down an anti-solicitation ordinance in Los Angeles County by finding it unconstitutional and in violation of First and Fourteenth Amendments.

In spite of these victories, there are other cities that have been able to successfully pass policies that restrict day laborers' ability to seek employment. Specifically, anti-solicitation ordinances have passed in cities where the courts have ruled that the content of the ordinance was neutral or did not target one group unfairly. For example, in the case of ACORN vs. City of Phoenix (9th Cir. 1986), the court held that the ant-solicitation ordinance was content neutral and did not single out a particular group or content of the speech and therefore supported the city in regulating traffic and prohibiting what the city considered as harassment of occupants of vehicles, including day laborers' solicitation of work. In case of Xiloj-Itzep v. City of Agoura Hills (Cal. Ct. App. 1994), the court decision was similar as it held the anti-solicitation ordinance to be content-neutral because it specifically prohibited vehicle addressed solicitation and was not concerned with the actual message or speech of the solicitor. Therefore, cities that have been successful in passing ordinances have largely done so by establishing a civil traffic offence whereas the real motivation may have been to deter illegal immigrants.

Such anti-solicitation ordinances place a heavy toll on day laborers as it not only restricts their ability to procure work by criminalizing the action of seeking work but it also has a deeper impact on their social vulnerability. LDLs who live in a context where perceived punitive and discriminatory policies are being implemented or even being discussed may develop further distrust or fear of local authorities. This is particularly compelling as research indicates that while the criminal victimization of Latino immigrants in the U.S is on the rise; it remains underreported to authorities (Martinez, Lee, & Nielsen, 2004). This underreporting of crime can be attributed to LDLs' perceived threat of deportation as well as their general distrust in U.S. authorities (Bucher, Manasse, & Tarasawa, 2010). As a result, many street level criminals often target LDLs, with some even referring to them as "Walking ATMs" due to the perception that this population is an easy target for crime as they are not likely to report victimization (Negi, Cepeda, and Valdez, in press). The creation of such marked disenfranchisement has broader societal implications that call for the need for social justice initiatives.

The intent of Arizona SB 1070, for example, has been to close all options for immigrant day laborers or workers to work and thus drive them to more vulnerable situations and exposing them to further exploitation and abuse. Since Arizona SB1070 passed, 36 other states have tried to pass similar tougher immigration control laws. Except for five states (including, Utah, Indiana, South Carolina, Georgia, and Alabama) that have passed laws similar to Arizona, 31 states have rejected or declined to advance their bills (Immigration Policy Center: American Immigration Council-Special Report, 2012). Many of these have a provision that makes it a state crime for unauthorized immigrants to solicit work or to hire unauthorized day laborers. The truth of the matter is that we may be seeing more states attempting to pass similar bills in future. While it is encouraging that many states and cities have been unable to pass restrictive policies that may have a disproportionate negative impact on day laborers and other undocumented immigrants, there is evidence that fear pervades immigrant communities during times in which restrictive immigration policies are being enacted or even being discussed (Hagan et al. 2003). This fear has an impact on even those who are legal immigrants as they become fearful of deportation or harassment by police and other authorities which leads them to avoid social activities (Aborna et al. 2010). The impact of restrictive ordinances has then an impact on LDLs' economic but also psychological well-being. We illustrate how a city's attempt to pass an ordinance that criminalizes the procurement of work by day laborers from the vantage point of those who will be the most affected, the day laborer themselves. This vignette is based off field work of day labor corners from 2007–2008 and is comprised of an amalgamation of participants rather than one person's account.

Vignette: The Case of a LDL in a Large City in the Southwest

Beto crossed the border from Mexico into Texas when he was 25 years old. He was married and had two daughters. One was five years old and the other was nearly three years old. He tried to make ends meet in the small village in Mexico that his family lived in but, unable to find a job in months, he decided to take his chances and cross the border. He left his family behind and promised them that he would send them money every fortnight and call them every day. He told his wife not to worry and his daughters not to miss him too much. Beto was fortunate to be able to cross the border successfully without being caught and without being killed by the extremely dangerous conditions of the route into the United States. Once in Texas, Beto headed towards a large city in the state where his cousin Alfonso waited for him. Alfonso had been living in this large city for four years and happily showed Beto around and introduced him to his friends. He also explained to Beto that their lives might become more difficult soon as he had heard rumors that the city was going to make looking for work illegal. When Alfonso took Beto to the day labor corner, he saw signs posted on walls around where other workers stood, "No Loitering" and he wondered what that meant since they were all actively looking for work. As the months passed, Alfonso's suspicions seemed to be realized as security began to patrol the corner and asked day laborers to move if they were too close to the Home Depot or Walgreens by the corner. Beto now became concerned. He did not want to get deported. What would he do? He needed to continue to send money to his family or how would his daughters continue at their school? The other workers at the corner were similarly worried and began to hear rumors that Immigration and Customs Enforcement (ICE) may start making surprise sweeps of the day labor corner. One man that Beto met even claimed that he had seen a sweep of the corner and that 10 or 12 people had been picked up. Every time Beto saw one of the security officials he wondered if they were ICE and if he should run. His level of stress increased. But when he spoke to his wife, he did not tell her any of this. He did not want her to worry or burden her with concern for him. He could handle it, he thought, and as long as he could keep on sending money, he would. One day he was picked up for a roofing job that involved 20 hours of work. After the job, Beto and a couple of other workers, approached the patrón (employer) for their wages but to his surprise the patrón said that their work was shoddy and refused to pay him. This demoralized Beto and he did not go back to the day labor corner to look for work for three days. He just lay in his bed and watched TV. He did not call his wife or daughter for over a week and when they called him to check in on him, he avoided their call too. He was stressed out and worried and now he was hearing that people were beginning to receive tickets for loitering or trespassing, he wasn't sure which, and he wasn't even sure for what amount. He just kept on hearing this from the guys at the corner. He was angry at the patrón and couldn't believe that his wages were stolen this way. He felt stuck and taken advantage of but never even considered calling the police as he was afraid that they wouldn't believe him as he was an illegal.

Discussion

The case of Beto represents many other day laborers who are caught in the similar quandary of having to navigate facts versus rumor when it comes to immigration enforcement. In the above case, the proposed anti-solicitation ordinance was eventually withdrawn. However, the accompanying anti-immigrant sentiment by community members and the ramped up security present at day labor sites created uncertainty and insecurity for many day laborers. Without a relationship of trust with police and other officials, many day laborers continued to feel criminalized despite the fact that no current law was criminalizing their solicitation of work. Therefore, it is important to consider that even in the absence of punitive anti-immigrant policies at the local level, without federal immigration reform, day laborers as well as other undocumented immigrants may continue to experience deportation fear which has an impact on their well-being.

Quesada's (1999) ethnographic study of LDLs in San Francisco explains that the day labor corner place LDLs into a homogenous stigmatized social category of "illegal aliens"—which often renders them vulnerable to scapegoating, repression, and exploitation by employers. Being segmented into marginal and unskilled jobs opens them up to employer abuse, lack of labor mobility, and lack of job security (Taran, 2000). Effective policy development is crucial as day labor continues to grow on a national level. It is clear that the unregulated nature of day labor work places its majority Latino immigrant workforce under considerable risk for workplace injury and workers' rights abuses. The violation of labor standards prevalent in day labor is especially compelling as many day laborers are undocumented workers who have immigrated to the United States to find work to support themselves and their family. On the margins of society, workers are often unaware of their rights or too fearful to complain to authorities about the workers' rights abuses that they face. Subsequently, many crimes against day laborers remain unreported. Significant outreach to workers is needed to inform day laborers of their rights as workers and the resources available to prevent their further victimization. Outreach is especially important as a national study of day laborers reports that approximately 70% of them do not know where to report workers' rights abuses (Valenzuela et al., 2006).

Social Service Implications

Policy plays a significant role in shaping the agenda and funding human service organizations. In the case of day laborers, immigration policies, in particular, significantly impact services. Recent anti-immigrant policies have severely impacted social service agency's abilities to provide services to day laborers as monies available for services to undocumented people are often sparse, mired in controversy, or outlawed. For example, Proposition 200, a proposed Arizona immigration law if implemented would require human service providers employed in the public sector to deny services to their undocumented clients. Many such similar policies are being implemented nationally. Consequently, the few organizations or agencies that are providing services and outreach to day laborers are often operating on shoestring budgets with minimal staff. In fact, a study of day laborers in New York found that only 10% of day laborers turned to community organizations to address workplace concerns or potential action against an abusive employer (Valenzuela et al., 2006).

Many cities have dealt with this uneasy tension between their city's need for labor and the community's opposition to day laborer corners through worker centers. Nationally, there are approximately 63 day labor centers in 17 states (Valenzuela et al., 2006). Both day labor scholars and activists seem to largely agree that worker centers are the most comprehensive and effective response to address both workers' rights and the community's concerns regarding day labor. Social service providers are uniquely equipped to utilize a strengths and client driven perspective. To this end, social service providers can be instrumental in the assessment of this community's needs and the implementation of a day labor center that is participatory and conducive to the psychosocial well-being of this population. This will necessitate bringing all community stakeholders including day laborers, day labor activists, various organizations and agencies involved with day laborers, residents or community representatives, businesses, state representatives, and governmental agencies to one table to initiate discourse (Pritchard, 2008). Community alliances between stakeholders, for example, government organizations (i.e. Department of Labor or State Labor offices) and community advocacy groups for day laborers or agencies could work toward crafting and implementing regulations that not only protect day laborer's rights to fair wage and health and safety conditions, but also support exemplary legislation that fulfills the needs of this vulnerable population.

Human Rights Implications

The rise of anti-solicitation policies and backlash against day laborers from community members is also a major issue that policymakers should address. Social service providers and other advocates who work with LDLs must be aware that their right to seek employment can be embedded within the larger discourse of human rights. In fact, there are specific acts that protect the rights of day laborers without regard to their documentation status. The United States Department of Labor (USDOL) implements the Fair Labor Standards Act (FLSA). The FLSA requires employers to pay covered employees a minimum wage and time and a half an employee's regular rate of pay for overtime hours (United States Department of Labor: Wage and Hour Division, 2008a). The Migrant and Seasonal Agricultural Worker Protection Act (MSPA) is yet another act under the U.S. Department of Labor that protects migrant and seasonal agricultural workers by requiring employers and farm labor contractors to pay the wages owed to migrant or seasonal agricultural workers and create other employment standards reacted to housing, transportation, and disclosures and record-keeping (United States Department of Labor: Wage and Hour Division, 2008b).

Furthermore, according to the Article 23 of the Universal Declaration of Human Rights, every individual has right to secure employment, has the right to equal pay for equal work without facing any discrimination, ensure a dignified existence for himself and his family through just remuneration, and a prospect for progress in the society. Similarly, the United Nations International Convention on the Protection of the Rights of All Migrant Workers and Members of Their Families adopted in 1990 but not ratified by United States enforces "a series of obligations on governments to promote 'sound, equitable, humane and lawful conditions' for the international migration of workers and members of their families" (United Nations, 2013).

These fundamental human rights are applied to all migrant workers, both documented and undocumented. The convention further ensures that the migrant workers and their family members are entitled to equal treatment in all areas such as employment, legal and social. Article 7 of the convention advises "governments/states to respect and to ensure to all migrant workers and members of their families within their territory the rights provided for in the present convention without distinction of any kind such as sex, race, color, language, religion or conviction, political or other opinion, national, ethnic or social origin, nationality, age, economic position, property, marital status, birth or other status" (United Nations, 2013). Article 45 of the convention recommends that members of the families of migrant workers shall, in the State of employment, enjoy equality of treatment with nationals of that State in relation to access to educational institutions and services, vocational guidance and training institutions, social and health services, and access to and participation in cultural life. Unfortunately, the enforcement of specific human rights has been particularly "selective" within the United States (Reichert, 2006, p.13). It behooves advocates to continue to underscore the importance of human rights and to leverage specific acts when arguing for day laborers' rights as workers. It also remains to be seen what President Obama's immigration reform will mean to the lives of LDLs and if his immigration policy will provide an opportunity to many to build a better life for themselves and their family. Regardless, President Obama's leadership on this issue and the bipartisan support are encouraging. As President Obama stated in his recent remarks on comprehensive immigration reform, "Remember that this is not just a debate about policy. It's about people. It's about men and women and young people who want nothing more than the chance to earn their way into the American story" (The White House, Office of the Press Secretary, 2013).

Discussion Questions

1. What assumptions did you make about day laborers that were corrected by this chapter?
2. If you were devising services specifically for male day laborers, what would they be?
3. How might police officers be trained to better deal with day laborers?

References

Abel Valenzuela, J. (2003). Day Labor Work. Annual Review Sociology, 29, 307–333.

Aborna, C., Olvera, N., Rodriguez, N., Hagan, J., Linares, A., & Weisner, M. (2010). Acculturative stress among documented and undocumented Latino immigrants in the United States. *Hispanic Journal of Behavioral Sciences*, 32(3), 362–384.

ACLU of Nevada v. City of Las Vegas, 466 F.3d 784. (9th Cir. 2006).

American Civil Liberties Union. (2013). Federal Appeals Court blocks Anti-Day Laborer, anti-speech ordinance. Retrieved from http://www.aclu.org/immigrants-rights/federal-appeals-court-blocks-anti-day-laborer-anti-speech-ordinance.

ACORN v. City of Phoenix, 798 F. Supp. 869. (D. Ariz. 1985), aff'd, 798 F.2d 1260. (9th Cir. 1986).

Berger v. City of Seattle, 569 F.3d 1029. (9th Cir. 2009).

Campbell, K. M. (2010). The high cost of free speech: Anti-solicitation ordinances, day laborers, and the impact of "backdoor" local immigration regulations. Georgetown Immigration Law Journal, 25(1), 1–46.

Buchanan, S.N., Nickels, L, and Morello, J. (2005). Occupational health among Chicago day laborers: an exploratory study. Archives of Environmental and Occupational Health. 260(5): 276–80.

Coal. for Humane Immigrant Rights of Los Angeles v. Burke, No. CV 98-4863. (C.D. Cal. Sept. 12, 2000).

Feere, J. D. (2007). Curbing day laborers: Anti-solicitation ordinances, commercial speech, and hiring centers: A user's guide to protecting municipalities from day laborer-related lawlessness and litigation. Retrieved from http://works.bepress.com/jon_feere/1.

Fischer, H. (2013 March 5). Day laborer part of SB 1070 ruled unconstitutional. East Valley Tribune.com. Retrieved from http://www.eastvalleytribune.com/arizona/immigration/article_75adc718-8601-11e2-b3a4-001a4bcf887a.html.

Immigration Policy Center: American Immigration Council-Special Report. (2012). Q & A guide to state immigration laws: What you need to know if your state is considering anti-immigrant legislation. Retrieved from www.immigrationpolicy.org.

Hagan, J., Rodriguez, N., Capps, R., & Kabiri, N. (2003). Effects of immigration reform on immigrants' access to health care. International Migration Review, 37, 444–463.

Lopez v. Town of Cave Creek, 559 F.Supp.2d 1030. (D. Ariz. 2008).

Mershon, E. (2012). Arizona immigration law ruling: Supreme Court delivers split decision. The Huffington Post. Retrieving from http://www.huffingtonpost.com/2012/06/25/arizona-immigration-law-ruling_n_1614067.html.

Negi, N.J. (2012). Battling Discrimination and Social Isolation: Psychological Distress Among Latino Day Laborers. American Journal of Community Psychology. doi: 10.1007/s10464-012-9548-0. First published online: August 3, 2012.

Negi, N.J. (2011). Identifying psychosocial stressors of well-being and factors related to substance abuse among Latino day laborers. Journal of Immigrant and Minority Health, 13 (4), 748–755.

Pritchard, A. (2008). "We are your neighbors": How communities can best address a growing day-labor workforce. Seattle Journal of Social Justice, 7(1), 371–420.

Quesada, J. (1999). From Central American warriors to San Francisco Latino day laborers: suffering and exhaustion in a transnational context. Transforming Anthropology, 8(1&2), 162–185.

Reichert, E. (2006). Understanding Human Rights: An Exercise Book. Thousand Oaks, CA: Sage Publications, Inc.

Sáenz, R., Menjívar, C., & Garcia, S. J. E. (2012). Arizona's SB 1070: Setting conditions for violations of human rights here and beyond. In Judith Blau & Mark Frezzo (Eds.), Sociology and human rights: A bill of rights for the twenty-first century (155–178). Thousand Oaks, CA: Pine Forge Press.

The White House, Office of the Press Secretary. (2013). Remarks by the president on comprehensive immigration reform [Press release]. Retrieved from http://www.whitehouse.gov/the-press-office/2013/01/29/remarks-president-comprehensive-immigration-reform.

Turnovsky, C. P. (2004). Making the queue: Latino day laborers in New York's street corner labor markets (pp. 1–29): University of California, San Diego.

Turnovsky, C. P. (2006). A La Parada: The social practices of men on a street corner. Social Text, 24(3), 55–72.

United Nations. (2013). Universal declaration of human rights. (2013). Retrieved from http://www.un.org/en/documents/udhr/.

United States Department of Labor: Wage and Hour Division. (2008a). Fact sheet #48: Application of U.S. Labor Laws to immigrant workers: Effect of Hoffman Plastics decision on laws enforced by the Wage and Hour Division. Retrieved from http://www.dol.gov/whd/regs/compliance/whdfs48.htm.

United States Department of Labor: Wage and Hour Division. (2008b). Fact sheet #49: The Migrant and Seasonal Agricultural Worker Protection Act. Retrieved from http://www.dol.gov/whd/regs/compliance/whdfs49.pdf.

Valenzuela, J., Abel. (2000). Working on the margins:Immigrant day labor characteristics and prospects for employment. Working Paper 22.

Valenzuela, J., Abel. (2003). Day Labor Work. Annual Review Sociology, 29, 307–333.

Valenzuela, J., Abel, Theodore, N., Melendez, E., & Gonzalez, A. L. (2006). On the Corner: Day Labor in the United States: University of California's Center for the Study of Urban Poverty.

Walter, N., Bourgois, P., Loinaz, H. M., & Schillinger, D. (2002). Social context of work injury among undocumented day laborers in San Francisco. JGIM, 17, 221–229.

Walter, N., Bourgois, P., Loinaz, H. M., Walter, N. n. i. u. e., Bourgois, P. b. i. u. e., Bourgois, P. D. o. A. H., et al. (2004). Masculinity and undocumented labor migration: Injured latino day laborers in San Francisco. Social Science & Medicine, 59(6), 1159–1168.

Xiloj-Itzep v. City of Agoura Hills, 29 Cal. Rptr. 2d 879. (Cal. Ct. App. 1994).

Chapter Nineteen

The Impact of Detaining Immigrants on a Detention Officer: An Autoethnography

Doug Epps

Introduction

Most discussions of the criminalization of immigration rightly focus on the various ways in which immigrants or their families are harmed. However, the various policies, practices and bureaucracies created to deal with the "problem" of undocumented immigration not only affects immigrants, but those who work within the institutions designed to contend with them. In this auto-ethnographic narrative, I present reflections upon the ways in which the criminalization of immigration impacted me in my role as a guard within an immigration detention center. To meet its aims, I will focus on three themes: The emotional costs, my changing views of immigration, and an exploration regarding my experience of "othering." Each theme will contain explicit excerpts from various interactions that occurred both internally and interpersonally during my employ as a detention officer. While I have broken this narrative into different sections, it is important to note that each of these themes intersect and elaborate different aspects of my experience. Breaking them into discrete sections in some ways is arbitrary; they represent the key aspects of my lived experience and how being an immigration detention officer impacted who I am as a person. Prior to this, I will briefly present a discussion of the context of my work, the Northwest Detention Center and my motivations for seeking out a career in law enforcement, as a way of helping the reader understand the intersection between my motivations and this experience.

Becoming a Detention Officer—
Motivations and Consternation

A long story of strife and survival led me to seek out a law enforcement career, one too long to fully express here. I did not know at the time of my pursuit of glory and honor that there were many different motives driving me besides the desire to protect the community from bad guys. Contrary to many of those in law enforcement, I was never in any branch of the armed forces nor did I have special training in weapons or security. At the time, I knew I wanted a career that would garner respect from greater society and possibly fulfill the boyhood fantasy of becoming a hero; a hero that saves the day, gets the girl, rides off into the sunset and all the other fantastic cliché benefits that come along with Hollywood heroism. What I didn't know at the time was that I had absolutely no clue of who I was, what I stood for, or what kind of person I wanted to be, and there was a much greater chance that I was merely trying to prove what I was not. I am just now beginning to explore the possibility that I was more likely trying to demonstrate to my family, my home town, the entire world and especially myself that I was not my father; I was not a criminal and should not be associated with one. This history profoundly intersected with what I would come to learn about myself, about others and those considered "criminals" I encountered in immigration detention.

I can recall several instances throughout my years as a detention officer at the Northwest Detention Center (NWDC) which forced me to take a step back and question my place in such an institution and the way I made a living. I didn't realize it at the time but my experiences at the detention center were slowly unveiling the true nature of what I was becoming. They forced me to ask myself questions like "What am I doing here?", "What makes me different than the people I am confining?", "Is this really something I want to be a part of?", "What does this occupation mean about myself?" and "Am I a bad person for doing this?" Perhaps most central on my mind: What happens when you get a job to gain the respect of your peers and greater society but lose respect for yourself in the process?

Psychosocial Repercussions

These people are criminals. They are 'Detainees,' not 'Americans' and are therefore undeserving of the same liberties reserved for those rightly 'made in the USA.'
This mantra is never taught in the academy, it's not printed anywhere in the 6 inch thick book of policies and procedures manual, nor is it spoken by

the institution's stoic, scar-faced warden, yet this is what is conveyed in the mannerisms, expressions and interactions between officers. It is imbedded within the system.

"It's a mental game," Academy Training Commander George Franklin once said. A giant of a man in his late 40s built like an NFL linebacker, standing over 6 feet four and tipping the scales well over 300lbs., he came from Texas and had a friendly exuberance about him but there was a sense that if he was messed with, there would be serious consequences. "It's either you or them, y'all. Take a look around the room. A year from now, a third of your fellow cadets won't be here, maybe more. You know why that is? It's 'cause they will forget that these people aren't like you and me, they're detainees. You let 'em get to ya, you let a detainee make ya feel sorry for 'em and you're on your way out of the facility for giving favors or something worse. Seen it happen countless times and I'll see it happen a bunch more. They don't care about the bills you gotta pay or the family you are providin' for," he said in his cowboy-like voice. "All they care about is trying to one-up ya, trying to get that edge. Don't let 'em get to you." A fellow academy cadet and experienced corrections officer recommended a book to me during the following lunch break, *Games Criminals Play: How You Can Profit by Knowing Them*, which I dutifully read from cover to cover. It explains the antithetical relationship of jailer versus prisoner in explicit detail, verging on the edge of necessitated paranoia, but designed for the benefit of those serving in all kinds of corrections institutions.

Unfortunately, the nature of such a situation places one group against the other. It is only natural that the officers on duty become the enemy of those being confined and therefore become the face of the plight of those in confinement. The prisoner's natural inclination is to survive, at any cost available. It's human instinct. If that means tricking a guard into getting them to provide a favor to them, then so be it. It's survival. Once that favor is given, the roles are reversed. The prisoner now has the leverage over the guard. It starts off as a favor, like mailing a letter or bringing in some food from the outside. Before the unaware guard knows it, the favor is used as leverage to get even more things, from drugs to weapons. It's a sad set of circumstances for all involved and can deeply influence the way a person views interpersonal relationships inside and outside of the institution.

Not only does being in a state of constant interpersonal paranoia cause a strain on one's psyche while in the detention environment but it lingers throughout a person's interactions well after the time clock is punched. When going to a restaurant, I find myself sitting in the corner within clear sight of the exit and a view of the patrons surrounding me. I avoid having people walk behind me with a need to look over my shoulder and will avoid any sort of gathering

or show that involves large crowds since I can become extremely claustropho-
bic and agitated when immersed in large groups of people. Going to a crowded
mall is often a difficult and stressful experience. A pervasive mistrust of the
environment constantly nags at the back of my mind when placed in situations that I am unable to monitor, feelings of anxiety and frustration build exponentially within me. This heightened awareness of surroundings may not
be completely blamed on the detention center and I imagine it does not affect
each officer the same as shown in life's inconsistencies. We all interact with
our environment in a diverse range of ways and adapt to extreme conditions
in avenues not fully understood, yet it would be inaccurate to claim that the
detention center atmosphere has left no residual imprint on who I am today.

*

Why am I in this cheap polyester uniform with a dull badge over my breast
and these other people, whom I do not know, are clad in bright unicolor jump-
suits? What gives me the right to be free? Is it because I have never made mistakes or because I am a better person? That is highly unlikely. It's impossible
to go through life mistake-free. Mistakes are as much a part of growing up and
life as breathing and falling in love—a very different kind of mistake in itself.

I still wonder, why do I get to be on this side of the law and not the other?
Maybe it's because I'm white? No, that can't truly be the answer. A large majority of our officers are immigrants, or children of immigrants themselves,
and many people that are locked up here are Caucasian from Eastern Europe.
Maybe it's because they are all intentionally coming to our country to exploit
our social services and deplete our resources? That doesn't sound correct to
me either, since millions cross the border each year in search of work, to support their families by spending long hours in the field in order to provide a
less than meager living in undesirable conditions. It makes one wonder what
conditions they are leaving behind in their home country to go through such
a great hardship for so little in return. It's disconcerting to say the least. I
thought our country was built upon the poor and mistreated immigrants that
came to this new world seeking freedom and a better life, as it says below the
Statue of Liberty: "Give me your tired, your poor, Your huddled masses yearn-
ing to breathe free, The wretched refuse of your teeming shore. Send these,
the homeless, tempest-tost to me, I lift my lamp beside the golden door!"[1,2] I

---

1. Lazarus, E. (1883). "The new colossus." Statue of Liberty, Liberty State Park. NY.
2. Statue of Liberty National Monument. US National Park Service. 2013-04-03. Retrieved
2013-04-27.

can't help but think this sounds like false advertising to those in need … maybe they knocked on the wrong golden door?

But all of this should not affect the officer that is in charge of enforcing rules and regulations and restricting the basic freedom of these individuals, right? A person's choice of employment does not necessarily have to reflect their world views or their personal beliefs. Just because you work at McDonald's doesn't mean you have to love hamburgers, after all. It's a job. A way to put food on the table, pay the bills and raise your family. It's like a military mission. Don't ask questions, don't think about your actions in the grand scheme, just complete the mission every day and report to duty when needed. It's about the greater good. Maybe that is why most correctional and detention facilities are paramilitary organizations and a large majority of their employees are ex-military. I, however, was never in the military. I never went through boot camp and was never torn down and rebuilt as a soldier. It became very difficult to silence the questions that breached the surface. Compartmentalization became a tediously draining effort and the walls of denial that I had so arduously fortified my conscience with, began to slowly erode. I struggled to look at these people as nameless numbers instead of human beings with spouses and children. Humanity continued to tear through the veil I had constructed and my inner voice grew louder.

*

In my second year at the detention center I encountered a detainee from South Africa named Smidt, who upon admittance was set on taking his own life. He had made at least one prior suicide attempt while being held at a local jail before his transfer to the immigration facility and had fresh stitches in both wrists to prove it. He was a quiet and respectful 19-year-old Caucasian man with short red hair and freckles who spoke with the vocabulary of the formally educated. He had moved to the States a few years prior with his family when they decided to leave Cape Town. Due to his current psychological condition he was taken to segregation immediately after he was booked into the facility to prevent disruption and to allow for closer surveillance. I happened to be the segregation unit officer when Smidt was transported from intake.

I usually liked to make my rounds as soon as I got on shift to get a visual idea of each individual and assess any possible situations for the evening. After securing Smidt into his new cell I spent some time out in the dayroom speaking to him through his cell door. It was not hard to tell that he was agitated as soon as we began conversing.

I asked him how he was feeling but he didn't answer. "I want to go home," he said in a defeated tone, devoid of emotion, even despair.

"That's just not possible, Smidt, but I know the ICE (Immigration and Customs Enforcement) officer is working on figuring out the details of your situation," I said. "All we can do is wait at this point."

He was clearly in a depressed state of mood and at first glance appeared to be in a trance. I found him gazing into the distance, not making eye contact and exhibiting a consistent flat affect.

It was around seven o'clock that evening when Smidt started tearing at his stitches. I did everything in my power to talk him out of hurting himself. I tried to command, I tried to persuade, I tried to reason and I ultimately tried to plead with Smidt to stop hurting himself. I tried to get him to realize that there was life after deportation and that he didn't need to do this. The problem was I didn't really know what that life would be. I didn't know what South Africa was like and I couldn't imagine being sent to a country all alone, with no family, no job and no money, without the possibility to move back to the country where your family lives. Smidt was luckier than some who couldn't even speak the language of their "native" country, yet he was likely doomed to homelessness at the least.

Smidt would later be strapped to the steel bed in his cell with leather four-point restraints since he would take every chance he could get to rip at his wrists. It would take days to get him medicated enough to inhibit his suicidal tendencies, or at the least postpone them until he was out of custody. Who knows what he was like when he wasn't in detention. Maybe he was the same kid, fed up with life and depressed to the point of self-destruction, or maybe he was a typical 19-year-old emerging adult with endless possibilities in front of him. Either way it's irrelevant. Thinking about a detainee's life outside of the facility is trouble in itself. As far as an officer is concerned, there is no other entity besides the detainee in custody and all other possibilities cease to exist. The struggle to isolate a human into miniscule snapshots of personalities was less difficult for some with more extensive experience but it often left me in a state of emotional exhaustion. A constant internal vigilance was required to monitor my thoughts in order to prevent them from traveling down the path of empathy and concern; two emotional weaknesses and enduring nemeses to the detention officer. I struggled to narrow my vision to the person that was detained and filter out the thoughts of who the "free" individual was. I looked to my colleagues to see how they approached these issues without implicating myself as a sympathizer.

I overheard two officers talking in the locker room about detainees in their unit.

"Can you believe Abdallah's got a Ph.D.? I got a doctor on my unit, all you got is gang bangers and cholos!" Officer Serrano boasted amid laughter.

"Shit, I would rather have cholos and gangbangers any day over some know-it-all doctor from the university of who-knows-where. He's just gonna cause more problems and manipulate the system," replied Officer Johnson.

"I hear that. Them jailhouse lawyers are a pain in my ass. Just the other day we had to delay rec because some of the Ethiopians put in grievances for not getting enough law library time. Completely fucked up the day's schedule!" Officer Serrano agreed. "Abdallah may or may not have a real Ph.D. but he ain't smart enough to stay outta this shit hole. Anyways, I'm sure he's here for getting caught up in some kind of criminal activity. They all are breaking the law if they are here without papers. All they had to do was apply for citizenship legally. If they didn't, they are probably up to no good anyways."

Officers Serrano and Johnson's dialogue that day was one among many others of similar nature that took place in the detention center over the years. I was able to distinguish specific elements within these types of discourse which would serve to alleviate my conscience as I dutifully performed my occupational obligations. By labeling every single individual confined in the detention center as a criminal, whether by failure to attain citizenship or perpetrating felonious activity, created less of an internal struggle to restrict the rights of those which it was my job to confine. Since it was their "fault" for being locked up in the institution, the blame for their situation now lay upon them.

The job became significantly easier when this became natural. However, there is a problem in training yourself to think and interact in a certain way. For most of us personality traits are not pliable attributes that can be switched on and off like a light switch It's more akin to getting a tattoo on the core of your being. It's a long lasting change of who you are and how you view the world. It can be removed or altered but it takes a conscious effort and the accompanying discomfort often associated with changing characteristics of the permanent nature. I saw this come to light when attending the local county fair with a girlfriend after I had been at the detention center for over a year. Coincidentally, we happened to be attending on "Hispanic Day." As luck would have it, I was also wearing a t-shirt commemorating my participation as a staff member during the opening of the detention center. This event would never have been an issue before becoming a detention officer, but this day's coincidence created a unique situation that had not crossed my mind. I found myself in a confused worry, not only about being recognized by a past detainee or family member, but being in the midst of so many individuals I spent my days labeling criminals. I immediately turned my t-shirt inside out and walked through the fair anxiously scanning the faces of all I could see. I didn't seem to comprehend the fact that the faces I tediously inspected could care less about my presence and were much more concerned about having a good time with their families and friends, which I was neglecting to do. Needless to say I was not able to enjoy the day and my companion could not quite understand the apprehension and discomfort I was displaying. The psychosocial weight of this final passage is evident but also, and perhaps more importantly, relates by foreshadowing the following section on changing views of immigration and immigrants.

Changing View of Immigration and Immigrants

"Detainee Hernandez-Martinez! Ven aqui!" I heard booking officer Chacon shout his aggressive cadence into the crowded holding cell. A tan, freckle-faced, red-headed young man sheepishly lumbered out of the cell and sat on the cold stainless steel stool in front of the booking desk, revealing a look of lost bewilderment. I was about to escort some detainees to their new housing units when I caught sight of Hernandez.

"Where's he from?" I asked the intake officer, motioning towards Hernandez.

"Mexico, like all the rest," said Officer Chacon nonchalantly. I tried to conceal my shock at seeing a red-haired Mexican man in the detention facility but Officer Chacon took notice. "Not all Mexicans have to be brown, Epps," he playfully chided. He's right, and I knew that, I think to myself. But why was I so shocked?

*

I found my outlook towards immigrants, especially Hispanic immigrants, changing as I continued to work at the detention center. Hispanic immigrants comprised the greatest percentage of the detainee population which consisted largely of Mexican nationals. Before I began working at the detention center, I was not exactly accustomed to diversity. I grew up in a small, dairy farm town in the shadow of the Cascade Mountains with mostly Caucasian residents. Trucks emblazoned with confederate flag stickers were commonplace on the small town's streets. As far as I knew, Latin Americans were people that worked at Mexican restaurants, drove around the green landscaping trucks and worked the farms as laborers. Even though I did not hold a clear picture of a people I knew little about, my homogenized ignorance could be considered benign for the most part, apart from the perpetuation of common stereotypical viewpoints. Once I became a detention officer, a large portion of the Hispanic population that I came into contact with changed drastically and the stereotypes I held shifted to mirror this. The substantial amount of detainees that came from the criminal justice system aided in the modification of my seemingly innocuous suppositions. Immigrants were collected and corralled from jails and prisons all throughout the northwest and other outlying states, then shuttled to the Northwest Detention Center, the 4th largest immigration detention center in the US.[3] The nature of the detention atmosphere forces detainees and officers into opposing roles, creating a captive versus keeper mentality inherent to the penal environment. The stereotypes I had previously formed were beginning to mutate into something quite different than the simplistic ones of my youth. These people had gang tattoos, teardrops under their eyes and an immediate disdain for me, due to the uniform I wore on a daily basis signifying allegiance with those that kept them from freedom.

I learned about gang culture and what to look for in tattoos. I learned of the Mexican mafia and that Nortenos and Surrenos had to be separated or there would be bloodshed. I learned of the infamous Mara Salvatrucha, or MS-13, and the fear that accompanied the El Salvadorian gang. I learned that every single minority, Mexican, Guatemalan, Russian, Samoan, etc., had some sort of set, clique or other gang affiliation which was also a form of survival within lock up. These were the immigrants I came to know. In all actuality, I learned that detainees were considered criminal, and detainees were immigrants. Therefore, whether gang tattoos were present or not, these individuals were deemed by the federal government enough of a threat to be confined in a medium security jail.

Othering (Structural Dehumanization)

Detainee Cortez was scheduled to see his wife and two children in visitation room number two and it was my job to make sure that all rules were to be followed according to policy. For example, at the facility I was employed, the contact visit policy strictly stated that a husband and wife were allowed only one closed mouth kiss and one hug from their significant other. This was to be monitored and enforced by the officer who is constantly observing the visit.

His wife and children were respectful and kind even though it was apparent that they were overtaken with emotion. They appeared to be conflicted between the happiness of seeing the man they cared so deeply for and the realization that it may be a very long time before they saw each other again. Cortez had lived in the US for almost 20 years and been married to his wife for over 10 years, and he was now being forced to leave them behind for a country he struggled to remember. He would be banned from legally entering the US for another 10 years, which is customary for immigrants that have been deported by ICE. It

---

3. Gavett, G. (2011). Lost in detention; map: The US immigration detention boom. PBS Frontline.

quickly became apparent that gauging this visit would be much more difficult than checking off privileges as they occur between visiting participants.

As is natural when loved ones meet after being apart for long periods of time, they immediately embraced one another at first sight. Does this count as their one hug that I am supposed to be controlling? Am I supposed to keep them from touching each other for the rest of their hour visit? It is policy, after all. These people may not see each other for several years from now, possibly never again, and I am supposed to tell them that they cannot hug, kiss or show physical affection towards one another. After all, I am the enforcer of rules who keeps order within this highly secure detention facility. I can still recall the visceral emotion surging and building within my gut. Was it pity, compassion, or sadness for what these people have to go through for losing or never obtaining American citizenship? Or was it a result of my own culpability from not only being the face of this everyday American family's separation and the part I have played in the grand scheme in this painful ordeal they have been forced to endure? It was nothing more than a nagging in the back of my mind but it clouded my ability to compartmentalize my emotions, a dangerous position to be in for any law enforcement/corrections officer. We were always trained to not let our emotions get the best of ourselves: 'That's how they get you.' It's a part of the job that has sadly resulted in more than a few officer terminations, but something told me that ignoring these feelings could eventually become much more destructive.

The look of desperation and sadness on their grown adult faces was difficult to bear but it was the look of their two small children that inevitably destroyed my will to strictly regulate the family's affections. The two daughters couldn't be more than 4 and 6 years old perched on each of their father's knee, both clinging to one of his arms as if they were afraid I was going to pull their father away from them. It was painful to watch and even more heartbreaking to be a part of it. My heart sank into my stomach like I was flying down a rollercoaster. I tried to ignore the feeling. I knew I had a job to do and it was so important to prove to everyone that I could be a good officer. Yet which is more important, to be a good officer/employee or to be a good person? This question was surfacing much more frequently than I would have liked and becoming harder and harder to ignore.

"Officer? May I hug my wife again?" asked Cortez, his voice soft with suppressed emotion.

My conscience took over, forcing my head to nod in affirmation before I could think about policies and procedures. The undeniable gratitude on their faces made the internal wrenching even worse. I could no longer stand fast as the cold hearted overseer of affection as cracks of light began to shine through the crumbling walls of my fortitude. I looked at my watch. Five minutes left until control would call to terminate the visit.

"Cortez," I said, "It's about time to say your goodbyes. Only 5 minutes left." A look of emotional terror struck Cortez and his wife's face as they realized that only a mere matter of minutes stood between them and long-term separation. Tears began to well in their eyes and the children began to sense the strength of their parents fading.

"Cortez," I said quietly, "You have 5 minutes left … make the most of it. Just keep it PG, ok?" His confused expression quickly faded into one of gratitude as I stepped to the side of the door and recognition took hold. "Thank you officer!" Cortez and his wife said emphatically. Any previous disagreements, arguments or stresses that may once have inhibited affections between the couple when in the daily monotony of outside life were completely dissolved as they embraced each other and kissed repeatedly. There was only 5 minutes left of a world where they could see and touch each other and feel the warmth of their lover's skin and the heat of each other's breath. I could not stop them from this last experience, whether due to weakness or strength I do not know. I just know that it felt good to let this family express their love to one another because that's what families do!

That heart-warming feeling of doing the right thing and helping someone when there is every reason not to took over me and forced my stoic fortitude into a compulsory smile. Yet, I couldn't shake the nagging guilt in the back of my mind. I cannot help but worry about what my past co-workers would think if they ever read this and I still have a sense of delinquency and shame for not being tough enough to do my job as it was instructed. The mental and emotional toughness that is inherent to the subculture of corrections makes it a necessity to not discuss feelings that could be considered weak with other coworkers. Officers are formally and informally required to exhibit stoic emotionless responses to situations that would normally cause an individual anger, disgust or fear. If you are unable to control these emotions there is great likelihood of becoming labeled as a detainee sympathizer or a "hug-a-thug" which is similar to being classified as a traitor in the military. You risk possible harassment from co-workers, intense scrutiny from supervisors, manipulation from detainees and shunning from all. Sadly, I feel there was no "right" way to do things in this kind of situation, leaving guilt an unavoidable outcome of either decision: either betray your supervisors and fellow officers or betray your conscience.

Conclusion

The writing of this autoethnography has brought about more questions and concerns than answers. Taking the time to delve into my personal history has brought about a time of deep insecurity and internal struggle that continues to conflict within me. To this day, I still feel shame and guilt from being a part of such an institution responsible for dissecting so many families. I carry a stagnant guilt for not only playing a part within the system that inescapably contributes to the institutional oppression of immigrants but also for trying so hard to be good at what I did. The shame still lingers from what I did and didn't do. More often than not, I didn't always adhere to my conscience and obediently followed my supervisor's orders. When I did listen to that intrinsic sensation of righteousness, I let fellow officers down, some of whom were and still are considered friends. I cannot help but cringe at the thought of some of them reading these confessions and brood over their possible reactions. Will I be shunned, disregarded and written off as some sort of overly sentimental hippie? Or will they find themselves analyzing their own part in a much grander scheme and relate to my purged experiences? Maybe they will embark on their own pilgrimage of integrity and question what it truly means to be an American by examining how they choose to make their paycheck as a willing component of the US immigration detention system. By writing these words I have placed honesty above personal friendships, my masculinity and self-image and instead placed my faith in that of human decency.

Discussion Questions

1. How might the process of writing an autoethnography help you in your work or studies?
2. What did you learn about yourself from reading this chapter, and from reading this book in general?
3. What are the emotional costs to other "players" in the criminalization of immigration?

Acknowledgements

I would like to offer my sincerest gratitude to co-editor Rich Furman, for his selfless guidance, patience and friendship over the years, and without whom this project would not have been possible.

Index